HISTORIC GARDENS
of WILTSHIRE

HISTORIC GARDENS
of WILTSHIRE

Timothy Mowl

TEMPUS

For John Kendall and Michael Manser

Frontispiece: *Stourhead Landscape Gardens*. Chris Broughton and the *New Arcadian Journal*

First published 2004

Tempus Publishing Ltd
The Mill, Brimscombe Port
Stroud, Gloucestershire GL5 2QG
www.tempus-publishing.com

British Library Cataloguing in Publication Data.
A catalogue record for this book is available from the British Library.

ISBN 0 7524 2893 4

Typesetting and origination by Tempus Publishing.
Printed and bound in Great Britain.

Contents

Acknowledgements

I must begin my thanks with the staff of the Wiltshire and Swindon Record Office, and in particular to the County Archivist, John d'Arcy, and to Steve Hobbs. Everyone at Trowbridge has been extremely helpful and has made the archival research for this book a real pleasure. My thanks also to the County Archivist of Gloucestershire, Nicholas Kingsley, for his continued support of the series and for making available for study the Repton sketches of New Park, Roundway. The Devizes Museum has an important collection of documents relating to historic gardens in the county and Lorna Haycock was a most courteous and informed guide to these. I am also grateful to the Wiltshire Gardens Trust, particularly to Nicholas Hunloake, for advice and support.

Many close friends and academic colleagues have been ready to answer my queries and give advice. These include: Michael Liversidge, Stephen Bann, Michael Richardson and Hannah Lowery of Bristol University Special Collections, Mavis Batey, David Lambert, John and Eileen Harris, Andrew Eburne, Kate Felus, Neil Porteous, Bill Haxworth, Stephen Parker, Douglas Gillis, Charlotte Gale, Carole Fry, John Kendall, Michael Manser, Susan Gordon, Philip White, Jonathan Holt, Sarah Fitzgerald, Kate Harris, Gillian Sladen, Martin McNicol, Dianne Barre, Ruth Guilding and Fridy Duterloo.

Owners in Wiltshire, together with their agents, gardeners and archivists, have all been willing to allow me access to their gardens and estates and have been generous with information and advice about their grounds. During my research for a biography on William Beckford, the Hon. Alastair Morrison gave me a fascinating and invaluable morning tramping around every grotto, cavern and garden building at Fonthill. Lord Radnor offered some intriguing insights into his family's past relationship with garden designers. Then I must thank the following: Lord Talbot, Lord Pembroke, Ray Stedman, Carol Druce, Ros Liddington, Nigel Bailey, Heather Purvis, Lady Iveagh, Sarah Finch-Crisp, Annie Kemp, Lord Cardigan, Lady Weinstock, Sir Mark and Lady Weinberg, Andrew Denley, Paul Morris, Richard Morris, Ray Hutchison, Lord Lansdowne, Kate Fielden, Berendean Money-Kyrle, Paul and Caroline Weiland, Peter Bazeley, Lord Suffolk, Lis Greenaway, Roger Kivell, Robert Lumley, John Reynolds, Robin Andrews, Richard Higgs, Louisa Wayman, Garry Calland, David Cornelius-Reid, Joanna

Martin, Bob Louden, Adrian and Matthew Shipp, Ian and Barbara Pollard, Elizabeth Cartwright-Hignett, Leon Butler, Chris and Linda Ellis, Ed Cross, Joanna Parker, Suzy Lewis, Deborah van der Beek, Alvin and Judith Howard, Robert and Patsy Floyd, Antony and Sue Young, Kjersti and Halvor Astrup, Pete Beazer, Henry Keswick, Stuart Hume, Rhian Glover, Elizabeth, Douglas and Samuel Colvin, Rosaleen Mulji, Michael Wade, John and Terttu Cordle, Stephen and Amanda Clark, Bill Painter, Sir Henry Rumbold and Sue Daly.

Kate Robson Brown and her committee of the Bristol University Arts Faculty Research Fund have given valuable financial help with the illustrations and travel. With her usual professionalism, Ann Pethers has produced the photographs from my negatives, and Douglas Matthews has prepared a thorough and enlightening index. My agent, Sarah Menguc, has been as encouraging as ever, and Peter Kemmis Betty and Emma Parkin have produced the book with their usual care and efficiency.

Finally I should like to thank my close friend, Brian Earnshaw for his help at the editing stage and for his companionship on site visits, and my wife, Sarah, daughter, Olivia, and son, Adam, for their constant encouragement. Cornwall next.

Timothy Mowl
Bristol
Winter 2003

Abbey House Gardens
• Charlton Park
• Garsdon
● **Malmesbury**
• Cowbridge
• Cole Park

Warneford • Place
● Swindon
Lydiard Park •

• Grittleton

Easton Piercy •
• Castle Combe
• Bolehyde
• Ridleys Cheer
• Sheldon
• Bremhill

Biddestone •
Chippenham
Hartham •
• Bowood
Corsham •
• Whetham
• Lackham
Lacock •
• Bowden Park
Cantax
• Spye Park
Lucknam •
Outdoor Studio
• Hazelbury Manor
● **Bath**
• South Wraxall
● **Melksham**
Great Chalfield
New Park •
• Southbroom
• The Courts
● **Devizes**
Belcombe •
Bradford-on-Avon
Devizes Castle
Iford
• Westwood
• Seend
• Urchfont
• Keevil

• Avebury Manor
Littlecote •
● **Marlborough**
Little •
Bedwyn
Tottenham Park •

• Oare House

• Erlestoke
• West Lavington

Chisenbury
Priory •
Chute Lodge •
• Netheravon
Biddesden •

● **Warminster**
• Longleat
• Bishopstrow

• Amesbury Abbey
• Wilbury

• Heale

• Stourhead

• Little Ridge
Fonthill •
Wilton House •
• Little Durnford
• Compton
Chamberlayne
● **Salisbury**
• Hatch House
• Clarendon Park
Clarendon Palace
• Brickworth
Shute
• Wardour Castle
• Longford
Shaftesbury ●
• Norrington
• Trafalgar House
• Newhouse
• Ashcombe
• The Moot
Ark Farm
• Rushmore
• Larmer Tree

Introduction

Back in the seventeenth century John Aubrey described the clay vales of North Wiltshire, where he was born and bred, as 'a sour woodsere country'. Edith Olivier, writing in the first *Shell Guide* to the county, claimed that South Wiltshire 'belonged to the fairies'. So what kind of county entity is that, remembering that between sour north and fairy south lies the chalk wilderness of Salisbury Plain; not to mention the sandwich filling of greensand between clay and chalk that makes Bowood, or the slice of oolitic limestone around Box, filched from the Cotswolds?

There is no such thing as a typical English county carrying a representative profile of English garden development. No one, for instance, would ever suggest that the gardens of Bedfordshire stood as a useful mid-point between those of Northumberland and those of Sussex. For that reason any book claiming to be a history of English gardens will be a series of generalisations shot through with multiple exceptions.

Prehistory has run like a theme through Wiltshire gardens, Stonehenge and Avebury have cast their shadows: Stourhead, Wilton, Fonthill, Avebury Manor, Bremhill Old Parsonage, Hazelbury Manor, Little Durnford and Wyndham House, Salisbury, all made or still make some kind of Druidic reference. This is over a three hundred year period from the 9th Earl of Pembroke's proposal to raise a new Stonehenge at Wilton to the massive reproduction of Avebury's sinister rocks at Hazelbury (**1**) in the recent lively Pollard occupancy of that great, but little noticed garden.

Grottoes have been another Wiltshire garden specialism; their linear shell patterns persisting from the dry little cave in the grounds of Marlborough College to the brilliant complexities and crystal stalactites of Bowden Park. They do not stem, as some authorities suggest, from Painshill in Surrey. The Grotto at Painshill was created by Tisbury men, quarry workers in the Chilmark stone, who had learnt their trade applying shells from Jamaica and crystals in Alderman Beckford's Savage Picturesque grottoes and Cold Bath at Fonthill.

Wiltshire is, therefore, typical only in that it is disconnected, unexpected, various yet themed; and, as one of the great, leading garden counties, its inventions and its breakaways are of real interest. On two occasions, within Caroline formalism and then in early Georgian movements towards Arcadias, the county has been an engine for national change. Sir Philip Sidney and his forceful sister, the 'salacious' Countess Mary, set in train at Wilton that spirit of competitive garden design that resulted, in the next Pembroke generation, in Inigo Jones' obsessively formal garden of the 1630s. Longleat would vulgarise and popularise it once the Commonwealth was over.

Then it was in Wiltshire that the same sterile pattern of formal layouts began to break up. At Whetham House, the Chancellor of the Exchequer, Sir John Ernle's water channels, cascades, lakes and hexagon intersected so playfully in his woodlands that Arcadia was prefigured before the seventeenth century was out. In two layouts at Amesbury Abbey and Standlynch (Trafalgar House) and probably at The Moot, Downton, Charles Bridgeman played fast and loose with formal idioms, reconciling their geometry with the natural terrain. Lastly it was a Wiltshire landowner, the immensely likeable Henry Hoare II, who brought Arcadia to its pitch of perfection at Stourhead. William Kent, who usually gets the credit for evolving the style, had no connection with this, the most imaginative and influential of all such gardens.

When Edwardian gardens became the preferred mark of a gentry garden towards the end of the nineteenth century, Wiltshire went its own individual way, responding to its own open landscapes with open, terraced gardens rather than the garden rooms enclosed within high yew hedges that the Edwardians usually adopted. In possibly yet another response to prehistoric precedent these gardens, at Keevil Manor, South Wraxall Manor, Avebury Manor, Westwood Manor and others adopted an extravagant vertical emphasis in topiary, with spires and

1 *The prehistoric Stone Circle at Hazelbury was built of Scottish menhirs in 1985 and designed by Ian Pollard to accompany another henge of yews, now uprooted*

2 *The Cloisters, a consecrated chapel and museum of marble fragments, was completed by Harold Peto in 1913 at the east end of the Great Terrace at Iford Manor*

monstrous chessmen rising from the lawns. Harold Peto's own garden and his best creation is at Iford Manor (**2**), another exception, far more continental Italian than traditional Jacobean in feeling, memorably devotional with its chapel and its burning candles, just teetering on the right side of an architectural antique shop.

This is not a guide to gardens open to the public, any more than Nikolaus Pevsner's *Buildings of England* series was a record of opening hours. Some gardens are open regularly, many open for two advertised days in a year, many more are private. Without exception all my Wiltshire garden owners have been courteous and helpful. What was even more encouraging was how many of them have recently created new historic gardens whose influence is likely to last. Biddestone Manor exemplifies the dour north, Chisenbury Priory the smiling south. Try to visit and compare them both. The last and greatest garden event I leave for readers who persevere to my final chapter to discover.

1

Gardens of the English medieval vernacular

Where garden history is concerned Wiltshire has been desperately unlucky with Clarendon Palace. If only the Plantagenet kings who built it, Henry II in the twelfth century, Henry III in the thirteenth, had used solid Chilmark limestone for the infilling of its walls instead of chalk rubble and flints. More to the point, if only the later Tudor monarchs had not insisted on living close to London, deserting Clarendon to ruin, Wiltshire would have not just a royal garden of great antiquity, but also one with intense romantic association. Clarendon was not simply a favoured royal hunting palace, the venue for national parliaments and councils of state. Its gardens had been the solace of Eleanor of Aquitaine, successively Queen of France and then of England, the toast of the troubadours and the scandalous patron of the Courts of Love. As wife to Henry II she had been the virtual Empress of Western Europe, the most formidable yet poetic woman in English medieval history. For years she was imprisoned for rebellion in, so legend relates, the cramped unhealthy castle of Old Sarum. But it is evident, from Roger of Hoveden's record, that 'her prison was no worse than her palace at Winchester'[1], that she was actually kept in the luxurious confinement, appropriate to her status, of Clarendon Palace on the other side of the valley from Old Sarum. Her husband had rebuilt what had been a mere hunting box in 1176, giving it a great aisled hall with Purbeck marble columns and a good wine cellar. Both the King's and Queen's chambers on the upper floors overlooked gardens on the north-east sectors of the great complex. Such was the beauty of their planting that in 1250, under Eleanor's grandson, Henry III, a hall window was cut simply to afford a view of the Queen's garden that had been laid out in 1247. Sadly there is no mention of what trees or flowers could be seen through that window. Two years later a whole building was demolished in order to extend the garden and there would be further improvements in 1252.[2]

No pollen analysis has been conducted to determine what flowers and herbs grew there, but there are hints of a richer than usual flora on the present site. The sophistication of the Palace can be judged by the Afghan lapis lazuli used in its wall frescoes and by Richard II's dancing room, the 'Camera Tripudiancium'.[3] Most telling of all is the exquisite, almost Grecianly reserved and elegant head of a youth, a label stop of about 1230, preserved in Salisbury Museum. It suggests that, by the mid-thirteenth century, two buildings of extreme distinction faced each other across the Avon water meadows – the Cathedral and the Palace – twin symbols of lay and ecclesiastical refinement in Anglo-French Gothic, pared down and fastidious.

The way up from Salisbury is two miles long, with the downs closing in on the right and a tramp across stubble fields dotted with blue flints like scraps of Chinese pottery. It is only when the path hits the slope and buries itself in a chalk gully fifteen feet deep that a certain medieval authenticity closes in. Before pressing on to the top of the hill and the depressing ruins of the Palace, it is vital to climb the flight of steps leading up the left-hand side of the gully to the viewpoint where there is a seat overlooking a wide valley where, on my visit, three fallow deer were bounding.

The view is one that Constable would have died for and what matters is that this is the view that Clarendon Palace would have enjoyed from those gardens on the north-east side of the complex before the trees grew up. Apart from being a perfect grandstand for observing game, compellingly framed down the valley to the west is Salisbury Cathedral spire, tower and crossing, not looking, as the spire often does from the downs, like an absurd spike sticking up out of a field, but entire and supremely confident. Is this a coincidence or could the spire have been raised, later post-1334, as the very grandest of all garden buildings? At over four hundred feet high it was for many years the tallest man-made object on the planet, a fact that the English modestly tend to overlook. The visual link between the King's favourite hunting palace and the bishop's brand new cathedral on a virgin site of wet water meadows is to say the least fortunate; could it have been simply fortuitous?

The Park's function as the largest hunting ground for deer in England is better recorded than its gardens and is even remembered by local place names. At Clarendon Park House, a mile and a half to the south-east of the Palace site, a map is kept of the hunting forest with all its old royal divisions and subsidiary lodges.[4] It was drawn around 1640, before the Parliamentary survey was made, preparatory to selling up the estate. Unusually orientated east–west, rather than north–south, it shows the five main divisions of the royal Park: Ranger's, Theobald's, Fussell's, Palmer's and Hunt's, each based on a lodge, eponymous except for Theobald's, which was based on Queen's Manor Lodge, and each controlling anything from three to six coppices. The twenty-one coppices in all were divided from each other by open rides, which would have offered long satisfying chases once the deer had been beaten out of the woods. Two east–west sequences of rides would have given chases of up to two miles with two shorter cross rides running north–south. The woodland, together with a much larger area of rough downland, was enclosed within a park pale with gates. There was also an Out Lodge tenement of marshland for hawking and fishing that included Osier Island in the Avon, and royalty over the swans, with some pasture land. It was to serve this last area that, when the Old Palace had fallen into its Tudor decay, Sir Thomas Gorges built Longford Castle on the Avon as a seat for Queen Elizabeth to use when she hunted in the Park or hawked along the river. Study of the Ordnance Survey maps will reveal modern farm buildings on the sites of Ranger's, Queen's Manor and Fussell's lodges with some traces of the two long east–west rides; while Kennel Farm recalls the royal 'Kennells' of the map. Park Corner, incidentally, by Sir Thomas' Bridge and Broken Cross, was where King Charles II, escaping after the battle of Worcester, was met by Colonel Phelps with the spare horse of his hunting party to enable the King to ride on to the sea and safety at Shoreham with a boat to France.

The lasting influence of this handsome and entirely unfortified complex of buildings on other Wiltshire houses was that county landowners tended, following the royal lead, to build not castles, but manor houses with dramatically vast welcoming porches and, though this is speculation, possibly with at least vestigial front gardens. The earliest hint of one of these gardens comes at Sheldon Manor near Chippenham. There the cavernous porch, though very little else, dates back to the 1290s when Sir Edmund and Isabelle Lady Gascelin were presiding in a significantly quiet, and consequently prosperous, interlude in that family's usually stormy history. An Inquisition Post Mortem of 1287 referred to a 'garden and two orchards', so the garden is likely to be as old as the house.[5] Until a recent storm there were three yew trees in the forecourt of the Manor; two still survive and are thought to be more than eight hundred years old, which suggests that yews were being planted as topiary features as early as the late thirteenth century. It could hardly be a coincidence that Sir Edmund's son, another Edmund, and brother, Walter, both served as Custos of the Manor of undefended Clarendon.[6]

There was never a protecting gatehouse to Sheldon, nor apparently to another Wiltshire 'porch house', Norrington, built in 1377. However, Great Chalfield, a third porch house built after 1470, is different. Like two other manor houses, both in the Cotswold shadow – South Wraxall (1430-50), and that elusively multi-dated Hazelbury – it went up while the Wars of the Roses were making even Wiltshire vulnerable to wandering bands of soldiery. These three manor houses have surviving systems of walled gardens. The problem is that these walls proved irresistible to their late nineteenth- or early twentieth-century owners, who planted their garden rooms with ambitious schemes of clipped topiary in the confident, aristocratic Edwardian style, largely concealing any relics of medieval planting. Consequently they will be discussed in a later Edwardian chapter.

As the true line of medieval vernacular garden design was, however, precisely that system of clustered yet unrelated and unlinked walled garden rooms found in most Wiltshire manor houses of the fourteenth to the sixteenth centuries, it is worth considering the most complex of them all, the gardens of Avebury Manor (**colour plate 1**), if only to grasp the ground base from which the Franco-Italian gardens of the Renaissance would develop and to which, for romantic privacy, Edwardian gardens would return.

Some of the six garden rooms at Avebury may retain walls from the Benedictine priory that was confiscated as an alien establishment in 1378, but most of their enchanting claustrophobia dates to the time of the Dunch family, William, Walter and Debora Dunch successively, between 1551 and 1640; something, therefore, of a garden still in a medieval time warp. When a London lawyer, Sir Richard Holford, bought the Manor in 1692, he had drawn up in brown ink and with many informative captions a wonderfully precise and detailed plan of the house and its grounds (**3**).[7] Nothing had changed since the time of the Dunch occupation except for an ill-conceived dog-leg approach from the east, intended to add a little formal seventeenth-century dignity to the grounds. Remarkably that 1695 plan can serve as a reasonably accurate guide to Avebury's garden rooms today, three centuries later.

Situated in the heart of the chalk downlands. Avebury's garden walls should have crumbled away long ago, like those of Norrington's walled garden. But they are not made of frail clunch. Their almost mauve- or lilac-tinted stone came from the vandalistic destruction of the great sarsen stones of Avebury's prehistoric stone circles and avenues. They were cracked to pieces laboriously. William Stukeley, a pioneer in British prehistoric studies, recorded in his 1743 *Abury, a Temple of the British Druids* the process of ruin:

> The method is to dig a pit by the side of the stone, till it falls down, then to burn many loads of straw under it. They draw lines of water along it when heated, and then with smart strokes of a great sledge-hammer, its prodigious bulk is divided into many lesser parts.[8]

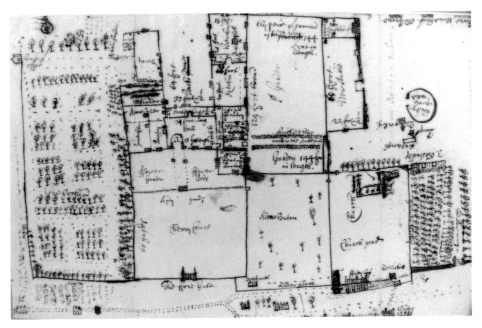

3 *The mid-sixteenth-century pattern of walled gardens shown on this 1695 plan of Avebury Manor survives intact today. Church and farm lie east of the house.* Wiltshire & Swindon Record Office, 184/4

15

When Stukeley made his plan of the village for the book, there were only twenty-four sarsens still standing within the village circle and many of the lost stones must have gone to make the garden walls of the Manor. Stukeley records with satisfaction that, if used to build a cottage, 'the stone being a kind of marble, or rather granite, is always moist and dewy in winter, which proves damp and unwholesome, and rots the furniture'.[9]

If the garden rooms are taken in their natural sixteenth-century sequence the first would be the Cherry Court on the 1695 plan, now the South Lawn. This was then the main entrance to the house from the 'Ffront Gate' on the village street. The Court was divided, rather more than half way up, by a fence of wooden palings beyond which visitors could not take their horses, and the protected section nearest to the Manor is marked 'Fflower Garden and Fflower Beds'. If we could be certain that this 1695 caption recorded Tudor or even medieval practice, it would be a valuable indication of just when a flowery front garden became a standard feature. It would also be some support for the antiquity of a similar front garden at Norrington, now ablaze with most un-medieval zinnias, border hibiscus and Tyrean purple lobelias. Here at Avebury the area has been turned into lawn. At its south-east corner the Great Parlour projects out with a window to overlook the flower beds. This suggests, though does not prove, that the Flower Garden is as old as that part of the house, around 1548, when a survey of William Sharington's manors by his steward, Stephen Cole, mentions 'a fair little parlour . . . new built with a chimney in him ceiled over with plaster'.[10] On the east side of the house is a 'Garden', marked in one sector as 'very poor ground'. This is now the East Garden and the modern way into the house. In the seventeenth century the path across it to the back entrance into the house from the farmyard and pigeon cote was lined on each side with pleached, quick-set hedges. This was the workers' way into the back premises, with the 'New Stables' and the 'Coach House' immediately east of the 'very poor ground'.

Returning to the southern gentry side of the Manor, the largest stone-walled garden room was then, as now, the 'Orchard' west of the Cherry Court, but the 'Sheare Barton' east of the Court and next to the churchyard was also planted with some fruit trees. Indeed the implication of the notes on the 1695 plan is that all these enclosures were for fruit and vegetables, except that portion of the Court between the front door and the paled fence. The others were pure, utilitarian gardens from the native vernacular phase of English garden design. Walls were for wind breaks to create fruit-ripening sun-traps.

Sir Richard Holford was, however, in 1695, giving rough and ready instructions[11] to a local Farmer Skeate to improve the privacy of his garden by planting 'some good elmes or okes in the corner of the sheere barton, between the dog kennel and wall, plant 6 or 8, probablie halfe may thrive. They must be taken up with as much of their rootes as conveniently may bee'. Skeate was also to 'pare' the 'syccomores' in the 'Sycommer Walk' and create a little bower. He was 'to plant 4 younge elmes or two elmes and two ashes or siccomores in the upper end of the

Bullwork in a square forme, and to preserve them, under which a bench or seate may bee hereafter placed'. This crude garden planning was taking place, it must be remembered, not in mid–Tudor times, but when William and Mary were on the throne. We are clearly in deep Wiltshire.

Hazelbury, a mystery manor house which never had a supporting village, has its share of stone–walled garden rooms but, for this chapter, their interest lies in their seeming to be on the cusp between a charming utilitarian chaos from the Middle Ages and a more sophisticated axial layout of garden sectors that owes something to Franco-Italian influences. The manor house with its attendant buildings lies like a substantial fort, curiously un–English when viewed from a distance, in high open fields on the county's western Cotswold borderland. Apart from the mysteries of its precise dating there is the mystery of its site. Built nearer to the edge of the steep By Brook valley it would have been more easily defended, but then who were the enemies so threatening as to require that sturdy line of walls with its two round bastions, and what strategic purpose did the house serve, isolated up there, well above Box village?

The Pevsner-Cherry *Buildings of England* volume concludes its account of Hazelbury airily with a question: 'To the N of the house a raised terrace with pretty corner bastions and an odd corbelled-out seat. What date may they be?'[12] Faced with Wiltshire's most impressive fortified garden, more formidable than 'pretty', an attempt must be made to answer that question. Hazelbury has preserved in its garden layout almost exactly the configuration shown on two maps: Francis Allen's 1626 survey, 'The Lordshipe of Colerne', and a more detailed map of 1832.[13] The big orchard shown on these to the east of the house has been transformed into the most extraordinary twentieth-century topiary garden in Wiltshire, out-pointing anything of the kind in Gloucestershire, so for this chapter the grounds are best approached from the west, the side where their fifteenth- or sixteenth-century character is best preserved. There are two ways up from the valley. One path leads up from Box, a village as handsomely built as many Tuscan hill towns, and this route gives tantalising glimpses of the two bastion towers on the north side of the complex. An even steeper path climbs up from the Thorn Wood, passes a quarry, where an attempt has been made to persuade scarlet acer bushes to grow, then a little conduit house, marked on both old maps, and lastly the service ranges of the Manor. This approach misses the bastions, but leads into what was, in 1626, the outer of two courtyards set axially in front of the main south entrance of the Manor. The dividing wall between the two courts is intact, but has eighteenth-century gate-piers of banded rustication topped with armorial shields where, in 1626, there was a gatehouse. Where the outermost wall of the second court once stood there are only giant eighteenth-century gate-piers at the start of a south drive. The long south front of the Manor is over-restored and disappointing, outclassed by the Steward's House linked to it on the right.

The inner court that fronts the Manor is laid to plain lawns with a thin show of flowers before the balustraded terrace. Formal layouts rarely have the charm of casual organic garden development and it is typical that Hazelbury's excitements and rewards have to be hunted out around corners to the left. Here, facing a picturesque ochre colour-washed west front, is the Croquet Lawn and above it two terraced areas. First comes a Wild Garden, modish but inappropriate in such an enclosed domestic space, then, higher up and cut off by a highly professional herbaceous border, is a long green terrace running along the inside of the fortified wall. To supply the views that this terrace lacks there are steps up to the westernmost of the two bastions, where ashlar upon rubble stone hints at later gentrification of an original military feature. At the other end of the terrace, where it is halted by a wall to a private garden with modern fountain and basin, is Hazelbury's best-known garden feature, the corbelled-out seat supposedly built for the teller (**4**), the scorer, in archery contests held in the forty-pace terrace below. Almost as far away again to the east is the second round bastion.

At the Croquet Lawn another direction could have been taken, down through bushes to the Kitchen Garden, which is a very technical, walled enclosure of disciplined beds and wicker training hoops. As it faces roughly south it is likely to be on its original site, but is nevertheless small for such an extensive complex.

Those are the Tudor or earlier walls of Hazelbury. A reasonable case for the dating of the bastions and the Teller's Seat would accept that the walls and the bastions are low, solid and not battlemented, so the influence was probably that of Henry VIII's coastal cannon forts like Camber. Then the archery trimmings have the playful air of having been designed for games to entertain the ladies; they are too intimate, too near the house to be for serious training. In Queen Elizabeth's reign there was an aristocratic fashion, one encouraged by the Queen, for games of the feudal period, a Spenserian romanticism perfectly exemplified in the *Faerie Queene* castle of Longford, built by a courtier, Sir Thomas Gorges. The Accession Day tilting in November was the high point each year in the rituals of the Court: a time for exquisitely wrought armour, witty armorial puns and mock violence. Hazelbury's upper terrace recalls those trumpets and toy conflicts.

The 3rd Sir John Bonham inherited Hazelbury in 1548, at the end of Henry VIII's reign. He built actively on the north and west sides of the house but died in 1551, too early for romantic Elizabethan gestures. There followed the minority of his son, which was unlikely to have been a building period; then the Manor was sold to Sir John Yonge who completed the building of the western range. That is the likeliest time for the building of the wall and for the archery contests on the terrace. The bastions were definitely in existence in 1626, clearly marked on Allen's survey.

Hazelbury looks backward in its walls, forward in its terraces and in its axially aligned entrance courts, but axially in a medieval spirit with that lost gatehouse, not axial in a Franco-Italian spirit with urns, statues and garden pavilions. It was sold to the Yonges around 1575[14] so, if this speculation over garden dates is accurate, the works would have been roughly contemporary with the far more advanced and Italianate gardens at Longford. However, the social gap between the

4 *The Teller's Seat corbelled out from the garden wall of Hazelbury Manor was for the judge of Elizabethan archery contests on the forty-foot-long terrace below*

two houses was considerable. Hazelbury was on Wiltshire's Cotswold fringe, an area with a very strong vernacular tradition of building, which would linger on as late as the nineteenth century. Its garden walls would, therefore, incline to traditional medieval patterns. The Avon valley around Salisbury was much nearer to London and it had, in Gorges at Longford and the Pembroke earls at Wilton, aristocrats with direct links to the Court and lively political ambitions. As a chalk area it lacked the tradition of masonry and design that characterised the Cotswold limestone belt; it had instead an experimental strain of polychromatic walling with mixed brick, flints and rubble stone. It would be here, in the south of the county, along the Avon that runs into the Solent, not that confusing northern Avon that runs into the Bristol Channel, that garden design would make its decisive move forward into Renaissance forms.

2

John Aubrey and the lady gardeners

There may well have been some rivalry between the parvenu Elizabethan courtier Thomas Gorges, who had bought the old manor house at Longford in 1574, and the lacklustre 2nd Earl of Pembroke, Henry Herbert, at Wilton. The Earl could be described as second generation Wiltshire, though the Herberts were really Welsh in their roots, but royal favour was everything. Gorges had bought Longford with the aim of raising a romantic fantasy castle on the Avon, which Queen Elizabeth could use when she came to hunt at Clarendon or hawk along the Avon's water meadows. Clarendon Palace had fallen into complete decay so this was a shrewd courtier's move, because Longford was midway between the royal forest and Wilton House. So, from the Herberts' point of view, Gorges' purchase was an aggressive intrusion; it cut their Wilton off from a forest which they saw as a natural Herbert territory, with their own Wilton as the proper base for any royal sport in the county.[1]

Whatever the two men, Gorges and Earl Henry, may have felt, the real tension and competitive drive came from their wives, two remarkable women, both with gardening interests. In 1577 Earl Henry married Mary Sidney who was by many years his junior and his third wife. The exact date of her birth is uncertain, but she may have been only sixteen at the time. An exceptionally beautiful souvenir of that wedding still stands in one of Wilton's many gardens, though not on its original site. It is an elegant Italian fountain of white marble with the Sidney porcupine and the Herbert wyvern carved into its middle basin (**colour plate 3**). Apart from that heraldry, it is wholly Mediterranean in feeling, a Renaissance artefact which would be at home in a Tuscan villa. The date of 1577 is usually suggested for it by the family. What matters is its entirely foreign sophistication. It is un-English, un-Tudor, an alien Italian artwork in what, under Countess Mary's direction, was to become the first of two innovative gardens following each other at Wilton under the 2nd, 3rd and 4th Earls.

The other marriage, the one that set up the pair of rivalrous lady garden fanciers, came seven years later, in 1584, when Thomas Gorges married Helena, the dowager Marchioness of Northampton. She was a formidable blonde from Sweden, a minor aristocrat of that country who had come over in 1565 in the train of Celia, Margravine of Baden, on one of the many European embassies attempting to interest Queen Elizabeth in a marriage partner, in this case a Swedish prince. Helena Suavenborg had taken advantage of the occasion to attract and marry the elderly Marquis of Northampton, a brother of Henry VIII's last queen, Catherine Parr. The Marquis soon died, but when she became plain Mrs Gorges, Helena retained her Northampton title and, apparently, her winning ways. Two years later her new husband was knighted and she, as one of the Queen's most influential ladies-in-waiting, persuaded Elizabeth to grant the Gorges the hulk of a Spanish galleon that had been driven ashore after the Armada of 1588. The ship, so the unproven story goes, had a cargo of silver bars, and it was with this treasure that the Gorges were able to raise Longford Castle next to the old manor house, which reverted to service buildings.

A map of 1579 shows the manor house in bucolic seclusion by the side of the river, which has been canalised to produce a defensive moat.[2] The riverbank has a 'Withybede' and a punt tethered for boating expeditions. Further out into the park there is the 'highe orcharde' and 'ye conygre', or rabbit warren. Inside the moated enclosure there were no formal gardens, merely plain grass lawns; but with the construction of the new triple-towered fantasy castle came an equally unusual garden.

It is generally assumed that Longford's three round towers with their symbolism of the Blessed and Indivisible Trinity were a whim of Thomas Gorges, likewise its odd garden buildings. His tomb in Salisbury Cathedral suggests a whimsical, allusive mind by its geometrical conceits and its general air of metaphysical references to be interpreted by the initiated. But that tomb must have been the creation of his wife, who outlived him by many years. He died in 1610, by which time Helena had a national prestige, having served as Chief Mourner at Queen Elizabeth's funeral in 1603. The fact that Gripsholm Castle in Sweden (begun 1537) with its triangular plan and three towers is the obvious model for Longford, virtually proves that Swedish Helena not English Thomas was responsible for the Castle design and also for the garden buildings, which were equally un-English.

There are no traces of that Elizabethan garden surviving on the ground at Longford, but fortunately its unusual features were recorded in eleven engravings of the Castle made around 1680 by Robert Thacker. Equally helpful is the post-Civil War account of the gardens written in a history of the house by the chaplain, the Revd H. Pelate. From these sources it is plain that Longford's grounds were as much of a challenge to the Herberts as was the Castle.

The first structure to impress a visitor riding in across the water meadows would have been the Cheese Gates. These were not gates in any normal sense, but a garden conceit implying power and antiquity, classical not medieval. Two enormous pylons, one on each side of the drive, were flanked by almost equally tall obelisks. If Thacker got his scale right, then, by the human figures he drew next to them, the pylons would have been about twenty-five feet high. Existing gate-piers of the early seventeenth century at Bolsover Castle in Derbyshire suggest that this is not unlikely. Beyond the Cheese Gates was an avenue of sycamore trees three hundred yards long and perfectly straight. Axial Renaissance forms had arrived in an English garden via a blonde Swedish Marchioness. Then came a balustraded bridge over the old moat and, instead of a Gothic gatehouse, there was a weirdly dramatic porter's lodge.[3] This, with its ogee dome supported by paired Doric pilasters flanking the round-arched entryway, was a preparatory conceit before the grand conceit of the Castle itself at the far end of a forecourt.

On the right, stretching below the balustraded terrace on the south front, were the gardens proper. First came a large walled garden, its little parterre lawns and paths set out as a circle within a rectangle, with a statue in each quarter and a punctuation of conical topiary (**5**).[4] This was one of several high-walled, and therefore old-fashioned, enclosures with fashionable planting that Pelate describes: 'my Lord had rebuilt, new modelled the Parterre, and with great cost, first chalked then gravelled the walks'.[5] In addition there was a long terrace walk beside the Avon with a continuous wall of arched topiary work on its landward side. It is just possible that the riverside terrace in the present nineteenth-century garden is a relic of this. The gardens, Pelate adds, had been encouraged to invade the walls of the Castle:

> The vines, before the house was garrisoned, climbed from the garden over the highest towers. The same having been cut down by the soldiers are notwithstanding got up again to the third storey and produce still infinite (and those as generous) grapes as (upon the verdict of many travellers and most exquisite palates) can be tasted anywhere in England. Under these vines (to wit up to the cornice of the first storey) were ingeniously planted the peach, apricot and fig trees to decypher the grace and plenty of the age wherein this house was raised. The variety of fruit and foliage thus weaved together upon one and the same wall looks like a stately piece of forest work hanging round that side of the house.[6]

Thacker's view confirms this description and explains why the entrance front has had to be restored twice since it was built. But it is surprising that fruit trees and vines should have been encouraged to cover walls intended for public show with their chequer-work of flints and Chilmark stone and the grotesque carving of the entry front arcading. Pelate explains unconvincingly that the sycamores of the avenue were 'then not common and (because foreign) much esteemed, though now trees out of fashion'.[7] By the time he was writing limes were popular for avenues.

Longford and its gardens were going up between 1584 and 1591. It would be helpful to have a similar dating for the rival garden at Wilton but, when John Aubrey is the chronicler, accuracy and precision fly out through the window and we are left with lewd anecdotes and spiteful gossip. It seems that, once the 2nd Earl had been made President of Wales and the Marches, he was only too happy to retreat to Ludlow Castle and his Welsh estates, leaving his young, forceful and

Visus Australis ædium Longi Vadi Fontanam Respiciens Simul, ac Floreta. | *The Southside of Longford House, with the Flower garden, & Fountaine.*

5 *Robert Thacker's late seventeenth-century view of the walled South Garden at Longford Castle shows a typical circle in a square formal layout of the period. The sixteenth-century Porter's Lodge is visible on the left and vines are trained up the Castle walls.* Bodleian Library, University of Oxford MS. Gough Maps 33, fol.32 (6)

culturally active wife Mary in charge of Wilton. She was, Aubrey admits, 'a beautiful lady and had an excellent wit, and had the best breeding that that age could afford', but 'She was very salacious', which, he implies, made her much older husband (probably twenty-seven years older) glad to get back to Ludlow.[8] 'In her time Wilton House was like a college, there were so many learned and ingenious persons'.[9] Most unexpectedly, 'she was a great chemist and spent yearly a great deal in that study'[10], though she is better known for her verse additions to her brother, Sir Philip Sidney's, *Arcadia*.[11]

'She kept for her laborator', Aubrey continues, 'in the house Adrian Gilbert . . . who was a great chemist in those days'.[12] Then he adds illogically, 'It was he that made the curious wall about Rowlington Park, which is the park that adjoins to the house at Wilton'.[13] Wall building is not an activity usually associated with chemistry and Aubrey may have got his facts confused. Adrian Gilbert, a half-brother of Sir Walter Raleigh, was Countess Mary's head gardener, the man responsible for Wilton Garden I. In another context Aubrey dismisses him as 'a man of great parts, but the greatest buffoon in England; cared not what he said to man or woman of what quality soever. Some curious ladies of our country have receipts of his'[14], which could suggest that Gilbert was a talented autistic. Our only account of his garden comes, not from Aubrey, but from a minor poet, John Taylor, writing in 1623, *A new Discovery by Sea, with a Wherry from London to Salisbury*. Taylor describes a garden at Wilton laid out 'by the pains and industry of an ancient gentleman, Mr Adrian Gilbert'[15], who would, in 1623, have been over seventy. That still leaves the date of the laying out of Wilton Garden I irritatingly vague, like Taylor's description of the garden.

One feature of Wilton Garden I is clear. Gilbert had taken Longford head-on in matters metaphysical. His grounds were rampageously symbolic, and symbolic, like Longford Castle itself, of the Trinity:

> There hath he made walks, hedges and arbours, of all manner of most delicate fruit trees, planting them and placing them in such admirable art-like fashions, resembling both divine and moral remembrances, as three arbours standing in a triangle, having each a recourse to a greater arbour in the midst, resemble three in one and one in three.[16]

Central to Gilbert's planting was a maze, a commonplace Elizabethan garden device and one most unlikely to impress visitors with any originality:

> He hath made his walks most rarely round and spaceous, one walk without another (as the rinds of an onion are greatest without, and less towards the centre), and withal the hedges betwixt each walk are so thickly set one cannot see through from one walk who walks in the other; that, in conclusion, the work seems endless.[17]

Taylor's last comment was equivocal: 'I think that in England it is not to be followed, or in haste will be followed'.[18] The garden was, as he said, 'every way curiously and chargeably conceited'[19], a moral garden full of horticultural precepts, reeking of religiosity, rather than of the open airs of Renaissance pleasure. Like Longford it was very much a fruit garden; neither flowers nor statues are mentioned, only shapes: 'turning, winding, circular, triangular, quadrangular, orbicular, oval'.[20] Gilbert called his creation 'Paradise', playing himself the role of 'a true Adamist continually toiling and tilling'.[21]

Was this metaphysical and very English-sounding garden of fruit trees and mazes the same garden for which that astonishing, supposedly 1577, Italian fountain was imported? If it was then Wilton was, in that respect, ahead of the Marchioness' clumsy pylons and obelisks at Longford.

One book which should throw light on Wilton's garden is *Arcadia*. Sir Philip Sidney was devoted to his sister Mary and spent much time at Wilton. Brother and sister would often retreat to the small seat of Ivychurch lower down the valley, to be alone and to compose *Arcadia*. This is an enchantingly artificial, pastoral Romance, best described as a prose equivalent of Spenser's *Faerie Queene*, with poems added by the Countess. Aubrey is confident about the interrelation between book and park:

> The *Arcadia* and the *Daphne* is about Ivychurch and Wilton; and these romancy plains and boscages did no doubt conduce to the heightening

of Sir Philip Sidney's fancy. He lived much in these parts, and his most masterly touches of his pastorals he wrote here upon the spot, where they were conceived. 'Twas about these purlieus that the muses were wont to appear to Sir Philip Sidney, and where he wrote down their dictates in his table book, though on horseback.[22]

Aubrey is insistent upon that point, repeating it with, 'This curious seat of Wilton and the adjacent country is an Arcadian place and a paradise'[23], thus echoing Taylor's claim that Gilbert 'called his creation Paradise'. This raises fascinating possibilities. Wilton Garden II, the 4th Earl's creation, was rigidly formal and artificial and his first action would be to destroy Wilton Garden I. So was Wilton Garden I truly 'Arcadian' as we interpret the term, an informal area of natural-seeming but 'improved' woods, fields and streams, with occasional lodges for recreation and privacy and, of course, that marble Italian fountain? Could it have been an anticipation of the Arcadian garden layouts of the mid-eighteenth century?

The assumption here is that Wilton Garden I was the creation, under Henry the 2nd Earl (who ruled from 1570 to 1601), of his wilful and dynamic Countess Mary. In his *Renaissance Garden in England*, Sir Roy Strong believes that Wilton Garden I was laid out for William, the 3rd Earl (ruling from 1601 to 1630). The evidence for both attributions is circumstantial. It is true that John Taylor's account of the garden was written in 1623, when the 3rd Earl had ruled Wilton for twenty-two years. But Taylor is quite certain that 'the pains and industry of an ancient gentleman, Mr Adrian Gilbert' were responsible for the garden's emblematic layout. Gilbert was 'ancient' in 1623, and he is recorded by Aubrey as having been the 'laborator' or assistant in chemical experiments to the 3rd Earl's mother, Mary, at a time far back when she had made Wilton 'like a college'. Aubrey is also quite exact in attributing Wilton's park wall to Gilbert's efforts in Countess Mary's time. Strong links the three-part emblematic planting of Wilton Garden I with Longford Castle's triangularity and with Sir Thomas Tresham's Triangular Lodge at Rushton in Northamptonshire. But both these buildings are of the later sixteenth century, the Countess Mary's time, not the early seventeenth century, the 3rd Earl's time. The Countess was sensitively aware of landscape; there is no evidence that the moody and melancholic 3rd Earl had any such leanings. So the argument must sway towards the earlier date.

There can be little doubt that there was hostility between Wilton and Longford, even though the 2nd Earl's father had been a nephew of the Marchioness' first husband. It was the Marchioness Helena whom the Herberts and the Sidneys really disliked. Sir Philip Sidney aimed sharp arrows of narrative fantasy at the rival house in his *Arcadia*. Longford was the Castle of Amphialus – the son of the wicked, contriving Cecropia, who was the Marchioness. In one episode Sidney's heroine, Pamela, and the other three princesses, her sisters, have been innocently picnicking in the clearing of a wood when a band of armed men seize, bind, gag and blindfold them before dragging them off to where Amphialus' castle 'stood in the midst of a great lake'.[24] There, by torchlight, 'the sisters knew their aunt-in-law Cecropia. But that sight increased the deadly terror of the princesses, looking for nothing but death since they were in the power of the wicked Cecropia, who yet came to them making courtesy the outside of mischief'.[25]

In fairness to the Marchioness another writer, Edmund Spenser, hails her as:

> *. . . the pattern of true womanhed*
> *And our only mirror of feminitee*
> *Worthie after Cynthia [Queen Elizabeth] to tread*
> *As she is nexte her in nobilitie.*[26]

But then Spenser tended to distribute his praise of various noble ladies indiscriminately; he also hailed the Countess Mary as 'Urania, sister unto Astrofell [Sidney] the ornament of woman kind'.[27]

To find out what exactly the topographical ideal of an Arcadian park or countryside was in the 1580s, it is difficult to better Sidney's account of the princesses' innocent picnic:

> There found they in the thickest part of the wood a little square place, not burdened with trees, but with a board covered and beautified with the pleasantest fruits that sunburned Autumn could deliver unto them .
> . . where they did sit and eat and drink a little of their cool wine, which seemed to laugh for joy to come to such lips.[28]

This is an important passage because it proves that gardens and elegant pleasures, enjoyed out of doors in poetically prepared settings, had already become an English upper class ideal. The countryside as a rough, rude and savage place, fit only for hunting and violence, was a fading concept. Another entire century, the seventeenth, with its rigid artificial gardens, all geometry and order, would intervene, and then in the eighteenth century William Kent, significantly an admirer of Edmund Spenser's Arcadian landscapes, would realise the casual, rustic charms that Sir Philip and his sister anticipated back in the 1580s. It is an irony that Philip Herbert, the 4th Earl of Pembroke, should have been the man who introduced the formal garden to England with his Wilton Garden II, when, if the malicious and lubricious Aubrey is to be believed, the Earl was the child of an incestuous affair between these two lovers of informal landscapes, Sir Philip and his sister Mary. However, Aubrey adds with characteristic spite that Earl Philip 'inherited not the wit of either brother or sister'.[29]

At this Elizabethan period it appears that, in Wiltshire at least, strong-minded women were more likely to influence garden design than men. At Amesbury Abbey, on the upper reaches of the Avon, two impossibly romantic 'lodges' or pleasure pavilions still stand, not in the sylvan depths of a leafy park, but alongside a busy main road, offering a rare instance of what the 'lodges' in Sidney's *Arcadia* would have looked like. Both buildings were created at the will and the whim of a dominant wife.

The Countess Mary may have been, as Aubrey claims, 'salacious', but the Countess Catherine of Hertford was a full-blooded femme fatale. She was a daughter of Lord Howard of Bindon, a Dorset branch of the great Howard family. Henry, her elder brother, was a moral monster and she married wilfully the first time a London vintner's son for love. He lasted only a few years and then his beautiful, childless widow became engaged to Sir George Rodney, only to drop him for the wealthier Earl of Hertford, who had become 'entangled of her fair eyes'.[30] Rodney was so distressed that he came to Amesbury, composed and wrote a poem in his own blood, and then fell on his sword like Mark Antony.

Unperturbed, or possibly flattered by his attention, the new Countess Catharine persuaded her husband to settle the enormous sum of £5,000 a year on her for life. With such a fortune she built out on the edge of Amesbury Park two romantic lodges, one inscribed over the door 'Diana Her Hous 1600', the other known as Kent House.[31] Diana's House (6) was probably used as a hunting lodge; Kent House may well have been a love nest or banqueting house. Of turreted charm, Gothic in style, not classical, they recall a passage from Sidney's *Arcadia*, where Basilius, Prince of Arcadia, safely returned from Delphos, 'brake up his court, and retired himselfe, his wife, and children into a certaine Forrest hereby, which he called his desert, wherein . . . he hath builded two fine lodges'.[32] Lodges, bowers and banquet houses also appear frequently in Spenser's *Faerie Queene*, particularly in the Bower of Bliss where Sir Guyon, representing Protestant Temperance, smashes down the 'pleasant bowres and . . .

> *Their groves he feld, their gardins did deface*
> *Their arbers spoyle, their Cabinets suppresse.*
> *Their banket houses burne, their buildings race,*
> *And of the fairest late, now made the fowlest place.*[33]

The Amesbury lodges do not stand as a twinned pair, but are sited around the bend of the road from each other. Both have a pleasing excess of ogee turrets with triangular and octagonal conceits playing around their ground plans. Each has a tall staircase turret with windows to view the hunt and the countryside beyond. Diana's House has three windows in its retaining wall, now blocked, but designed to spy upon visitors approaching from the road. Its principal front, however, commands views of the river flowing by its garden. Kent House acts more conventionally as a very early park gate lodge on a main drive to the Abbey.[34] The hexagonal drawing room at its side is an eighteenth-century addition built over a dairy by the Duchess of Queensberry.[35] Without their Gothic silhouettes it would be easy to imagine the 'lodges' in Sidney's *Arcadia* as small classical temples. In reality they would have been Elizabethan vernacular in form like this Amesbury pair.

If John Aubrey had been as precise and clear in his account of a garden layout as he was over a scandalous liaison, writing about the county's gardens would be easier. Unfortunately he has left garden historians baffled by his account of what was supposedly Wiltshire's last garden in the build up to Inigo Jones' Wilton Garden II. This is the garden that Sir John Danvers laid out behind his house on the main village street of West Lavington. Sir John was a known and influential figure in horticultural circles. His brother Henry, Lord Danby, founded Oxford's Botanical Garden and Sir John's own house and garden at Chelsea had been designed as one integrated unit, with the house facing down into a circular bowling green within a square, the Longford motif. The garden terminated with a grotto sunk into a raised terrace at the far end, between twin garden pavilions.[36] Danvers began that Chelsea garden in 1622; West Lavington came to him as his country seat by his second marriage to Elizabeth Dauntsey of a distinguished Wiltshire family. Aubrey considered the garden Danvers created at West Lavington to be purely Italian and, therefore, very influential, but Aubrey was related to Danvers and was, therefore, not impartial. He was, moreover, though an entertaining writer, hopelessly whimsical and often inaccurate. Aubrey's conclusion to his account of West Lavington says it all: 'It is almost impossible to describe this garden, it is full of variety and unevenness'[37], but enough survives today among the suburban retiree houses of West Lavington to make some sense of the original, 'full of irregularities, both natuyrall and artficiall, elevations and depressions'.[38] The Manor, in pleasant 1908 Jacobethan styling, fronts directly onto the pavement of the village street. Its grounds, covering only a few acres,

6 *'Diana her hous 1600' at Amesbury Abbey. One of two lodges built for pleasure by the wilful Countess of Hertford*

have been made smaller by the selling off of plots for modern housing. They lie north of the street in the shallow valley of a brook. 'Through the length of it', Aubrey wrote, 'there runneth a fine cleare trout stream; walled with brick on each side, to hinder the earth from mouldring down'.[39] Some sections are still walled in brick laid in English bond, as are the stout eight-foot high walls that enclose large sections of the original garden. In its lower reaches the stream has been expanded to create a lakelet, which Aubrey does not mention. Confusingly he does claim:

> a very pleasant elevation on the southside of the garden, which steales, arising almost insensibly, that is, before one is aware, and give you a view over the spatious corn-fields there, and so to East Lavington: where, being landed on a fine levell, letteth you descend again with the like easiness; each side is flanqued by laurels.[40]

If Aubrey had written 'northside' instead of 'southside' this might have made more sense. He has lost his bearings, but is recalling a path through a laurel grove to views of little distinction. What makes the garden interesting and possibly mildly significant, is his claim that in 'this stream are placed severall statues. At the west end is an admirable place for a grotto, where the great arch is, over which now is the market roade'.[41] The statues have gone but the 'great arch' is still impressive with fine grey ashlar spanning the trout stream, walkways on each side and a modern summerhouse beyond. It should be noted, however, that Aubrey writes: 'an admirable place for a grotto'. He does not actually write that a grotto had been created. Nevertheless, the effect of the arch in the great brick garden wall is quite Roman and suggestive of grand possibilities. Aubrey adds that 'About anno 1686', the Earl of Abingdon, who had inherited the house, 'built a noble portico full of water workes, which is on the north side of the garden, and faceth south. It is both portico and grott, and was designed by Mr Rose of Oxfordshire'.[42] There is nothing else of Aubrey's 'irregularities' in the remainder of the grounds, with their tennis courts and a sunken garden below a lawn.

If Sir John Danvers did not gain control until after his marriage in 1628, his improvements, such as they were, must have been almost contemporary with Inigo Jones' Wilton Garden II, but in no way comparable. All that can be said of West Lavington is that it may, by the pleasant lie of the valley land, have satisfied Sir Henry Wotton's ideal, proposed in his 1624 *Elements of Architecture*, that while 'a house should be *regular* a garden should be *irregular*, or at least caste into a very wilde *Regularitie*'.[43] There has to be a suspicion that if John Aubrey ever walked the laurel paths of West Lavington it was after he had dined well and drunk copiously. Sir John Danvers had returned from Italy in 1625 and may have brought some statues with him, but those, a brick-walled stream and a single fine arch, do not amount to an important Franco-Italian garden. Perhaps they were in the Arcadian spirit of Wilton Garden I.

3

Wilton Garden II –
a ghost that still haunts the park

Wilton Garden II is the great ghost that has haunted garden history and caught the imagination of garden enthusiasts ever since it was begun in 1632.[1] Its life span was short. Work on it was probably discontinued when the Civil War broke out in 1642, even though Philip Herbert, the 4th Earl, remained cunningly neutral before siding with Parliament when he was sure which side would win. By 1669, when Magalotti drew the site, the garden was a mere shadow of its original projection, with statues scattered over bare lawns, but the Grotto House was intact.[2] When Stukeley drew the park in September 1723 even the Grotto House had gone.[3] But the first vision of the garden, captured in detailed engravings, possibly drawn by the celebrated French engraver, Jacques Callot, was so vauntingly ambitious, so confident a break away from Tudor garden fashions to Italian and French models like Henry IV's garden layout at St Germain-en-Laye, that Wilton II has never been forgotten. Its memory is kept fresh by a number of sculptures, some naïve, some of an exquisite confidence quite new in English art, that are still to be found in areas private to the family.

Once Earl Philip had succeeded his brother, William the 3rd Earl, in 1630, he shrewdly assessed what was required to gain the royal favour in the new reign and gardened accordingly. He was not a sympathetic character by modern standards, but someone who had been familiar with Shakespeare, patronised liberally artists of the calibre of Anthony van Dyck and Inigo Jones, and flirted profitably with King James to gain the earldom of Montgomery to add to that of Pembroke, hardly needed to be conventionally sympathetic. He was quarrelsome, treated his wife, the stately Anne Clifford, badly, and betrayed his King. But he was a wise politician in exceptionally difficult times; he kept the Pembroke estates together, free from fines, and left Wilton house with one of the earliest and most satisfying Palladian façades in Britain. If an example of an English aristocrat in the good and bad senses of the term is needed then Philip Herbert fits that requirement perfectly.

King James I could be won by hunting, soft fruit and handsome young men. His son Charles was completely different. Small, sensitive, obstinate and a devout

Christian, he loved Italian paintings, a decorous, civilised lifestyle and, after an interval for assessment, he loved his French wife, Henrietta Maria, daughter of Henry IV, the first Bourbon on the throne of France. Queen Henrietta is the key to that second Wilton garden. A French Catholic princess would automatically despise the cultural levels of Protestant England. It is in the blood; no country loves its immediate neighbour. But Earl Philip had contrived to pass himself off to the King as a fellow art lover and Charles was inclined to visit Wilton most summers for its congenial atmosphere. As Lord Chamberlain, Earl Philip was anxious initially to encourage royal favour so he commissioned the King and Queen's favourite architect, Inigo Jones, to design a twenty-one-bay new range for Wilton, which would provide separate state apartments for the royal pair. This monster, one of Inigo's least impressive designs, was never built, but was fined down through two further design stages to something very near to the present, flawless South Front.

Unfortunately, as soon as the twenty-one-bay palace had been projected, though not a stone laid, the Earl began to lay out Wilton Garden II to fit that palace design in width (**7**). It was a near imperial scheme, but one that would eventually, after the economies, have only a modest nine-bay house at the head of it. Inigo's new garden never quite recovered from this false start, but the Earl went ahead. To be Italian, artistic and, at the same time, amusing to lesser spirits, it would have fountains and naked statues supplied by Nicholas Stone, who had trained in Holland, but carved better than his Dutch schooling might suggest. For

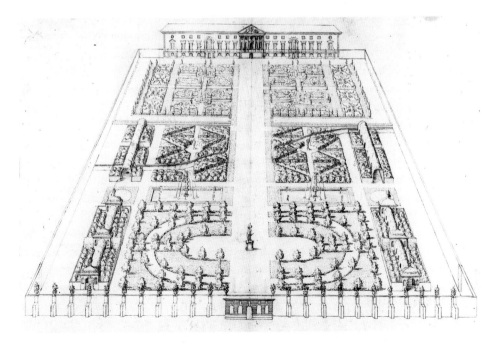

7 *In this 1632 drawing the proposed 'Grand Design' for Wilton House fronts the Parterres, Wilderness and Grove of Inigo Jones' three-part Franco-Italian garden, with a façade of Isaac de Caus' Grotto House in the foreground.* The Provost and Fellows of Worcester College, Oxford

fun and practical jokes there had to be an Italian-style Grotto House with all the latest hydraulic devices, birds that whistled tunes, figures that moved and appeared to chase each other, and a rainbow fountain.

Salomon de Caus, the author of the 1615 *Les Raisons des Forces Mouvantes*, had been the hydraulics expert in the previous reign. Now Isaac de Caus, his son or nephew (no one is ever quite sure which) was at hand to carry on the family business. Inigo designed both the new South Front and the garden but, being occupied in London, he left Isaac de Caus to act as clerk of works and to deliver a thoroughly entertaining set of hydraulic toys for the Grotto House.

The garden was designed with three sectors: parterres, grove and ornamental orchard, but the engravings for the layout in *Wilton Garden*, published haphazardly during the Civil War[4], are neither in Jones' fussy style nor Isaac de Caus' crude, incompetent hand. They are witty and assured enough, with their enchanting staffage of women and children, old men with walking sticks and dashing cavaliers, to have been drawn by Jacques Callot. Jones had copied a Callot engraving, 'The Parterre du Palais de Nancy' (**8**), etched in 1625, when he needed a garden scene for his masque *The Shepherd's Paradise*, performed before the Court in 1631. So it would have been in his mind when Wilton Garden II was begun in 1632. But, with a superior and highly critical French woman to please Jones may have gone directly to a French source and asked Callot to etch a truly French garden on agreed lines.

Sir Roy Strong in his *The Artist and the Garden* attributes the entirely professional and exquisitely detailed etchings of the garden in *Wilton Garden* to Isaac de Caus, whose only other known designs, those for the Wilton Grotto House illustrated in John Harris and A.A. Tait's catalogue of architectural drawings at Worcester College, Oxford, can only be described as incompetent scrawls.[5] Even more questionably, Strong attributes the design of Wilton's matchless South Front to de Caus while well aware that de Caus did definitely design the clumsy reshaping of the stables at Wilton on the other side of the river. Scholarship has moved on since Strong published his *Renaissance Garden in England* in 1979. This legend of Isaac de Caus as a major Stuart designer is slow to die, even though Sir Howard Colvin, who launched it back in 1954, has now disowned it.[6]

Grand as it was, there are some curious design faults to what Inigo projected for Wilton. Because Henry IV's garden at St Germain-en-Laye was on a steep slope, the trees in its middle 'Wilderness' or 'Grove' sector would not have obscured significantly the view from the chateaux's terraces of the third sector at the bottom of the hill. Wilton's garden, however, was laid out over an almost dead flat valley floor and the Grove in the second sector would have hidden the formal orchard of cherry trees in the third sector from the windows of the house. The Grotto House, constructed within a broad terrace at the end of that third sector, would not have been obscured because it lay at the end of the wide axial walk linking all three sectors. It was possibly to overcome a potential visual block in the Grove that Inigo Jones added, to his third, and actually realised, design for the house, two tall viewing pavilions or banqueting houses on the roof.

Ce dessein façonné des honneurs des printemps, . . Cest uostre aage, Madame où les douceurs encloses Qui pousseront sans fin des doux-flairantes roses
E moliue dobiech de diuers passetemps; 'Nous sont autant de Fleurs, ou 'Rosiers precieux Dont l'odeur aggrera aux hommes et aux Cieux

8 *In 1631 Inigo Jones borrowed many features from this 1625 engraving by Jacques Callot, 'The Parterre du Palais de Nancy', for a stage back shutter and then used it again in 1632 for Wilton Garden and eventually for Wilton House*

Another oddity in the garden design was the way it entirely ignored the best feature of the terrain, the clear flowing River Nadder. Instead of making a feature of the Nadder with cascades, canalised sections and basins, the design simply left the Nadder to wind its way, obscured from sight, among the trees of the Grove. On the west side of the layout a long covered walk of topiary is shown apparently bridging the river. How topiary could have been persuaded to grow and arch six feet high out of tubs on a bridge is not explained. That main axial walk crosses the Nadder, but not on an ornamental bridge. The river seems to be culverted, an impratical solution in a flood. It is almost as if the garden designer had never walked the landscape in person, but was designing blind. Callot, if he had been left to fill in the details, would have been in that situation. The three sectors are supposed to have had an iconographical programme. The first sector of parterres and fountains represented Love with statues of Cleopatra, Venus and other well-known love objects. Fertility was evoked in the Grove with its two large statues, the finest of Stone's works, of Flora and Bacchus representing wheat and wine. Bacchus carries a baby in his arms, which is not one of the god's usual symbols. Lastly, with its centrally placed statue of 'the Gladiator in brass the most famous Statue of all that Antiquity hath left'[7], the third sector represented War. Its two fountains, though considered great marvels

33

of ingenuity in their time, had unfortunate symbolic prognostications. They were in the form of tall columns with blocked rustication, each encircled by a coronet, denoting the power of the Pembroke earls, and those two coronets could be made to wobble uncertainly up and down the columns by blasts of water squirting out from the fountain basin.

In his account of Wilton's garden, with all its confusing factual errors, Aubrey explains the power that drove, not only the many fountains, but the hydraulic toys in the Grotto House next to Hubert Le Sueur's bronze Gladiator:

> By the kitchin garden is a streame which turns a wheele that moves the engine to raise water to the top of a cisterne at the corner of the great garden, to serve the water works of the grotto.[8]

It was the Grotto House that made Wilton Garden II so celebrated and so much visited. Facing down the central axial route with its richly rusticated, three-bay portico of niches and statues it must have concentrated the eye as soon as visitors left the house. Aubrey was clearly captivated by its watery drama:

> On either side of the said portico is an ascent leading up to the terrasse, upon the steps whereof, instead of ballasters, are sea monsters, casting water from one to the other, from the top to the bottome; and above the sayd portico is a great reserve of water for the grotto.[9]

But having reached the terrace the visitors would be standing on the roof of the Grotto House with most of the discoveries and marvels still to be explored. Descending the sea monster steps they would find in the shadowy, practical joke-ridden interior that, 'The grotto is paved with black and white marble; the roof is vaulted. The figures of tritons & etc. are in bas-relieve, of white marble excellently well wrought'.[10] This last remark is an understatement. Nicholas Stone's work is indeed of the very highest quality; Wilton was introducing the English to the true standards of Italian Renaissance art. It is likely, however, that anyone inspecting the tritons would suffer a thorough wetting from hidden pipes. 'Here', Aubrey continues, 'is a fine jedeau and nightingale pipes'[11], all part of the ritual of the visit. At the same time that they were being soaked, visitors were being forcefully introduced to the marvels of applied hydraulic science, which may have been some compensation. 'The grott and pipes did cost £10,000', Aubrey adds respectfully.[12] To put that into perspective the 4th Earl's annual income in 1638 would have been £30,000, from which he had to support 'one hundred and twenty Family uprising and down lyeing'[13]; so the Grotto House must have been considered an essential prestige symbol.

The wheel, mill, kitchen garden and a big pool for fish were all upstream to the west of the house. Across the Nadder from them were, and remain today, the clumsy Serlian Mannerist brick stables, Isaac de Caus' surviving monument.

Beyond the terrace and the Grotto House the garden continued with avenues of trees. Cut into the hillside just off the central axial walk was an Echo, an amphitheatre contrived acoustically to magnify and flatter the human voice. There was a famous example of such a feature in Paris in the gardens of the Luxembourg, home to the Queen Mother, so this would have been intended as a further device to charm Henrietta Maria.[14] An elegant flight of moonsteps led into the Echo on the engraving. At an unknown date in the seventeenth century, while formal gardens were still the fashion, a triumphal arch was built up on the hilltop to carry the equestrian statue of Marcus Aurelius, moralist, writer and almost Christian Roman Emperor. This now stands on the triumphal arch that Sir William Chambers designed for it in 1759. James Wyatt brought both arch and statue down in the first decade of the nineteenth century to serve as the grand entrance to Wilton house from the main Salisbury road.

Such was the scale, at least half a mile in length, and the complexity of Wilton Garden II. It will be seen that those four parterres in the first sector would alone have employed a whole team of gardeners. The sector was twice the width of the present South Front and stretched as far as the Nadder. But the whole philosophy behind such formal layouts was an assertion of Man's orderly and geometrically precise control over Nature, which could explain why the designer had ignored and hidden the course of the river. Accounts by visitors and their sketches still leave us in some doubt as to how accurately the garden teams of the 4th Earl actually carried through the grand design of the engravings. Magalotti's and Stukeley's views of a very pared down and modified layout have been mentioned. What is not in any doubt is that the 4th Earl spent a fortune on statuary. Nothing was skimped there, and it was for its daringly un-English show of 'nakeds' as much for its practical water jokes that the garden became nationally famous.

The first recorded tourist was Lieutenant Hammond, who visited in 1635 when the garden was laid out, but when work on the South Front was only just beginning and the hydraulic marvels of the Grotto House were not yet functioning.[15] Hammond did, however, have the privilege of being taken around, by Isaac de Caus in person. He describes him as 'the fat Dutch keeper thereof, a rare Artist'. As the de Caus family came from a part of France close to the border with Flanders the error is excusable; Isaac probably spoke English with a Dutch rather than a French accent; de Caus could be a French version of the Flemish de Kock. Hammond gives the impression of being in a state of lecherous excitement. In each of the four parterre squares was a fountain with a nude statue of a woman. He reported gleefully: 'in one is Venus with her sonne Cupid in her Armes (**9**); in another Diana with her bathing sheet; in a third is Susanna pulling a thorn out of her Foote; and in the fourth Cleopatra with the Serpent'. He added lustfully that 'with the turning of Cockes' there was 'washing and dashing the Eyes and Thighs of faire Venus and Diana'. He had little to report of the Grove so it may not have been planted out in 1635, while the 'fayre House of Freestone', the Grotto House with its marble reliefs by Nicholas Stone, was not yet working,

9 *The eyes and thighs of fair Venus were once dashed by a fountain in the parterre of Wilton Garden. Nicholas Stone was the sculptor. She now stands in the forecourt of Wilton House*

though Isaac promised that later there would be 'the Singing and Chirping of Birds and other strange rarities'.

Isaac de Caus was paid a pension to stay on at the house and demonstrate those 'rareties' to visitors. In 1644 he published an entirely plagiaristic book, *Nouvelle Invention de lever l'eau plus hault que sa source*, its text and its illustrations simply filched from Salomon de Caus' *Raison des Forces*.[16] At roughly the same time he brought out *Wilton Garden* or *Le Jardin de Vuilton*, with a brief text in English and French and many illustrations including the problematic engravings of the garden. At no point did he give any credit to Inigo Jones and his dishonesty has caused some confusion in twentieth-century accounts of what went on at Wilton in those years. De Caus died in Paris in 1648 and with him, the ever sentimental Aubrey noted, the secret of how to work the rainbow fountain of the Grotto House died too.

John Evelyn toured the garden in 1654 when it should have been in its prime. He was a great enthusiast for 'Ventiducts, Waterworks for Musicall especially and other motions (to ye Vulgar stupendous) devices by various casting reflecting and breaking of lights and shadows . . . and other Italian gloryes pompous beautys'.[17] But unexpectedly he gave Wilton a withering description:

The Garden (heretofore esteem'd the noblest in all England) is a large handsome plaine with a *Grotto* & Waterworks, which might be made much more pleasant were the *River* that passes through, clensed & raised, for all is effected by a mere force: it has a flower garden not inelegant: But after all, that which to me renders the Seate delightfull, is its being so neere the downes & noble plains about the Country & contiguous to it.[18]

These were fair judgements, but Evelyn still included Wilton as first among England's ten greatest gardens when he ranked them in 1660. In preferring Nature to artifice Evelyn seems to be anticipating the more relaxed garden fashions of the next century. Once Newton had demonstrated that Nature was God's perfectly functioning machine there would be no point in disciplining it with straight lines.

When Celia Fiennes, another active garden critic, reached Wilton in 1685 she was in no mood to appreciate the rareties of the Grotto House, though they were still clearly in good working order.[19] There were still many statues and 'many gravel walkes with grass squaires', but none of the flowers Evelyn had admired, and the topiary had all gone. When she entered the Grotto House she noted disapprovingly that 'a sluce spouts water up to wett the Strangers'. In the central

10 *Nicholas Stone's relief of a Triton was carved for an inner chamber of Isaac de Caus' Grotto House. It is now in the private Italian Garden at Wilton*

room water spouted up into 'the hollow carving of the roof', to descend 'in a shower of raine all about the roome', and, of course, all over Celia. Statues in the niches 'weep water on the beholders' and when the song of birds lured the unwary into another room to discover the source there was 'a line of pipes that appear not till by a sluce moved it washes the spectators'. It was, she wrote grudgingly, 'designed for diversion'.

What should not be forgotten is that all these seemingly childish devices – optical, acoustic and just plain wetting – were positive signs that science was coming to grips with practical realities that could be applied to machinery. There was a device for sawing logs in the de Caus books and another for fire fighting. The Industrial Revolution was being tried out in noblemen's gardens. Soon the new aesthetic approaches to Nature would make Inigo and Isaac's Wilton Garden II look childish, but in its time it was a true mirror to its experimental age.

While bowing to horticultural fashions of the new age and creating a garden in the liveliest spirit of the Rococo, the Pembroke earls, to their great credit, retained a wise respect for the statuary of Nicholas Stone and for the riotous grotesque work carved into the walls of the Grotto House. Unfortunately, for safety, most of Stone's carving is now kept in areas of the garden not open to the public, and that has prevented his oeuvre from receiving its proper due of praise. The Herberts had an impressive record of patronage in the arts before Wilton Garden II was projected. There had been that elegant marble fountain of around 1577 and, even earlier, at some time soon after 1548, when William, the 1st Earl, was given the Order of the Garter, the sumptuously decorated porch was built which Aubrey, inaccurate as ever, attributed to Holbein. That, for all its beauty, is English and mannered; the fountain is not, neither are the reliefs of nymphs, tritons and Europa on her bull that Nicholas Stone carved to the clumsy cartoons of Isaac de Caus (**10**).[20] These reliefs are of a truly assured and delicate Renaissance confidence like the carvings of the Quattrocentro that can be hunted out in Italian hill cities like Perugia or Orvieto. They are now inset into a wall in Westmacott's Loggia, facing the Elizabethan fountain at the centre of the late nineteenth-century 'Italian Garden'. A little further west towards the Holbein Porch, which was re-sited as a garden pavilion in 1826, are the two coronet columns from the third sector of Wilton Garden II (**11**). It is valuable to have these still with us as they give an exact impression of the scale of those seventeenth-century garden works. They are roughly sixteen feet tall.

Most impressive of all are Stone's Flora and Bacchus and Child. For protection, they have been built securely into the parapet of Westmacott's 1826 Image Bridge over the Wylye just above that point where the Wylye and Nadder meet. They gain enormously by the beauty and oddity of their setting. Bacchus, crowned with grapes, quite nude and carrying a naked child on his shoulders looks out up river. But the subtlety of Stone's composition is best seen from the Bridge where the handling of the child's foot as it presses into the concave of the god's back (**12**) would be world famous if it had been rescued from the sea and was a treasure of the Greek national museum in Athens. Being provincial work by an Anglo-

Dutchman of the early seventeenth century it has no fame. Flora, with her skirt split up to the thigh and her left breast exposed, has the same sensuous unpredictability of modelling. She holds a wreath of flowers, which she has taken from her head as if to salute the watcher.

If these are pure Attic invention, then the carving which has survived from the walls of the Grotto House is indigestible, but enjoyable, Mannerism. It was moved first to the Pavilion on an eighteenth-century dam made by the 9th Earl, who fancied a lake in the grounds. The Pavilion in no way resembled the original Grotto House; it was just a jumble of unrelated carved fragments on a three-bay pedimented structure. When the carvings were moved again to their present site, Park School House, their jumbled formation was retained intact (**13**). Vitruvian scrolls twine around the windows, bizarre women sit on top of its Corinthian capitals and lines of carving similar to those on Indian totem poles criss-cross its pediment. It may look like a lodge for deranged goblins, but it is also clearly now a most desirable single-storey residence tucked away in a leafy corner of the estate. If the interior decoration of the Grotto House was anything like the façade of Park School House then it must have produced a defiantly anti-classical atmosphere.

11 *One of the two coronet columns from fountains between Wilton Garden's Wilderness and its Grove. Water jets once forced a metal coronet up and down at the top*

12 *Nicholas Stone's Bacchus and Child, originally sited in the Wilderness, now stands on the Image Bridge over the Wylye*

13 *The façade of Park School House is set with Mannerist fragments of stone that were originally part of Wilton's Grotto House, then sited on the eighteenth-century dam Pavilion and finally jumbled up here*

In their usual thrifty style the Pembrokes have recently re-used some of those statues representing Love from the first sector of Wilton Garden II. The present Earl has re-assembled them in a curious rectangle of greenery immediately before his front door. The statues have nothing like the quality of the Grotto House reliefs or Flora and Bacchus, but they can be identified as seventeenth-century originals from the formal garden by detailed plates in *Wilton Garden*. To animate them all and remind them of their first watery setting, the Earl has dropped a violently whirling fountain into the rectangle as a memorial to his father. The resultant swirl of water may not be supremely aesthetic, but it is memorable, and for anyone to re-activate in the twentieth century the artefacts of a seventeenth-century ancestor is commendably traditional. Wilton's gardens are still alive and unpredictable.

There is one postscript that, in scholarly fairness, must be added to this paean of praise to Wilton and the Herberts. Wilton Garden II is not quite as ground-breaking and original as it is usually claimed to be. One advantage of researching the gardens of several counties is that one tends to make unexpected parallels. While researching my *Historic Gardens of Dorset* in 2002, I noticed that Lulworth Castle seemed to have had a three-part formal garden exactly like Wilton Garden II; parterres, wilderness, orchard and a building on an axial centre line, also a host of small pavilions. And while Wilton Garden II was not begun until 1632, Lulworth had its park, largely complete, by 1615 when King James I was being entertained there by its loveably villainous owner, his Lord High Treasurer, Thomas Howard, a most tremendous cheat in money matters, but a hero of the 1588 Spanish Armada.[21]

The question must be: did Inigo Jones have any knowledge of the Lulworth layout when Wilton Garden II was planned? Both gardens were designed to ensnare the favour of Stuart kings. Lulworth's problem was that it did not have a secure family like the Herberts to guard its fame. No illustration was made of its grounds until 1721, and then nothing to touch the Wilton engravings.[22] The Howards abandoned Lulworth in 1641 and the Castle fell into the hands of the recusant Welds. The Herberts kept a check on their expenses and stood firm; Wilton today is the proof of their providence and their taste.

4

Caroline formalism and the rude shock of Longleat

Between the Caroline gardens of Charles I and the Carolean gardens of Charles II's reign, there is the difference between the Italian and the Franco-Dutch influences. That may seem illogical as it was Charles I who had a strong-willed French queen; but it was in his reign that the great Gonzaga collection of paintings from Mantua came to Whitehall and Hampton Court. It was a Caroline aristocrat, the Earl of Arundel, the most prestigious peer in the land, who collected sculpture from Italy, toured that country with Inigo Jones, and set up the Arundel marbles in his London town house. Charles I was never in thrall to France as Charles II was; indeed for much of his reign France itself was in political uncertainty. It was Charles II who had to cope with Louis XIV at the height of his power, and accept a French mistress, Louise de Keroualle, a French pension and extravagant French garden gestures.

Because the gardens at Wilton were not only on a very grand scale, but laid out on level country, they tended to underplay their essential Italian structure of three separate areas with a Grotto House. Ideally they should have been on three distinct level terraces cut into a hillside. That is what the well-travelled Evelyn family had achieved at their seat, Wotton Place, Surrey in 1652, during the Commonwealth. Wotton, with its Doric Temple-Grotto in the middle terrace, was a gesture of loyalty to the exiled monarchy: a garden in a style King Charles I had approved, not in the Commonwealth model of horticultural experiment.[1] Wotton's garden is well known; what is much less known is that a royalist family in Wiltshire had, in those dark years before the royal cause triumphed, made another Italian-style garden of composed charm at Hatch House, near Tisbury. It can be seen as the climax and end result of a series of less successful gestures in the same direction in other parts of the country.

In the County Record Office and in various private collections there is a wealth of plans, drawings, surveys and paintings that illustrate how richly endowed the area once was in experimental, semi-formal garden layouts that could be described, politely, as 'bucolic', or, accurately, as amateur and amusing.[2] Most of these gardens have been swept away; in a few some traces remain.

In what survives of Wiltshire's formal gardens and in those frustrating maps and plans of lost layouts, it is possible to detect quite early a theme of rebellion against too much discipline. John Aubrey himself, in the last years of the Commonwealth, before he had to abandon Easton Piercy and flee his creditors, designed an eminently enjoyable garden 'al Italiano' as he would have called it, that rejected both French and Dutch formalism.[3] He is unlikely to have laid a single turf of it, but the careful picture which he drew for it makes a fascinating comparison with another Wiltshire garden of the same period that survives, virtually intact, at Bolehyde Manor, only a mile or two across the fields from Easton Piercy.

Aubrey drew a perfect Italian villa garden of three terraces (**14**). Steps led down from the *piano nobile* of the villa to a narrow first terrace of lawn bordered with conical shrubs. Below this, down a walled, fifteen-foot drop was the second terrace with a deep, arched recess and a small fountain. A sideways flight of steps brought visitors, who had apparently jumped down the first stage, to the third level. Here Aubrey had concentrated what he, thinking basically in a pre-flower stage of garden making, thought of as garden delights: two arched grottoes and a circular fountain pool lined with conical bushes. After that climax, further steps led down through a wilderness of low shrubs. It was orderly, manageable if a head of water was available, and would have provided diverting discoveries and places to sit at leisure. That was his ideal.

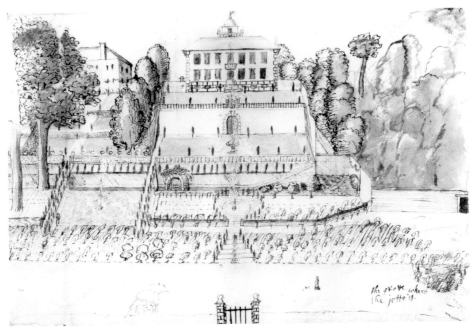

14 *John Aubrey drew his ideal villa and garden, 'al Italiano', for Easton Piercy, with three terraces, three fountains and three grottoes around 1660, just before his finances collapsed.* Bodleian Library, University of Oxford MS. Aubrey, 17, fol.5r

To appreciate the gap between Aubrey and reality it is only necessary to follow the rough field track west of that jaunty, high-stacked, seventeenth-century vernacular house, which he never got around to demolishing. It will become evident from the field behind it, where a long, shallow slope ends in a wet ditch, that to achieve his terraces he would have needed a JCB to change the entire topography.

At Bolehyde Manor we can experience true seventeenth-century realities, with charmingly picturesque features applied from time to time to an existing medieval chequerboard of walled enclosures, a truly organic garden growth. The sixteenth-century manor house was bought in 1635, the year when Lieutenant Hammond visited Wilton, by John Gale, and the Gale family, a squire dynasty of prosperous sheep farmers, lived in the house until 1927, which explains its happy survival. A bend in the lane brings the whole complex, house, garden and garden buildings into sight, open to the public gaze and welcoming inspection (**15**). Overlooking the lane are twin garden pavilions of around 1690 with a section of a medieval moat that has been retained as a mini-canal. Just visible behind walls and a tree to the south of the house is a second and earlier set of twin pavilions (**16**), jewels of formal misconception and dating, probably, to the 1630s.

Everything about this earlier pair is wrong. Whoever built them had heard that garden fashion required an axial line with symmetrical features, but an axial line to what? Instead of leading to the lane, this primitive pair point out south from the manor house courtyard into open fields. When first built they had an avenue of trees leading nowhere to give them a spurious significance. Such twin pavilions were a typical Elizabethan garden feature, but they are curiously rare in Wiltshire yet common in neighbouring counties. They offered privacy to the family, refuge

15 *The front garden at Bolehyde Manor with its late seventeenth-century pair of gazebos leading to the house. One has Dutch-style murals of ships*

16 *Privies or stables? The earlier sixteenth-century pavilions at Bolehyde – a bucolic attempt at formal gardening*

from servants' eyes and views of passing travellers. But the Gales had not grasped their function. These pavilions afford no views out over the lane and each small building has two doors on its inner façade to the courtyard. Christopher Hussey suggests ingeniously that the Gales used them as stables, but they could just as easily have been privies. Would four privies have been necessary?

Then, one Gale generation later, the proper function has been grasped. Overlooking the lane is the second pair of pavilions, more polite than vernacular in style with neat stone-tiled roofs and intended as gazebos. Inside one is a chimneypiece for road watching on cold days or assignations on cold evenings and very rare murals of seventeenth-century ships partly preserved on the wall plaster. Gale family tradition had it that these were the work of a Dutch artist who came over after 1688 with William of Orange, which is perfectly possible.[4] By 1688 the axial notion would have been understood, but to give this second pair a correct viewing line a little garden had to be created across the road. This originally had mulberry trees, but it has been abandoned.

The chequerboard of walled enclosures has, inevitably, been romanticised by post-1927 owners, but the original functionalism of these spaces, serving as orchard, vegetable garden, herb garden can be easily imagined. Bolehyde seems to have lived in a time warp of the unexpected. Though it is sited in open countryside a 500lb German bomb fell on it in the Second World War. Was it the HQ of an American general? Andrew Parker Bowles, his wife Camilla and their family lived here for a while, and at the end of one wall the statue of a lady, locally known as Anne Boleyn, looks out through a porthole in a beech hedge. Hussey, to complicate the attribution, believed that it was a Roman statue unearthed in the area.[5]

The present owners, Earl and Countess Cairns, have handled the grounds tactfully and on NGS days visitors can, if they ignore the admirable flower borders, experience a bucolic Wiltshire formalism in these grounds better than anywhere else in the county. The experience will make sense of several garden plans of lost layouts. Old Southbroom House, the Drew family home, was at the heart of just such an engaging confusion of formal gesture as Bolehyde.[6] An estate survey of the very early eighteenth century (**colour plate 8**) shows the house standing, for all its 286 acres, right on the edge of a public road, just like Bolehyde.[7] The urge for seclusion, the Stourhead 'Procul O Procul Este Profane' syndrome of the mid-eighteenth century had not yet set in. Landowners still relished belonging to the community they directed. South of the house are four elaborately geometrical parterres and a vast yew hedge clipped into castellations. In the late seventeenth century England was enjoying Marlborough's victories over the French and military reminders were popular.[8] At one end of the hedge is a high-domed garden pavilion overlooking a lane on one side and, on the other, tall gate-piers to a long double avenue of trees leading to nowhere. Avenues became common after John Evelyn published his *Sylva* in 1664, emphasising not only the beauty of a handsome lime avenue, but its value as a future investment. Those early pavilions at Bolehyde would look more rational if their avenue had been replanted after felling. The Drews of Southbroom were as obsessed by gate-piers as the Gales were by pavilions. There are three sets of gate-piers on the survey, all polite status symbols. Between the four parterres and a fifth parterre closer to the house is a pavilion with four 'poles' around it, probably four clipped yews, also a formally planted orchard and a bowling green. As at Bolehyde, an Elizabethan garden complex has been given formal touches, but no grand scheme has been applied, though there is a suspiciously symmetrical array of six hedged fields around that long tree avenue.

Bolehyde began to evolve into uncertain formality in 1635; Southbroom with its avenues and gate-piers has a Caroline feeling, of perhaps 1670, but rustic and unsure. In between the two, firmly dated to 1659 on its garden seat, is the layout at Hatch House and here the garden is in no way uncertain or fumbling, but a resolved, confident and attractive composition in the Caroline Italian style of the old reign. It was the loyal creation of the Hyde family which, like Sir Robert Shirley, who built a church at Staunton Harold, Leicestershire in 1653, did 'ye best things in ye worst times and hoped them in the most calamitous'.[9] But whereas Sir Robert died miserably in the Tower in 1656 for his daring, the Hydes would be abundantly rewarded. One son of the family, born at Hatch, became Earl of Clarendon and the grandfather of two reigning Queens of England: Mary, wife of William of Orange, and Anne, the last Stuart.

Their house is one of a line of country seats on that favoured south-facing slope above the Sem and Nadder valley, almost a suburb of gentry with Pythouse next door, Fonthill nearby and Wardour just across the way. Hatch's approach drive is the same now as it was in 1816 and a visitor arrives alongside the back garden before struggling to find the front door. In 1908 Detmar Blow completely revised and revamped what had become by then an L-shaped farmhouse.[10] He also restored the Commonwealth garden, which is probably why its originality and importance have not been as widely recognised as they should be. But an early photograph at the house proves that Blow only tidied up and repaired the steps to the perfectly scaled garden that had survived the years.[11]

Hatch House garden is quite simple; its designer knew exactly what was wanted. Here are no boxy walled enclosures opening one out of another. A wide exact rectangle faces the west garden front of the house (**17**). It is divided precisely in two by a path with low rusticated piers and steps climbing up to a three-sided terrace whose supporting walls are lined at regular intervals by the time-worn busts of Roman emperors (**18**).[12] One of these last reveals its early date, like a contemporary at Waterston in Dorset, by its Cavalier-style moustache. Central to the tripartite terrace is an arched summerhouse, Hatch's equivalent of a grotto. It is set back, cave-like, into the garden's rear wall and its details are completely classical with an acanthus frieze and a waterleaf carved cornice. In its overall aspect the summerhouse is perhaps more grim than welcoming and its 1659 wooden seat is crudely carved, as if by a Jacobean rather than a Caroline joiner. The real pleasure of the garden, and one that needs to be experienced in order to appreciate its harmony, is the way in which the green lawned terrace commands the views down into the valley and across to Wardour. It is a 'pleasaunce' in the true sense of the word.

Detmar Blow made a Croquet Lawn, hedged with yew to the north of this garden, but around the north-east of the house is the wreck of a very old yew hedge, probably dating back to 1659, which has grown quite out of control. After the two yews at Sheldon Manor this could be the county's oldest garden hedge.

The question immediately arises: how did the rural Hydes achieve a garden of such good Italian manners? The answer must be through Henry, third son of Lawrence Hyde. Pay no attention to the bronze plaque attached to Blow's loggia. All its facts are incorrect.[13] Lawrence Hyde, founder of the family fortunes, was born at Norbury in Cheshire and died in 1590 at Hatch. He made his money as an auditor at the Treasury working for Sir John Thynne of Longleat. The third of his six sons, Henry, travelled extensively in Italy and became friendly with Cardinal Allen, an English member of the Sacred College. This suggests, at the very least, strong Catholic sympathies. He settled first in Dinton, then at Purton in 1625. He would have gained first-hand experience of Italian gardens and advised his elder brother Edward on how to plan one.[14] His own son Edward, the future Earl of Clarendon, was born at Dinton in 1599, and it was Edward's daughter Mary who married James, Duke of York, the future King James II, producing two daughters, Mary and Anne. If that branch of the Hydes had Catholic sympathies, inherited from Henry, it would help to explain why James was persuaded to make an honest woman of Mary, as he was himself militantly Catholic. The daughters, however, inherited the throne purely on the strength of their Protestantism – an odd paradox.

17 *Looking east to Detmar Blow's reconstructed Hatch House from the terrace of its 1659 formal garden – Caroline design surviving into the Commonwealth*

18 *One of the time-worn Caesars on the terrace at Hatch House*

Hatch House garden is entirely un-Carolean in that it had no associated avenues until much later. King Charles II set a disastrous example at St James' Park in 1661 and at Hampton Court a year later, laying out long straight canals and long straight avenues of trees, all based on his experience in the years of Commonwealth exile of French and Dutch garden practice. A grand canal gesture impresses for a few minutes and then bores for hours. An elaborate parterre reduces the individual impact of a flowering plant and requires a troop of gardeners to weed, snip and coax it into order. It was all misconceived and it was generally to England's national credit that we led the Continent out of this authoritarian tedium into the 'English Gardens' of wandering sylvan paths, casual lakes and diverse picturesque garden buildings for discoveries, picnics and alfresco living.

A telling example of the sterility of formal gardening in Wiltshire was recorded in the view Sir William Pynsent, who died in 1719, had made of the entrance garden to his trim William and Mary-style manor house at Urchfont.[15] This was no place for discoveries or alfresco living. Two straight lines of cypress trees led from a rectangular pond to the east front of the house. Between them were five equally straight gravel walks separated by narrow lawns and punctuated by bay bushes in urns set on stone pedestals. There the Pynsent garden inventions ended. A garden house was half hidden by the cypresses. Such was the eighteenth-century reaction to seventeenth-century rigidity that by 1763 everything had been swept away.

If a pseudo-Freudian analysis is applied then the fashion, post-1660, for planting long formal avenues out into the countryside from a house could have been a knee-jerk assertion of territorial control by squires and aristocrats badly shaken in their landed authority by the late Civil War and so many expropriations. A long axis laid out in 1686 for Earl Thomas, the 8th Lord Pembroke is more likely to have been a gesture of royal sympathies from a family with an anything but loyal record. This was Carolean in style, a ruler straight canal running east from the house towards Salisbury. It utilised the waters of the Wylye, Wilton being blessed with not one, but two clear trout streams; a gaudy Japanese Garden now covers the site. But even this addition was not enough to qualify Wilton, which in 1660 John Evelyn had described as the first garden in England, for inclusion in Leonard Knyff and Jan Kip's prestigious *Britannia Illustrata* published in 1707 as an assertion of Britain's ability to rank alongside France in the grandeur and invention of its formal gardens.[16] Yet on the count of invention at least, Wilton deserved inclusion as the 8th Earl had built on the west end of his new canal a trick fountain ingenious enough to rival de Caus' hydraulic devices (**19**). The water came pouring out from a sluice halfway up a mound raised dramatically in the level lawns before the great South Front. A statue of Pegasus rose above it and the water seems to have disappeared, between two statues and some conical yews, as mysteriously as it first appeared. Clearly a hidden head of water was involved in the mechanism. The device was still in place on mid-eighteenth-century engravings showing the celebrated Palladian Bridge, built in 1737.[17]

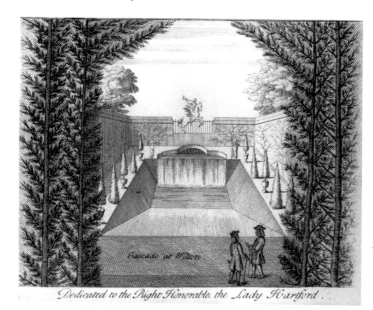

Cascade at Wilton.

Dedicated to the Right Honorable the Lady Hartford.

19 *The short-lived trick fountain of Pegasus was built on the South Lawn at Wilton by Thomas, 8th Earl of Pembroke, who reigned from 1683 to 1733, as a riposte to Longleat's new gardens.* Bristol University, Special Collections

Constructed in 1686, the fountain could well have been a counter stroke of the Herberts to balance the new fame of the vast formal gardens being planted for the Thynnes at Longleat. Sir Thomas Thynne had been created 1st Viscount Weymouth in 1682 and, to celebrate the honour and establish his new county status, he had in 1683 signed a contract with the four directors of the Brompton Park nurseries in West London whereby for the ultimate cost of £30,000 they would create the grandest formal layout in England.[18] This was to stretch east from the house, across the valley floor of the Leat and then up to the top of the neighbouring hill. Such an enormous sum of money would have built a new Longleat House and it is an indication of the role that applied horticulture had come to play under the Stuarts that the Thynnes should have paid so much for gardens that would be swept away and completely reshaped before fifty years were out.

For the money the directors took their duties seriously. George London, Roger Looker, Moses Cook and John Field took it in turns to spend a month on the site supervising the operations, a section at a time, with London in overall charge. Longleat would make the Partnership's reputation nationally and establish George London as the country's leading garden designer. In 1689 Moses Cook would sell his share to London's assistant, the young Henry Wise, who would take over the firm after London's death in 1714.[19]

The capitalist cunning of the Brompton Park Partnership's scheme was that not only would their team install the various garden enclosures, but that thereafter they would continue to service them with plants, trees, pots and installations. In garden history terms, Longleat's evolution is interesting because, over the years the formal geometry on the valley bottom and the lower slopes would be abandoned, while the Grove, the pleasure ground at the top of the hill, gradually developed most of the characteristics of a mid-eighteenth-century Arcadian garden. Longleat's account books from 1687 to 1788 record the process over a hundred years.[20]

Kip and Knyff's view in their *Britannia Illustrata* show Longleat's gardens in their over-ripe prime (**20**). Visitors would drive up the valley on a straight drive between double avenues with glimpses to the right of a chain of rectangular basins of the canalised Leat. The entrance front of the house was quite austerely handled with two fountains in two plain lawns. All the visual attention would be drawn away to the right where a prodigious regiment of squared enclosures became instantly visible climbing up the hillside to the woods of the Grove. These are shown in a detailed plan of the gardens (**21**) in the third volume of *Vitruvius Britannicus*, which labels them precisely, although there are some minor changes to the original layout.[21] Immediately east of the house was the 'Long Stone Terras' 215 yards long lined with 2,500 flower pots. Below this were four quarters of simple parterres: grass cut into patterns outlined by coloured sand. Centring this was a canal with the largest and most multiple-spouted 'Great Fountain'.[22] A wide axial 'Avenue' swept up the hill Grove-wards with an oddly disparate group of enclosures on every side, as if each of the four directors had gone ahead with a pet project regardless of what the other three were doing. On the level to the left of the four cut-grass parterres were ranks of vegetable beds (the 'Kitchin Garden'), but on the right was the 'Flower Garden' (**colour plate 4**) with a fountain in an elaborate *parterre de broderie*, the most complex in the whole layout and the first to meet a visitor's eye. On the first, sloping level were originally seven fruit orchards, two with fountains, and one Bowling Green. At the last level before the Grove were, from left to right, an orchard, a geometrically planned garden around a central pavilion, two small orchards and the Wilderness with box hedges, gravel paths and yet another fountain. After an exedral lawn came the Grove, increasingly a world in itself, walled, ditched and gated, but still on the main axial line. As first planned, this pleasure garden had a star-wood, fountain centred as usual, with eight rides, one of which led to the reservoir serving the fountains. Beyond the star-wood was the Hexagon, a clearing with, in its centre, six terraces leading up to a modest summerhouse.

Brompton's profits can be judged by the orders from Roger Looker's nursery for one year alone, 1684: 7,000 'asparagrase' plants, 2,000 tulips, 4,000 crocus roots and 177 choice auriculas.[23] Lilies were popular: 200 *Lilium candidum*, 200 *Lilium bulbiferum* and 200 Martagons, a mere 50 'Pioneys'.[24] But after 1689 London and Wise retired to a watching brief and James Vane, the Thynnes' head gardener took over the shaping of the Grove.[25] In 1693 his labourers planted 1,262 trees in the Hexagon; in 1694 the pleasure element was taking shape with a 'hen house' (pheasantry), duck baskets in the pond and an arbour.[26]

By 1704 the Viscount had decided that the Grove was the social success of the new layout. In a major operation he filled in its ha-ha and built the wall with a gated entrance visible on the Kip–Knyff view.[27] The ironwork was being painted

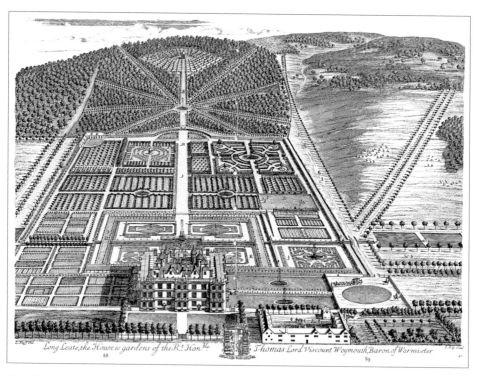

Long Leate, the House & gardens of the R^t Honble Thomas Lord Viscount Weymouth, Baron of Warmister.

20 *The vast, post-1683, formal layout of Longleat made the fortunes of the Brompton Park Partnership. It cost £30,000 and lasted barely fifty years. Floods, frosts and labour costs were its undoing*

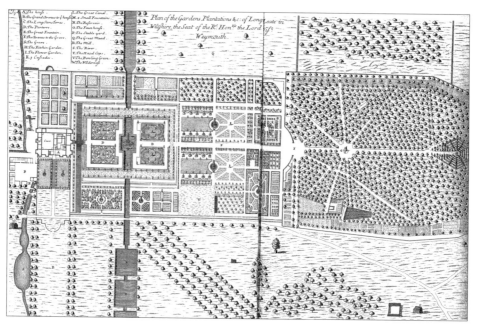

Plan of the Gardens Plantations &c: of Long-Leate in Wiltshire, the Seat of the R^t Honble the Lord V^{ct} Weymouth.

21 *A plan from* Vitruvius Britannicus *of the formal compartments of Longleat Garden climbing the hill up to the Grove, a pleasaunce which proved more popular than the repetitive geometry* and the garden within a garden was complete by 1707.[28] By that time the late frosts and occasional floods on the valley bottom were having a disenchanting effect and in a letter of 22 January 1709 Vane told the Viscount:

> What wants to be done in ye grove – 1 Acer of ground to be didged for Turnips, hallf Acer for beans, hallf acer for pease, hallf acer for Cabbages and Cale, half acer for onions, carets, parsnips, halfe acer for straberys and potatoes, ye wall borders to be dunged and didged and an Edging of Straberys ye old Edging is worn out.[29]

If Longleat House had been newly built in 1683 it would probably have been sited up on the healthy hilltop, not down in the valley. So now the vegetable gardens were being brought up out of the frost area to join the 1712 summerhouse in the Grove. A carriageway 'euan for a Coach or Sheas to go' had been laid in 1710[30], and twelve peach trees and nectarines, twelve apricots and three standard cherries were needed. By 1711 in the Grove, 'a division within a pale for flowers' appeared.[31] Few household accounts in England have a clearer record of the move in garden fashions from geometrical pomp to casual pleasure grounds. In the end the nation would go where the Thynnes had led; but in 1714 the 1st Viscount died leaving Thomas, a four-year-old, his heir. Over the subsequent long minority, these labour intensive grounds fell into inevitable decline.

In 1691, near the end of his life, John Aubrey held forth, still with his usual Toad-like self-confidence, on the gardens of Wiltshire. He ended: 'As for *Longleate Garden* it was lately made. I have not seen it, but they say 'tis noble'.[32] Whether it was noble is a matter of opinion; it was certainly revolutionary – gardening as a way of maximum consumption. For the second time in one century Wiltshire had set the national trend in gardens.

In this half century gardeners could always choose between the Franco-Italian: geometry with a grotto, or the Franco-Dutch: geometry with canals. Technically, despite its steep topography, Longleat should be classed, from its long chain of five rectangular basins, as Franco-Dutch. Lacock Abbey went the same way though on a more modest scale. While it is hard to regret the disappearance of the Brompton Park Partnership's layout at Longleat, sufficient remains of the late seventeenth-century garden at Lacock to create a real sense of loss. The house had, since 1550, the most exquisitely furnished banqueting room and garden viewing tower in the country, its stone table supported by John Chapman's grinning satyrs (**colour plate 6**). Whether in the first Sir William Sharington's time (he died in 1553) it also had complex gardens to be viewed from above is not known; indications are that there was only a narrow strip of grass within bastion-like walls before marshy fields succeeded.

It was Sharington Talbot, who died in 1677, and his son Sir John, who died in 1714, who changed all that, swinging the focus of the gardens decisively around to the north, where the Kitchen Garden was already using the marshy water meadows of the Avon to advantage. Ultra royal during the Civil War and rewarded for their loyalty by the King's visit in 1663, the Talbots could hardly garden any other way than that which their monarch had established at St James' Park and Hampton Court. When an 'Exact Plan of the Demean and Manor of Lacock' was drawn in 1764 those water gardens were still splendidly intact and mature (**22**).[33]

On the north and east sides of a broad rectangle ran wide terrace walls with a bastion at each of the north-east and south-east corners. Enclosed within the rectangle were two bold water features: a long canal with a short right-angled extension to the south-east end and, next to it on the west, an irregular informal lakelet beset with small islands, on one of which there was a summerhouse. Even further west was a large circular basin and to the south-west the 'Old Orchard' and 'Kitching Garden'. Slicing decisively across the water features, but not bridging them, were two north–south walks and one unexpected diagonal.

All that remains of a garden William of Orange would have recognised as Dutch is that short right-angled length of the main canal, still well watered, but with its banks now planted with fine trees. Dull conventional woodland and winding gravel walks cover the rest, but the shape of that circular pond is preserved in a

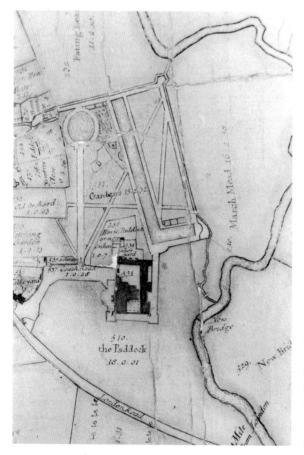

22 *This 1764 'Exact Plan of the Demean and Manor of Lacock' shows the Franco-Dutch formal canals, which the ultra loyalist Talbots, Sharington and Sir John, had laid out by 1714. The bottom right-hand canal survives.* Wiltshire & Swindon Record Office, 2664

circular 'Rose Garden' overlooked by an alcove seat. It was this last that William Henry Fox Talbot photographed in June 1840 on salt and silver nitrate covered paper, making several prints from the negative.[34] This was, unless the French dispute the claim, the first ever photograph of a garden. Since 1990 the garden has been reverently restored to that first early-Victorian condition, by the Head Gardener, Simon Taylor.

There is one other curious feature on the 1764 estate map, also shown on the later 1773 Andrews and Dury *Wiltshire* map. Across the road from the Abbey is a square of woodland called 'Inwood' within which is a tree called 'The Fair Sister'. Straight rides criss-cross it with never a serpentine curve, but there is a summerhouse at its heart. It would be interesting to know how it functioned, perhaps for shooting, or possibly for solitude.

Last in this group of pre-1714 formal gardens comes Littlecote. Like the others its grounds have an engaging experimental quality, an air of hit-or-miss, of geometry as a device rather than a ruling force. After 1714 the geometry in the remaining formal grounds of the county seems to have become more predictable and deadening. Uncertainty is a positive quality in a garden, and one very present in Littlecote's garden history. It is an impressive but unloveable Elizabethan house with earlier building in its rear portions and the painting of it by Thomas Wijk[35], dated roughly to 1700, proves that by that time the park had already been laid out with avenues of very young trees. The walled areas immediately around the house were still semi-fortified with a three-storey gatehouse leading to bare lawns. On the left was a walled privy garden with a high viewing terrace and a central sundial.

When the two maps of the grounds were made in the 1770s, possibly versions from the same survey by Thomas Smith of Shrivenham, one simply of 'Littlecot Garden'[36], the other a part of Andrews and Dury's *Wiltshire*, a far more complex pattern of gardens had been laid around the house and the defensive walls had gone (**23 & 24**). The gardens in front of the house now brimmed over into half the stable yard and a long flower garden at the back linked the house to a canalised reach of the River Kennet. However, these gardens were so formal as to suggest work of the seventeenth century, so no Capability Brown or even Arcadian broom had swept over that deeply conservative house with its grim Commonwealth chapel and 'murder' room.

Out at the far western area of 'The Park' is a star-shaped wood with its eleven radiating avenues, a favourite formal pattern with no softening, despite the late date, of winding paths or surprise clearings. Easily the most intriguing feature of the grounds is a little pleasure ground with a summerhouse sited on one of the ten islets created by the wandering streams of the Kennet. Smith's map shows the pleasaunce as a square with intersecting paths and marks the nearby islet as a small wood. Andrews and Dury's map is equally interested in this poetic garden feature, but clearly marks it as a round mound within a square and puts the island wood further downstream. Both maps mark a bridge linking the pleasure island to the mainland. There is a farm close by on the riverbank. Nothing remains today of

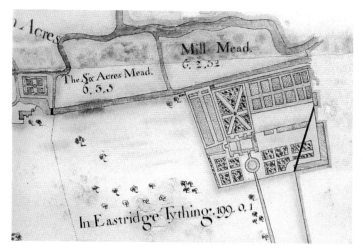

23 *Thomas Smith of Shrivenham's survey of 1775 shows the grounds of Littlecote trapped in clumsy, pre-1714 formal geometry, but the imaginative island garden at the far left may hint at a movement towards the informal.* Wiltshire & Swindon Record Office, 2027

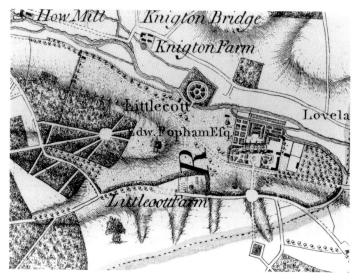

24 *Andrews & Dury's 1773 map of Wiltshire illustrates the whole disconnected reach of Littlecote park from the house to the star-wood of Park Coppice. It was this kind of challenge that made Capability Brown a celebrity. He would have dammed the Kennet.* Bristol University, Special Collections

the 1775 layout except Park Coppice, stripped of its star of avenues, so we may have lost an Elizabethan pleasure island with wilderness attached or perhaps a brief flight of mid-eighteenth-century Arcadian invention.

Garsdon Manor, a gaunt but elegantly attenuated house of the late 1630s, lies in Aubrey country within the sound of the M4. Because its garden was laid out before 1720, with a gazebo and with all the hesitant bucolic formalism of the previous century, it will make an appropriate mid-point to the chapter. At the same time it may persuade some readers to enjoy the pleasures of tracing on the ground, in ditches, earth banks and surviving walled enclosures, what is shown on the many estate maps of the period held at the County Record Office. The maps in question here are one of 1720[37], and a revision of the original carried out in 1746.[38] Both illustrate, in varying detail, the same conservative garden features (**25**). Below the house is an Italian-style three-terraced formal garden. To the side, below a large orchard, a stream has been harnessed to create a canal with two little orchard islands and one smaller basin. In the 'Cunningrey' or rabbit warren field on the other side of the terraced garden is one large tree, obviously revered for its age; there is another by a small pond at the bottom left-hand corner of the orchard. Immediately behind the house and its service ranges is a round formal lawn edged with conifers. As a mark of unsophistication there is no obvious carriage approach; visitors simply rode into the stable yard. A garden house or gazebo stands on the corner of two garden walls enjoying views over the gardens and warren rather than passing traffic.

Every feature of this map has left some kind of imprint today: a marshy field where the lines of the canals can be traced, a ridge in a slope indicating a causeway walk, two walls of the terraced garden; even the stone circle that guarded the ancient tree in the orchard remains to protect a sapling successor. It is unlikely, from the maps, that even in the 1730s the owners of Garsdon, the Shirley family, had troubled to plant a parterre or flower bed. They were absentees from at least 1711 and sold the property in 1758.[39] Their last simple reshaping of the grounds, as recorded on these maps, may be as late as 1720, though the date 1701 is carved into the lintel of a door giving onto the walled enclosure with the garden house.

Some reservation has, however, to be made on the assumption that an absentee family would neglect a garden which they never visited. Sir Walter St John of Lydiard Tregoze and his wife, Johanna kept up such a stream of correspondence between 1659 and 1664 with their steward, Thomas Hardyman, instructing him and the gardener, Richard Rudler, exactly how to plant the gardens at Lydiard House, that we know more about the homely practical side of the seventeenth-century formal layout at Lydiard than at any of the county's more celebrated gardens, Longleat excepted.[40] The St Johns' country seat remained the larder for the London house. 'I hope you will provide all manner of garden stuff for us', Johanna wrote, requiring peas, asparagus, barberries, skirrets [carrots], nuts, live muscovy ducks to

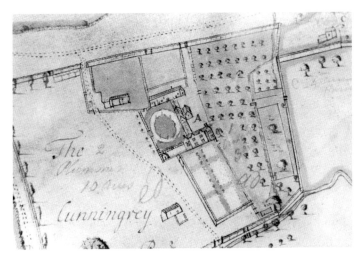

25 *A 1720 estate map of Garsdon Manor in north Wiltshire shows a conventional late seventeenth-century layout with a three-terraced garden, rectangular canals on the right, a pavilion on the wall of the entry court, carriage turning circle, orchard and rabbit warren or 'Cunningrey'.* Wiltshire & Swindon Record Office, 135/1

give to King Charles and dead deer as presents for friends. She sent oranges and lemons for cordials to be made, also 'oak bud and red rose water and concerve of red roses' with requests for coltsfoot, borage, plantain and mint from the Wiltshire herb garden.[41]

Flowers featured regularly. She wanted 'slips of the austrian rose set betwen the lawrel tre in the court', and wanted woodbines planted about the larder and stillhous cort'. From London she 'sent Rudler downe some seeds and some poppy Eminy [anemone] roots', but the seed must not be s[own] till next yere . . . I would have all the white and yelow crowns planted in the outward garden as wel as thos that are turned plaine red or yalow or white bid him also save some of his white stock seed for us'.[42] The implications of her interest in colour seem more in keeping with those of Gertrude Jekyll than of seventeenth-century formal beds; but this is speculation. Soon Johanna intended to send Rudler 'some Crocuses', meanwhile 'he should all this time of our absenc have planted Harry choks [artichokes] and parsnips . . . I hope you git a good stor of Hors radish planted'.[43]

Melon seeds 'that come out of Franc last week', together with 'Portingal Melons' and 'rare Musk Mellon' suggest a passion for soft fruit, but in with instructions for these Johanna mentions 'the stertion' and 'Lark spur 2 sorts'. With interesting and almost herbaceous-border precision she orders 'let him [Rudler] plant flowers of the sun and Hollyhocks on the bank under the rails and balesters', clearly a reference to lost formal terracing, 'next the bowling green'. Then 'let him compass the lawrel round the cort wth pole as he did the woodbine by the Hal dore to fenc it from the children'.[44] Lastly and with the note of a genuine flower lover, she orders:

> Git violet roots out of the woods and Plant them in the orchard under the wal that gos from Dr Dewels garden to the great Pond and that wall by the mil for thos violet planted in a garden wil be far blewer and better for my use.[45]

The letters were written mostly in the first five years after the Restoration of King Charles II. Very little remains at Lydiard of the three long formal avenues of this period.[46] The walled garden to the north-west of the house was laid out in the eighteenth century, when kitchen gardens were considered unaesthetic and lowering. The 'stillhous cort' would have been between the house and the stables, while the parterres for flowers and the bowling green would all have been south of the house, gently terraced. Mention of Dr Dewel's garden recalls that lost village with its pond that once clustered between the church and where the crumbling dam now stands across the course of the Shaw Brook. Johanna's instructions give an impression, not so much of formality, as of a diverting picture-postcard garden scaled to human needs with potager, flowers and vegetables in relaxed confusion. One of the more controversial themes of this book is that Capability Brown-style aesthetic simplifications of parkscapes, carried out in the eighteenth century, often destroyed gardens that were far more visually arresting and often more beautiful than what succeeded them.

John Aubrey's account of the natural history of Wiltshire was written in 1691 and has its predictable store of inaccuracies and amusing generalisations, but it also has some value as being broadly representative of the views of his squirearchic class and age. Of gardens he writes:

> The pleasure and use of them were unknown to our great grandfathers. They were contented with pot herbs, and did mind chiefly their stables . . . in the time of King Charles the second gardening was much improved and became common. I doe believe I may modestly affirm that there is now, 1691, ten times as much gardening about London as there was anno 1660; and wee have been, since that time, much improved in foreign plants, especially since about 1683, there has been exotick plants brought into England no lesse than 7,000.[47]

Aubrey attributes this information to 'Mr Watts, gardener of the Apothecary's garden at Chelsey and other botanists'.[48]

The truth is that the Tradescants were introducing exotic plants and trees in large numbers as early as the reign of Charles I, chiefly from America; though Aubrey's account may have been true for the average Wiltshire gentry, and 1700 to 1714 is a fair time to fix for a change in the mood of Wiltshire's formal gardens. The really interesting question is why, when England, at Colen Campbell and Lord Burlington's bidding, dropped Baroque architecture for Palladian after the Hanoverian succession in 1714, did formal garden design become softened into more relaxed Arcadian forms when the Palladian was such an austere, doctrinaire style, eminently suited for formal gardens? With Burlington active in the design of the grounds of Tottenham Park, Wiltshire can throw valuable light on this question.

Briefly though, before engaging with those gardens, some mention has to be made of gazebos, a favoured Wiltshire garden type. Wiltshire ladies apparently loved to spy on travellers. Would it, therefore, be right to generalise and describe the gazebo as a response to a walled-in formal garden, a building type that, consequently, largely faded away once wide open, though usually still park-walled, Arcadian garden fashions set in? Do gazebos represent an instrument of purdah, of female isolation? A whole collection of these miniature stone and brick boxes for curiosity could be made around the county. The pair at Bolehyde, with their Dutch-style murals, has been mentioned earlier. Biddestone has two, one for the farm overlooking the village green (**26**), another, extended by an eighteenth-century brick bow, at Biddestone Manor. A saucy round gazebo at Pickwick Mansions spies on the main road to Corsham and the level, rather dull, green fields of north Wiltshire may have produced more gazebos than the livelier southern half of the county.[49] The biggest and grandest must, however, be that tall brick gazebo with its gallery and inner room, more Roman than English, in

26 *Biddestone is a village of gazebos; this one at Pool Farmhouse overlooks the village green. With a fireplace for heating it would have offered privacy even in winter*

the far south-east of the county at Manor Farmhouse, Little Bedwyn. It has attractive eighteenth-century plasterwork inside. The farmyard of the same establishment has what looks like, and surely functioned as, a second gazebo in the form of an octagonal game larder sited strategically on a street corner of the village. Perhaps the gazebo was a subliminal protest by the gentry classes against the loss of privacy caused by employing a large domestic staff. Only in a gazebo could the lady of the house escape eavesdropping maids and spying butlers. Gazebos may well have been a foreshadowing in the Baroque garden of those eclectic garden buildings: Gothic summerhouses, classical temples and Chinese kiosks that are the mark of the next, Arcadian, garden phase. Sociologically the formal garden was failing to be functional, failing to relate flexibly to the ordinary needs of social life in the country.

5

Burlington, Bridgeman and the evolution of a garden for the Palladian

This chapter covers the pivotal years in English garden history when the formal layouts of the Stuarts gave way to the informal Arcadias of the Whig aristocracy under the Hanoverians. It is a fascinating period because, when the Whigs brought back Inigo Jones' Palladian as their architectural house style, there was no ready-made formula for Palladian gardens to go with their new houses. As a result England went ahead, insular and experimental, to create an entirely new style, 'the English Garden', which would be widely admired and imitated on the Continent later in the century. In Wiltshire it was a particularly innovative and exciting time.

Charles Bridgeman, who died in 1738, but whose origins and birth date are unchronicled, was the last and most unorthodox of the formal gardeners.[1] He was a designer unable to rid himself of geometrical garden thinking yet often tottering on the edge of informality, his gardens at Stowe and Rousham needing only a few softening strokes from William Kent, breaking his axes and cloaking his amphitheatres, to become ravishing Arcadias, perfectly responsive to their natural topographies. Bridgeman is, therefore, a key figure in English garden history; the possibility that he was not only Wiltshire born, but that he was initially influenced by Sir Orlando Bridgeman's gardens at Bowood and tried out his own garden ideas on the next door park of Whetham House sometime around 1715, is of real significance.

Bridgeman's proven gardens in the county, Standlynch (Trafalgar House) of 1733, and Amesbury Abbey of 1738, together with a probable Bridgeman layout at The Moot, Downton, all came late in his career. By that time Lord Burlington had intervened to suggest a simplistic and unoriginal garden layout at Tottenham Park, the estate of his brother-in-law, Lord Bruce, in the south-east of the county. If Bridgeman had begun to liven up garden design several years before that on the other side of Wiltshire, then Whetham is a site that garden historians will have to take seriously. To follow the natural consequences of chronology, Bridgeman's probable work at Whetham will be considered before Tottenham Park and Marlborough; then a return will be made to his later gardens at Standlynch, The Moot and Amesbury.

To confuse any investigation into Charles Bridgeman's possible and quite probably illegitimate birth into the Bridgemans of Bowood, there were no fewer than five Orlando Bridgemans in four generations of that family. What matters is that the founder of its fortunes, the first Sir Orlando, who died in 1674, had three legitimate sons, Sir John, Sir Orlando the Second and Sir Francis.[2] Sir John's line became, several generations later, Earls of Bradford; Sir Orlando the Second remained at Bowood, died in 1701, and was succeeded by his son, the third Sir Orlando, who died in 1745, predeceased by his son, Francis, and the last in that line.

Sir Orlando the Third was a profligate who committed suicide in the Thames, so the formal garden at Bowood, recorded in an oil painting at the house of around 1725 and still relatively untouched as shown on John Powell's map of 1763[3] made just before Capability Brown began his works at Bowood, was a fairly standard early eighteenth-century affair. Straight vistas were cut through woodland to give controlled views from the house; there were long north and south-west avenues, a bastioned rectangular terrace and lawn, taking the fall of the land and leading to a rectangular pool immediately east of the house. On the 1763 map this pool is overlooked by a square viewing mount. The 1725 oil painting shows, however, more casual serpentine pathways in the woodlands, and one watercourse appears to make a deliberately sinuous course through a Wilderness.

If Charles Bridgeman was a Bowood man, as this chapter tentatively suggests, this formal layout may well have been his introduction to garden design; indeed he may have contributed some of the features to it. To appreciate the difference between the two properties, Whetham and Bowood, which march together for a quarter of a mile, it is necessary to walk them both. They are threaded by the Marden stream, but whereas Whetham park is a cluster of moist dingles, small irregular valleys, by the time it reaches Bowood the Marden valley has become far more open: an area readily adaptable to long avenues or, when Brown arrived much later, the usual Brownian recipe of sweeping landscapes around a large lake.

In the time of the original Sir Orlando, the father of the family, his Bowood was neighboured by Sir John Ernle's Whetham. Both Sir Orlando and Sir John were Barons of the Exchequer, a significant coincidence for next door neighbours. Sir John died in 1685, his son, Sir John, in 1697. The estate was inherited by his grandson, John Kyrle Ernle, who died in 1725, leaving Whetham to his daughter Constantia. It was for Constantia that the revealing map of the estate was made in 1728 by John and Ian Overton, Surveyors of Devizes[4], presumably to record the young Charles Bridgeman's early attempt to adapt garden geometry to a promising, well-watered, but exceedingly irregular site. Today the park of Whetham is a mixture of rough woodland, mostly new growth, and pasture; but in its 1720s prime it must have approached very near to the Arcadian landscapes, which William Kent would be creating, often around Bridgeman's basic frameworks, in the 1730s.

The 1790s turnpike road cut through this layout and Whetham House stands north of the road with what the map calls 'A Large Pond' on its east side. This pond was created by a dam at its north end and served Whetham Mill. The Marden stream then runs on to swell the great Capability Brown lake in Bowood Park, where, incidentally, Brown originally proposed a second mill on a second dam. Immediately west of this reach of the stream the map shows a fascinating system of ornamental water gardens. High up on the left is a three-sided pavilion or seat, overlooking a little 'Pond'. Four straight 'Water Works' or rills run down the hill from this, the northernmost into a 'Pond' on a straight 'Walk' on a north–south axis running through Whetham House itself. This axis terminates at its northern end in a circular 'Grove'. The axial walk has gone, but the pond seems to survive in what is now called the 'Wishing Well'. Out to the west of that three-sided pavilion on the hill the map shows a 'Water Carridge', possibly an underground system of hollow elm pipes bringing water from ponds further back up a little tributary of the Marden. On the slope above these was a 'Vine Yard'.

The evidence for Charles Bridgeman's authorship lies south of the house where that same north–south axis is shown running along a walk into one of those distinctive Bridgemanic design favourites: a stepped, rectangular clearing flanked by the 'Parke Walk'. These stepped rectangles are found in Bridgeman's park at Sherborne in Gloucestershire and on the approach to the Temple at Eastbury in Dorset.[5] At an exact right-angle to this feature the map sites 'The Ring', with two more stepped Bridgemanesque recessions cut into the wood on each side of it. All this area now lies south of the main road and is completely overgrown. While today Whetham offers a most rewarding if muddy field trip for garden enthusiasts, and traces of the 1720s layout can be made out, easily the most memorable feature of the grounds is Cowage House, which rises more like a natural stony exudation in the woods than a real seventeenth-century yeoman's house, with rough rubble textures, blocked and open cross-mullioned windows, massive chimneystacks and staggered rooflines.

After Whetham of the many waters, the park at Tottenham will come as a less stimulating experience. The earliest of a whole chain of Tottenham Park estate maps, drawn between 1710, when Charles, Lord Bruce was still only Baron Whorleton, and 1825, when the Bruces had become marquesses of Ailesbury, shows the old house and its garden as Lord Whorleton was absorbing his inheritance.[6] At that time the gardens and the park ran east–west, not north–south as they do today. There is no hint on the map of a link up with Savernake Forest to the north. Three modestly sized formal pools flank the house and there is a small parterre south of the house where the gardens now spread out generously. A small pleasure wood has a clearing at the centre of four curling paths, the walks in Durley Wood to the west are winding, but the main Durley Avenue is straight. It is a layout that could be paralleled at any number of middling gentry parks in the county that were nervously experimenting with casual curves.

Next comes a map of 1716 by Charles Price, with the first north–south hint in a straight canal east of the house, with a garden wood on each side of it.[7] But all the emphasis is moving south, not north, without any suggestion of that six-mile axis through Savernake that makes the park so impressive today. Instead a broad straight avenue has been driven south to another, equally straight, running east–west and marking the park boundary. To the north the house looks out over pasture and farm buildings.

Then in 1720 Lord Burlington, with his tame architect Henry Flitcroft, was called in to build a new house for Lord Bruce. Burlington was just back from his second, fact-finding Italian tour of Venice and Vicenza; he created a pretty villa-like house with corner towers in 1721, one of the earliest buildings of Whig Palladianism.[8] The next estate map, undated but of the mid-century, can be assumed to illustrate Burlington's directions to his brother-in-law on garden design.[9] Predictably Tottenham now shadows the grounds of the villa at Chiswick, which Burlington built between 1723 and 1729, with classical park buildings set as focal points at the end of straight radiating avenues. By 1743 Burlington had designed a three-bay 'Banquet House' for the end of the Durley Avenue; this was demolished in 1824. A second straight avenue has been cut north–west of this to an octagonal clearing centred upon an octagonal pavilion; this is also to Burlington's own design. That north-south canal has been filled in and turned into a drive heading north to 'Iron Gates'. All these features are shown on Andrews and Dury's map (**27**). So far the mood is tentatively formal, but with a scatter of pleasure buildings on that formal framework. Even more Rococo in tendency are the

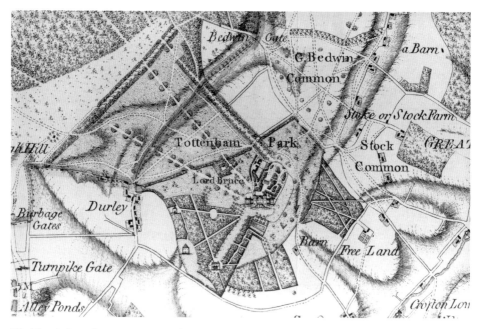

27 *The Andrews & Dury 1773 map showing Tottenham Park captures both the ambition and the confusion of the grounds. Lord Burlington's avenues lance out left to garden buildings. Other avenues reach up north to try to bridge the gap between house and Savernake Forest. A few woodland walks are informal.*
Bristol University, Special Collections

28 *William Stukeley's 1723 bird's eye view of the Duke of Somerset's 1699 garden at Marlborough; formality reigns. Stukeley has misplaced the Grotto high up on the side of the Norman motte. It should be at the bottom, facing the wood.* Bristol University, Special Collections

wandering paths through the Durley Woods and the 'Menagerie' next to the farmyard. But there is still a gap about a mile wide, between the house and Savernake Forest. Capability Brown will not be commissioned to bridge that gap and pull the whole complex, six miles long and three miles wide, together until 1764; but, very cautiously, a less formal garden, one set with surprise events and retiring places, is emerging; all that is missing is a show of still or moving waters.

As a result of what it is tempting to call benign neglect, the last twenty or thirty years have given the grounds at Tottenham an accidental Arcadian air. In the spring of 2003, with permission from Lord Cardigan and the tenants of the house, I was able to walk the grounds in their deliciously dilapidated decay, a romantic experience of drifts of daffodils, jungles of dark rhododendron, a ruined kitchen garden large enough to have fed a regiment, and sudden burning bushes of brilliant forsythia. The house was just holding on, a refuge for a few young people with the usual twenty-first century problems and run by a young, positive team.

The experience was the more enjoyable as there was a scheme to turn the lumbering place into a hotel and leisure complex, a destiny for which it seems entirely suited. Soon the lovely air of overgrowth and neglect will be lost, the gardens will be shaven and trimmed, organic vegetables will grow within that vast brick-walled enclosure and there will be neat houses for a large staff. So I congratulated myself selfishly on having got to Tottenham just in time, when there were only, it seemed, two horses in that gigantic quadrangle of stables. What had survived of Lord Burlington's time, apart from a room or two digested within Thomas Cundy's lengthy façades, was that little octagonal pavilion, forlorn in the long grasses of its octagonal clearing, but still a witness to Burlington's huge influence and limited talents.

Estate maps and bird's eye views illustrate another garden of the county in this uncertain stylistic condition of the 1720s. William Stukeley, the antiquary, was naturally drawn to the sixty-foot Norman motte of Marlborough Castle, with the added lure that he supposed (wrongly) that Marlborough had been built upon the Roman town of Cuneto.[10] So between June and July 1723 he drew a bird's eye view of the thirteen-bay house and garden that the 6th Duke of Somerset had created next to the motte in 1699 (**28**), together with an overhead view of the motte and the surrounding formal gardens.[11] The twenty-four year interval had done little for the grounds. They appear unimaginative but labour saving. A standard tree-lined turning circle has a plain grass lawn in its centre, a few curly box hedges surround the south lawn, otherwise the three grass plats are simply quartered; the canal is straight and un-fountained with a very dull 'Somer house'. The Wilderness betrays a faint yearning towards eccentric patterning in its paths, but all the patterns are geometric.

Marlborough's puzzle is its Grotto. Stukeley draws the great motte circled by a winding path that leads to a small viewing pavilion on the summit, but quite clearly draws the grotto, which Lady Hertford, the Duke's daughter-in-law had created, together with a cascade, on the path immediately below the top. Today the Grotto (**29**), a pleasant, bat-haunted, three-cell structure, is quite firmly sited at the foot of the mound. Stukeley probably heard, in 1723, that a grotto was proposed, drew it in the wrong place and failed to correct it when Lady Hertford built it at the foot, with at least the possibility of some water from the stream circling the motte. Shell grottoes take time to create and Marlborough's was not complete until 1739. Its round pool is dry today, but its vault is dark with flints, pebbles and shells through which wriggles a very Rococo line of white pebbles, writhing in a random pattern. An alcove is outlined by a broad band of white shells and a massive conch basin waits to collect water that no longer flows. This is not Wiltshire's finest grotto. It faces due south and is far too brightly lit. In its first state it would have been shaded and flattered by the Wilderness. With a motte as dramatic as that towering above the house and a generous supply of water Charles Bridgeman would have been far more creative.

Where Bridgeman's dates are concerned there are usually uncertainties, but two plans for Standlynch, one at least in his drawing style, can be confidently dated to 1733, the year when the London merchant, Sir Peter Vandeput was rebuilding the old house on his new estate.[12] The first plan illustrates what Bridgeman would have to liven up (**30**). The Avon flows north–south between treeless banks, below a U-shaped courtyard house of Tudor date. Three square kitchen gardens overlook the river, but the main formal garden lies well away from it to the north, sheltered from any western views by two straight lines of trees. Diamonds and triangles of paths criss-cross the formal planting of the rectangular space.

29 *Lady Hertford's Grotto in the Marlborough motte was completed in 1739. The white tracery running lace-like through crystals and shells was a favoured county idiom*

Bridgeman's response in the second plan is an interesting compromise (**31**). One small quartered rectangle of the formal garden has been retained, but planted thickly with trees to make a Wilderness with a central clearing, not unlike that on the 1716 map of Tottenham. All the emphasis, however, has been thrown onto the park's best natural feature, the Avon. Its steep banks below the new square brick house have been thickly planted with trees. Through them runs a winding carriageway that opens into four or five geometrically-shaped glades or lookout points. These lead, at the park's northern limit, to Bridgeman's favourite figure, an amphitheatre cut boldly out of the steep hillside overlooking a point where the Avon widens out naturally and turns briefly westwards. This sloping half-circle is bare of trees, but topped with a huge square viewing mound, like those Bridgeman had used to orient the sight lines of the gardens he laid out around George Bubb Dodington's house, Eastbury in Dorset.[13]

At such a strategic point Kent would have built a classical temple and planted enough trees to open a gracefully framed view down to the Avon; Bridgeman thought instinctively in hard outlines. Lower down the Avon, where it leaves the park boundary, a mill and its race have created a long island or peninsula. On this confused and marshy area Bridgeman was proposing a second tiered amphitheatre, though to what purpose it is not clear. A visit to these steep tangled woodlands today is most rewarding. Bridgeman's layout has been abandoned for the usual Brownian solution of woodlands parted to give long vistas out to the west, but in those woods,

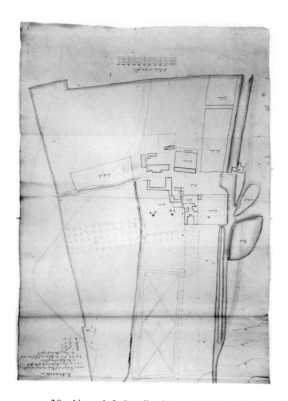
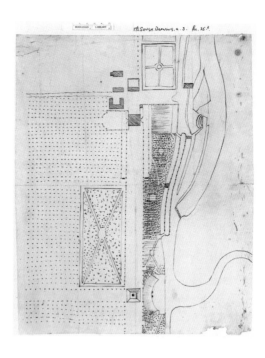

30 Above left *Standlynch (now Trafalgar House) as the Tudor house and its formal garden lay when Sir Peter Vandeput bought the estate in 1733; there is no sign of terracing to the river. The map has been rotated to align with figure* **31**. Bodleian Library, University of Oxford MS. Gough Drawings, a.3, fol.24r

31 Above right *Standlynch as Charles Bridgeman proposed to enliven its static geometry with his characteristic animation of amphitheatres, square viewing mount and geometric clearings on winding paths. He has thrown most of the emphasis onto the Avon.* Bodleian Library, University of Oxford MS. Gough Drawings, a.3, fol.25r

just before they topple down steeply to the river, it is still possible to find traces of Bridgeman's carriageway, well cambered and eight feet wide. There is much box and yew in the otherwise deciduous tree growth, and that southernmost clearing before the way drops down to the Avon is still open. Once down at the mill a wonderfully Arcadian path leads back up the river along the bank, the clear water providing a non-stop garden of reed beds, roaring sluices, clean gravel and delicate water weeds until the river bends sharply to the west. Here it is still possible to see, through a thick growth of trees, the inward curve of Bridgeman's amphitheatre. Facing as it did, when it was bare of trees, a wide reach of water, the aim could have been to create an Echo, an acoustic marvel like that at Wilton. It may be wishful imagination, but there still seems to be an amplifying effect to speech at this point of the bank, even though the trees have to some extent deadened it.

At Amesbury Abbey, where he was working five years later, just before his death in 1738, Bridgeman had much the same topography to enliven.[14] The Avon flowed at the foot of a steep hillside, this time facing east, not west, which looked directly across to Amesbury Abbey House down on the valley floor. This time, instead of his usual amphitheatre he planted the woods on the slope to produce a huge diamond shape facing the house (**colour plate 7**). The Diamond of bare hillside was centred by a stone arch leading into a grotto that could be reached by a narrow terrace cut across the exact centre of the Diamond and reached by a path rising up gradually from the river. Six statues were placed to dramatise the Diamond, two at its top, two at its foot and two at the points where the path entered and left the Diamond. Through the woods on the hilltop Bridgeman laid out drives, as at Standlynch. These connected open glades, two round, one square and one amphitheatric. Each of these glades was to have its rotunda or statue as a point of focus and interest, very much as Lord Burlington planned his straight avenues leading to garden buildings at Tottenham Park.

Down on the level valley floor near the house, Bridgeman had inherited the two long straight avenues: church to house and church to Kent Lodge as shown on Henry Flitcroft's 1726 map.[15] Here his response was not to naturalise and soften, but to suggest nature tentatively in exactly the same exedras and rectangles of stripped-back recession that are present at Whetham and which he laid out at Sherborne, Gloucestershire in 1729. Within a rectangle of woodland he permitted natural tree planting, but the perimeter lines of his groves are all geometric and straight. Even the millpond was to be made into an exact circle and another garden building was to centre precisely the big exedra proposed for the end of the avenue to Kent Lodge. Around a kite-shaped Kitchen Garden near the house trees were to be planted in a military bastion shape. If it was ever realised as he planned it in 1738, it would have been the archetypal cusp garden, poised between seventeenth-century formal and eighteenth-century Arcadian. The Andrews and Dury map of Amesbury of 1772 (**32**) shows that the groves were planted, but the garden buildings and statues were not.

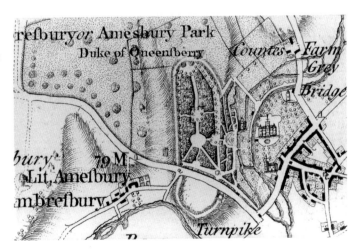

32 *Amesbury Abbey grounds caught by Andrews & Dury in 1773 before Bridgeman's park outlines have been softened. There are geometric clearings in the wood and the Diamond, one of the three, faces the house. The building to the left of the house seems to be the mill, still sited on its race.* Bristol University, Special Collections

The Diamond was still intact and clearly visible in photographs taken for *Country Life* in 1902. Now unfortunately the woods have grown over it completely and it takes a determined garden fancier to battle through fallen trunks and undergrowth across the crumbling chalk soil. But the pedimented grotto still survives among the bushes. It was here, so house legend credibly relates, that John Gay composed *The Beggar's Opera* when he was staying as a guest of his patroness, the Duchess of Queensberry. Some tree felling and re-pointing of stonework to the arch of the Grotto might merit national support, though the hillside probably looks more attractive without the Diamond artificially sliced out of the trees. Bridgeman's aesthetic and our own do not accord; we are closer in taste to an observer of the grounds at Amesbury quoted in John Britton's *Beauties of Wiltshire*: 'diamond walks, and other reliques of the frippery of false taste, prevent the lover of native simplicity from bewailing the neglect. In a picturesque point of view, desolation itself is preferable to the spruceness and affectation of artificial scenery'.[16] There would, however, be real interest in preserving Bridgeman's earlier vision as the National Trust has done in his gardens at Claremont in Surrey. Just a little way upriver from that lost lower point of the Diamond is Amesbury's Chinese House, which has its place in the next chapter, further still up the Avon Diana's House overlooks the stream in this unusually rich and positively endowed park.

Bridgeman is very likely to have been the unconventional designer of the gardens at The Moot, a quietly elegant Carolean house, brick built, in Downton village. Downton is the next parish down the Avon from Standlynch where Bridgeman's work is recorded. Before considering his authorship it is worth

33 *Newhouse in Whiteparish was already standing in 1619 when it was bought by Sir Edward Gorges of Longford to use as a hunting lodge. It lies more than half way up one of the longest axial projections in the county and could itself have served as a stand commanding a wide open area and two canals*

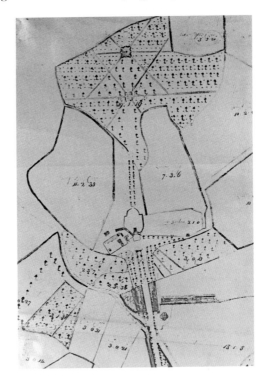

34 *This 1734 map shows little more than half of the extraordinary axial layout created by Kingsmill Eyre for Newhouse. It included eight deer traps and a stand at its top end for ladies to view the hunt.* Wiltshire & Swindon Record Office, copy map

remembering an even more individualistic, even obsessive, garden of the period that, at one time, pointed its extraordinary axis downhill, straight to the centre of Downton and The Moot.

Newhouse lies in Whiteparish, immediately to the east of Downton, a well wooded, hilly region. The *Victoria County History* believes that Sir Edward Gorges of Longford Castle bought Newhouse ready built after 1619, one of two matching hunting lodges raised for William Stockman of Barford.[17] However, with its three wings, part of an incomplete hexagon, the house smacks of the Trinitarian fixations of the Gorges family (**33**). To complicate the matter, Pevsner and Cherry in their *Buildings of England* Wiltshire volume add the gnomic fact that Newhouse Farm in Goodrich, Herefordshire, built in 1636, also consists of these three Trinitarian ranges.[18]

What is not in dispute is that the primary function of Newhouse was that of a hunting lodge. One of three very crude estate maps drawn between 1730 and 1734 by the surveyor Richard Joliffe for Robert Eyre of Ven House is entitled 'A Plan of Newhouse Farme' (**34**).[19] This actually places Newhouse in the centre of a remarkable axial drive called 'The Walke'. North of the house an avenue leads to woodland crossed by diamond and triangular rides like those on the earlier of the two plans of Standlynch. In the heart of these woods is a circular structure with four semicircular extensions at its imagined corners. It seems to be a stand from which ladies or the infirm could view the hunt. South of Newhouse the axial drive passes through woodland cut by radial rides and then between two long canals. After reaching a public road it continues through a sequence of seven or possibly eight exedral and gated deer traps before ending in the last of these. This section was presumably intended for the men of the household riding to the hunt. Half way along this axis and a quarter of a mile to the south is another curious piece of possible symbolic geometry. In a small wood a circular island appears to lie within a square pool. Two short and three long rides radiate out from the shores of the pool. Could this have been the fishing lodge of some sport-fixated Eyre? Was Bridgeman involved? Robert Eyre's brother was Kingsmill Eyre, who was baptised in 1682 and who died in 1743, and their father Samuel was a political crony of the Prime Minister, Sir Robert Walpole.[20] In his *The History of the Modern Taste in Gardening*, Horace Walpole writes that 'Mr Eyre, an imitator of Bridgman', presumably Kingsmill, was responsible for the very long axial layout of the grounds at Sir Robert's Houghton Hall in Norfolk.[21] We may, therefore, have here a relatively unnoticed garden designer in the same rough mould as Charles Bridgeman, and the strange axial way at Newhouse could have been a work by Kingsmill for his brother Robert.

Newhouse now stands proud above a great sloping fan of rough lawns, but the axial drive still runs between two sinister canals of black water with drowning trees and sedge before reaching a public road where it comes to an end. No trace remains of the hunting exedra or of the other two geometric structures in the woods. Eyre's Folly, also known as the Pepperbox, a three-storey hunting stand on a hill to the north, was built by Giles Eyre in 1606.[22] Andrews and Dury's map shows the Pepperbox connected by formal avenues to Brickworth House, also in Whiteparish. All this area of country was once a part of the greater royal hunting ground around Clarendon Palace and the deer hunting tradition obviously lingered on into the eighteenth century in the various houses which grew up after Clarendon's ruin.

If Newhouse's odd park must go to Kingsmill Eyre then Bridgeman has a much better claim to The Moot; but what is interesting is how wildly the garden designers of this pivotal period are flailing around for direction. Fifty years ago The Moot had one of Wiltshire's greatest and most atmospheric gardens, but to recover the intensely individual beauty of its prime when topiary and topography combined in a dream-like fantasy it is necessary to consult an early issue of *Country Life*.[23] Its photographs illustrate a classic instance of H. Avray Tipping, the magazine's country house writer, holding a semi-scholarly debate with himself over the style and dating of the site. In his day the strange undulations of the ground, towering mount and deep-delved ditches were still covered in mature trees, the lawns were closely mown, the Temple of Mercury still stood, seven bulging box bushes surrounded the sundial on the Sundial Lawn and a unique Doric Ombrello stood under a spreading beech tree on the summit of the motte. Sale particulars of 1870 capture its atmosphere precisely: 'Upwards of Seven Acres of Charming Pleasure grounds . . . Intersected in every direction by a labyrinth of shady walks, and beautifully diversified with terraces, avenues of lofty trees, massive yew hedges, and yews cut into fanciful shapes'.[24] It was a concentrated instance of early eighteenth-century garden design from that time when Bridgeman was livening up the predictabilities of the formal.

Now, thanks to the spirit and vision of a local conservation group, something has survived if only as an intriguing curiosity, a public open space where lovers meet and families have picnics. But the loss of topiary and temples and trees is heartbreaking. A notice at the entrance to the garden, across the road from its parent house, tries to make sense of the garden's obscure chronology. The Moot spawns antiquarian myth. Towards the end of the nineteenth century a Scandinavian expert proclaimed the garden's amphitheatre to be the most perfect and the largest folk meeting place of the Dark Ages that he had ever seen. From that time onwards the obvious derivation of the house name from the motte, or keep mound of the motte and bailey earthworks dug in 1138 by King Stephen's brother, Henry of Blois, Bishop of Winchester, has been dropped. Instead the legend has taken root that the eighteenth-century amphitheatre of eight terraces was a place where the Saxons held their Moot, or open-air meetings. The sale particulars, already mentioned, record 'an almost Unique and Perfect Specimen of an Ancient Saxon Court Terraced on the side of a Conical Hill, nearly surrounded by a deep double Entrenchment, supposed to be Roman'.[25] Bridgeman was, however, working at Standlynch (Trafalgar House) with his riverbank amphitheatre, and he created further amphitheatres, at Stowe in Buckinghamshire for Lord Cobham, at Claremont in Surrey for the Duke of Newcastle and at Chiswick House for Lord Burlington.[26] What made The Moot's garden so precious was that it had preserved its geometry and never collapsed into Kent's softenings or Capability Brown's visual generalisations. The sheer size of those Norman earthworks which did most of Bridgeman's work for him deterred any attempt to lessen the garden's compulsive charm.

There were improvements. In the 1750s the Rococo-style Ombrello to the god Mercury, one of the handsomest garden temples in England, went up for the ease of view connoisseurs. At the same time a Gothick Alcove was built along the trilobal lake at the foot of the eight terraces completing a fine, entirely unnatural garden composition. Sadly, this was replaced in 1850 by an Italian-style Loggia. More regrettably still both Ombrello and Loggia were allowed to decay completely in the philistine late twentieth century. If vandalism could be controlled it would be an eminently worthwhile project to restore them both and, above all, to let great trees mature again.

The garden can still be enjoyed, partly as a self-indulgent exercise in melancholy, partly as an exploration of completely unpredictable spaces. Bishop Henry's fortress must have been a formidable place. Wrought iron gates lead in opposite The Moot House. These were brought by Mr Pitts Squarez in the late nineteenth century. He obtained them from a dealer, Mr Binns, who was cashing in on the Edwardian taste for formal gardens. Mr Squarez was an antiquary whose book *The Moot and its Traditions* possibly created some of its traditions. He may also have planted the box balls around the sundial in what was the castle's bailey or outer ward. Its earth walls make a fine promenading terrace, but all the topiary has gone except for the Giant's Chair, a vast yew bush lowering over a seat.

A path leads inconsequentially away dividing into an outer south terrace walk and a broad grassy way that crosses the motte's dry ditch on a single arch of brick. Here Bridgeman, or whoever, has divided the motte into two. The left-hand hill once had the Mercury Ombrello and a surprise view down the amphitheatre to the trilobal lake and the Loggia. Untidy yews show that the amphitheatre once had topiary walls (**35**). The other half of the hill was just a wooded viewpoint.

Between the last terrace of the amphitheatre and the lakeside is a flat area so perfect for amateur theatricals that it is curious why so few eighteenth-century records recall any such events. Possibly the acoustics would have favoured musical picnics like the one Horace Walpole describes at Esher Place, Surrey in March 1763: 'the scene transporting, the trees, lawns, concaves, all in the perfection in which the ghost of Kent would joy to see them'.[27] After dinner, taken off earthenware for bucolic peasant simplicity, the ladies of the party formed a circle of chairs before the mouth of a grotto,

> which was overhung to a vast height with woodbines, lilac and laburnums, and dignified by those tall shapely cypresses. On the descent of the hill were placed the French horns; the abigails, servants, and neighbours wandering below by the river – in short it was Parnassus as Watteau would have painted it.[28]

The Coles family, who built The Moot House and paid a gardening genius to transform an earthwork, must have held many such Watteau-esque functions by the lake. Now what remains are the grassy terraces and a wall painted with a pathetic memory of that lost Loggia. The dates offered for the creation of the gardens are between 1690 and 1705; one closer to Bridgeman's engagement at Standlynch around 1733 would be more acceptable.

The other well-known and influential garden designer of this experimental period between two styles is Stephen Switzer. Hampshire born and trained at London and Wise's Brompton nurseries, he published *Ichnographia Rustica* in 1718, arguing persuasively for more fluid forest garden designs where an axis was present, but partly concealed behind a swirling pattern of driveways and a virtually random scatter of lakelets and coppices. Quite how much of a say he had in the overall planning of Spye Park, near Lacock, for the Baynton family is not clear, but there are descriptions of one, or possibly two, complicated water features which he designed for that exceptionally well-watered park.[29]

In his *General System of Hydrostaticks and Hydraulicks* of 1734, Switzer describes an oak in Spye Park 'through the Roots of which there issues out at least 200 Hogsheads of Water in a Day; and there are in that beautiful, (though

35 *This tiered amphitheatre at The Moot, Downton was, until recently, topped by an elegant classical Ombrello. Charles Bridgeman was probably the designer of the grassy theatre though local legend claims it was a Saxon gathering place*

now forlorn Place,) at least thirty or forty of such Springs'.[30] There was in the park what John Evelyn had described on 19 July 1654 as 'a precipice of an incomparable prospect'[31]; and it will have been upon this feature that Switzer devised a cascade,

> sometime since made at Spy-Park . . . which though done with very poor materials, yet admits of such a Variety, as some good Judges who have been Abroad seem to like, and think equal, at least, to any in the French Gardens, the Falls of the Water being over Steps and rough Work of different Kinds and different Heights, of about 30 or 40 Foot Fall.[32]

There was also another Switzer water work, probably linked to this cascade, several square basins, 'not only designed for little stews for fish, but at each corner there are clay or elm pipes, with plugs to them'. When the plugs were removed a whole chain of 'adjacent divisions' would fill quickly with water, though to what purpose Switzer does not make clear.[33] It is apparent from the variant garden designs, which he offered in his *Ichnographia*, that the cascade would not have been part of a rigidly formal layout. By 1734 Switzer himself writes of the place as sadly 'forlorn', so the complex water works may well have only lasted a decade; there is nothing left on the ground at Spye Park to suggest their siting.

Andrews and Dury's map in its satisfying clarities of the ground catches a number of formal gardens that have been edged towards informal Arcadias. At Warneford Place, Sevenhampton, east of Swindon the owner, Francis Warneford, has left the early eighteenth-century nine-bay house surrounded by eighteen dull rectangular beds. The lake, however, which began life in a neat horseshoe shape, has had its shores roughened up, though only delicately, to imitate nature, and its island planted with trees, while all the woodland around its head has been threaded with a wandering, winding path, like that which William Kent threaded through the groves in the grounds of Frederick, Prince of Wales' Carlton House in 1734.[34]

The most satisfying survivor of the Andrews and Dury formal layouts is at Biddesden House in the south-east quarter of the county (**36**). Biddesden's chief garden attractions are its Art Deco statue and swimming pool Gazebo, which will feature in a later chapter, but the bright, pink and lilac-blue brick building, like some giant doll's house designed by a gifted amateur, was originally surrounded by formal gardens of topiary work laid out, presumably by General Webb, who designed the military-style tower on the east side wall. A house wide open to the public road and set in quite limited grounds appears in Andrews and Dury to be surrounded by a tight supporting system of garden compartments. Until recently there were yews at the point where the drive meets the road, and there is still a straggle of yews to the west. On the east side of the house a dense sweep of yew hedge survives from the General's time, and on the west side is a short avenue of straggling overgrown yew trees close to the back of the house, intended originally to have grown no higher than a few feet. Above these and cut into the steep hillside below the walled garden are three terraces, General Webb's gesture in a Bridgemanesque direction, as the date of the garden's creation, 1711-12, would indicate.

First come two broad terraces, either of which could, and probably did, serve as a bowling green for tournaments with fellow retiree officers (**37**). They are now linked by central stone steps. The terrace above them is much narrower and, if the

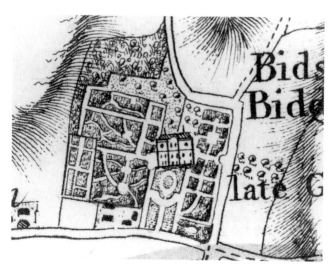

36 *Andrews & Dury's 1773 map of the grounds of Biddesden shows a semi-formal Bridgemanesque Wilderness to the right of the house, but more relaxed walks and woodland cover all but the lower terrace on its left-hand side. The Walled Garden is bottom left.* Bristol University, Special Collections

37 *The terraces at Biddesden are now back to lawns as they must originally have been when General Webb built his house between 1711 and 1712*

1773 map is any guide, was laid out to parterres. The three terraces offer a lively bird's eye view of the confident house below. Then trees close in, one a remarkable Dawyck Beech, which obviously thinks it is a poplar. House and garden are best described as serene and relaxed for all their formal pretensions. It took a military man to devise a formal garden with casual, human-scaled episodes.

Before moving on to Wiltshire's matchless group of fully achieved mid-eighteenth-century Arcadias there remains Compton Chamberlayne, a house of the Penruddocks in a side valley of the Nadder above Wilton. That, so John Seagrave's estate map shows (**38**), still retained in 1769, long after the tide of Arcadian informality had risen, gardens of the late formal period which were crying out for transition into Arcadian charm.[35] That would be effected soon after the map was drawn, but Seagrave had already recorded tentative movements of earlier Penruddocks towards relaxation with four oddly assorted pools in need of a unifying lake. A visit to Compton Chamberlayne today will reveal what is, in the author's experience, easily the most attractive and varied village in Wiltshire, far superior to tourist charmers like Castle Combe. It will also illustrate how much the alterations in style to a garden landscape can change the social geography of the community around that garden.

Seagrave marks the drive, from what was in 1769 the village street, as part of an axis from a 'Summer House' in the 'Park' running straight through, between two large square pools, to the front door of the house. There the geometry ends. Each of the other two pools beyond these has been tentatively irregularised, striving

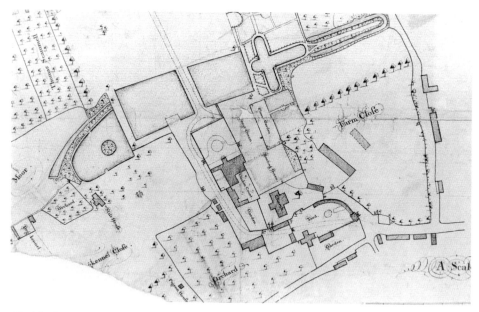

38 *The formal gardens and lakes at Compton Chamberlayne still survive in John Seagrave's map of 1769; only the curved wall along the church path remains today after a radical reshaping in the Brownian manner with one long 'natural' lake.* Wiltshire & Swindon Record Office, 332/284

towards the natural. Within the left-hand pool of the four is a wooded island and a curious wooded isthmus walk lies between the pool's upper shore and a curving crescent-shaped canal. On the right the fourth pool is cruciform, edged by walks which, from its longer arm, extend into a peninsular walk bounded by a U-shaped canal. Around the old house a vernacular clutter of enclosures has hung on with a 'Bowling Green', a 'Great Green' and a 'Flower Garden', from which last a narrow walk divides another square pool into two, adding to that varied pattern of paths between waters which is a feature of Charles Penruddock's property.

Very little on Seagrave's map is a useful preparation for the village and the house today. On a cloudless October morning the village street was in harvest festival mood with windfall apples and pears strewn across the road and the leaves colouring with unusual brilliance after a dry summer. But it was not the street Seagrave marks with cottages for Widow Weller, John Livelong and S. Snook. That has been completely swept away to give the house, now a chunkily aggressive castle of Regency Gothick, an idyllic view of tastefully wooded hillside without a house or even a right of way. As for the semi-formal pools, they now form one long dark lake to fill the valley bottom and give the Penruddock castle-house a dramatic foreground.

What does survive from Seagrave is that long curving wall which he marks as bounding a 'Yard'. This now forms one side of a perfect instance of the upper class desire for privacy at all costs. Between the wall and an even taller wall of topiary runs the villagers' way to the church, St Michael. At the end of this theatrical and, it has to be admitted, enjoyably claustrophobic path, lies the churchyard, inconveniently almost hugged by the battlemented house. A big vine drooped over the wall of one outbuilding into the graveyard, loaded with dozens of bunches of ripe black grapes, increasing the harvest festival air of the place. Down a few steps from the church were the lawns with a round pool and a cherub, then the lake. It was the quintessential aristocratic ambience, appropriately autumnal as the last ninety-six hereditary members still cling on desperately to their seats in the House of Lords. Within the church that same Charles Penruddock who commissioned Seagrave's map had put a memorial to his ancestor, the 'fighting' Penruddock, John 'beheaded at Exeter the 16th buried the 19th May 1655' for a gallant but vain revolt against Cromwell.

It seems churlish, looking down from Compton's churchyard to the perfect English ideal park of lake, woods and rising downland, to query the merit of what the Penruddocks effected so ruthlessly and so tactfully just after the village-scape was recorded. Yet it is a basic question that should be asked once the diverse charms of surviving vernacular gardens like Bolehyde, or half preserved like those of The Moot, have been enjoyed. Which were superior for pleasure, interest, variety and charm: those time-textured congeries of paths between waters, of enclosures beside jostling enclosures, of unexpected glimpses around wooded corners that the 1769 Compton map reveals, or this simple perfection of a lakeside park that Capability Brown would have approved and that Oliver Goldsmith, poet of *The Deserted Village*, would have condemned?

Compton Chamberlayne is still the most seductive community for retirement in the entire county, but the question should remain in the reader's mind over subsequent chapters.

6

Arcady on Avon – pioneering gardens of the mid-eighteenth century

These are the years, from roughly 1730 to 1780, when Wiltshire achieved mature gardens in a style best described as Arcadian; one where classical temples and a lively mix of garden buildings in eclectic styles were set, apparently informally, though actually with precise art, among casually planted woods and natural-seeming lakes. These would be so successful in capturing an aesthetic mood for a century weary of formal planting that they would be copied, not just in the county and the country, but all over Western Europe. Stourhead was the epitome of the 'English Garden' as imitated in France, Germany, Sweden and Russia. It becomes, therefore, a challenge to trace exactly how the post-1714 Palladian revival in house architecture managed to develop these Arcadian gardens – parks of exquisitely groomed Nature – around country seats that were anything but relaxed in their carefully proportioned classical façades. It was obvious in the previous chapter that a Bridgemanesque semi-informality was becoming acceptable, with randomly linked and geometrically shaped clearings cut out from woodland. The next step was the Arcadian, and the gently dramatic valleys of south Wiltshire were the ideal sites for Arcadian planting, lake creation and temple building.

It is natural to expect to find the first of these innovative evocations of the paintings of Claude Lorrain in the parks of the county's leading lords and super-rich banker-merchant classes. It is no surprise therefore to find, in 1735, Henry, 9th Earl of Pembroke beginning a complete Arcadian make-over of what remained of formal Wilton. In 1736 the black sheep of the Thynne family, the 2nd Viscount Weymouth, set about imposing a double curved Serpentine, the S-scroll shape of the Rococo, on the decaying formal canals of Longleat. The 2nd Henry Hoare, known as 'the Magnificent' to distinguish him from his father, Henry, 'the Good', began in 1741 his inspired, hands-on conversion of the valley of the Stour into a templed Arcadia more Claudian than a real Claude painting. Only a year or two later Alderman Beckford, a sugar plantation owner from Jamaica and a leading Whig politician in the Commons, began a crude but enthusiastic campaign of grotto, temple and bridge building at Fonthill. That was the park which would shape the hectic imagination of his son William Beckford, resulting in the amoral Romantic novel *Vathek* of 1786, and ultimately in the legendary if short-lived Fonthill Abbey. It is no exaggeration then to describe Wiltshire in these years as the leading county in England for garden design.

Just two quite small gardens were exceptions to this rule of the lead being taken by the rich and the blue blooded – one was for a Bradford-on-Avon clothier, the other was for a young man who narrowly escapes description as a confidence trickster. Their gardens were Belcomb Brook Villa, built in 1734, half a mile downstream from Bradford, by John Wood the Elder of Bath for Francis Yerbury, and Wilbury, built in 1710, probably to the designs of its owner, William Benson, as a villa to serve him during his term as High Sheriff of the county. Set on open downland near the Hampshire border, Wilbury is the exception in that its setting does not greatly flatter its gardening. Consequently it is not well known; Arcadias always need a helping hand from a friendly topography. Wilbury's date, however, coming a full twenty-four years before any of its rivals, demands attention; and the fact that, from 1734 to 1741, it was owned by the 2nd Henry Hoare before he moved to Stourhead following the death of his mother, makes Wilbury all the more interesting. Was this where the Arcadian garden was first tried out around a Palladian house?

The answer has to be yes, but not convincingly, an uncertainty which could explain the gap between 1710 and 1734. William Benson is not one of the charmers of garden history. His father was a rich steel merchant and his mother was Prussian, which accounts for Benson's influence over George I, who spoke no English. By picking the brains of a local Amesbury curate, the Revd Thomas Holland, and by hiring a skilled mechanic who could construct Holland's chain pump, Benson was able to create a fountain with a spectacular 100-foot jet for King George's palace garden at Herrenhausen in Hanover.[1] That was in 1716, but he does seem to have had some personal flair for hydraulics as he supplied Shaftesbury with a water supply and was rewarded by being elected MP for the town even though the water in summer 'was seldom or never fit for nice uses, as for coffee and tea'.[2]

More impressively Wilbury's damp water meadows are still drained by an unusually solid system of leats and ducts with little stone bridges and channels that Benson installed.[3] While he was waiting for Wilbury to be completed, he had leased the nearby Amesbury Abbey for twenty-one years from February 1708. Henry Flitcroft's survey of the grounds, drawn in 1726[4], proves that Benson's ideal of garden design at that time was one of rigidly straight tree avenues pointing towards set-piece existing buildings, Amesbury church in one case, Kent House in another. The gate piers at Kent House, very tall with blocked rustication, are the only memento of Benson's lease. His layout completely ignored the Avon, which bounds two sides of the park.

At Wilbury, which he sold in 1734 to his nephew Henry Hoare, he gardened in much the same manner with two straight beech avenues at right-angles to each other, one from the house to the road, the other, and the more interesting, to an octagonal temple hollowed out underneath by a cavernous grotto, possibly used as a cold bath. The temple could, of course, be a post-1734 building by Henry Hoare, but the similarity between the blocked rustication of its Tuscan columns and that of the Amesbury gate piers indicates Benson's taste. This layout may not seem very impressive, but it contains the basic elements of an English Arcadia: a temple and trees. The terrain did not lend itself readily to a lake. There is another Grotto at the centre of a saltire of paths in Grotto Wood, but that, with its acutely pointed Gothic brick arches is probably a later work. What is significant is that Henry Hoare II would have seventeen years' residence in this setting, ample time to brood over the possibilities of landscape. At the end of it, after 1737, he spent two years in France and Italy travelling, not as a brash adolescent, but as a mature thirty-three-year-old, developing a feeling for Italian landscapes and for the paintings of Claude, Nicolas Poussin and Gaspard Dughet, as well as landscapes by Ricci, Panini and Canaletto. Between 1739 and 1740 he bought one or more examples of the work of all these artists to hang eventually on the walls of Stourhead, the desperately austere villa that Colen Campbell had built for his father in 1719-20. Somewhere between his visual experience of what Benson had left him at Wilbury and those paintings bought in Italy, lies the inspiration for Stourhead, the ultimate and definitive Arcadia. But that is moving on too far, beyond 1741. Much else had happened in Wiltshire gardens between 1734 and 1741.

Wilbury was the creation of a political adventurer. Belcomb Brook Villa was designed by John Wood, an eccentric antiquary and genius, the most inspired town planner of his time in England. While Benson seems to have adopted Palladianism as opportune to his career, for John Wood the Palladian, Inigo Jones and the largely mythical Celtic pre-history of his native city of Bath were near-religious obsessions.[5] This needs to be absorbed to understand his approach to Belcomb Brook. 'Bel' was the key. According to the, frankly crackpot, theories of prehistoric Britain and the Druids that Wood had picked up from his reading, particularly of John Toland's 1702 *Critical History of the Celtic Religion and Learning*, Bel was the name of the Celtic sun god, the equivalent of Apollo, whose shrine at Delphi, 'the navel of the earth', had a monopteric (circular) temple as its focus.[6] With his characteristic impetuosity, Wood decided that the Belcomb valley was a Druidic site that 'the antient *Britons* dedicated to their God *Belenus*; and, in all Probability, erected a Pyraea in the Comb'.[7] So, if Delphi had its monopteric temple, Yerbury's new villa had to have one too. Francis Yerbury was persuaded, but then shrewdly determined that a local builder would put a temple up for much less cost (**39**). Wood, understandably, was enraged. When the temple was built he fumed in print that 'It wants that Proportion which rendered such kind of Structures correct', the 'Working Mason' who designed it 'cannot be supposed to have ever heard of covered Monopterick Edifices, much less to have known the

39 *The years have evolved the Bradford-on-Avon clothier, Francis Yerbury's original, semi-formal 1734 layout at Belcomb Brook into the ideal eclectic garden with monopteric Temple, Grotto and Gothick cottage around a crescent-shaped pond*

Rules by which the Antients built them'.[8] Too late, it was built, but before considering the design of Yerbury's garden as it was first laid out, it will be helpful to look at the grounds as they appear today.

The impact is intensely concentrated as one leaves the road and walks past the elegant, golden stone, Ionic front that Wood designed with pedantic correctness for his client's villa. The garden is like some Arcadian stage set for one of Handel's operas. The intensity of the effect is theatrical because the temple on its little mound, the curving pond and the rugged rocks of the Grotto have been crammed together, with wooded slopes behind them and a diminutive Gothick cottage to the rear, all in a space no larger than a decent-sized suburban garden. It is a breath-catching demonstration of just what can be done to a pleasant, ordinary Wiltshire valley. Distributed across an average park the impact of the elements would be slight, laid out a few yards from the fortunate clothier's drawing room windows the grounds make a persuasive case for the evocation of the past in one's back garden.

The 1777 map by James Sartain in the Bodleian Library presents a different scene at Belcomb (**40**).[9] The circular temple was the eye-catcher at the furthest limit of the little garden. A pool, half the length of the present pond, curved along the wall of the road, whose course has since been entirely altered.[10] There was no Grotto; that was a Regency invention by John William Yerbury or his heirs. He was a great fossil collector and left 'all monies and goods, including a fossil collection' to his sons jointly when he died in 1824.[11] His great ammonites still

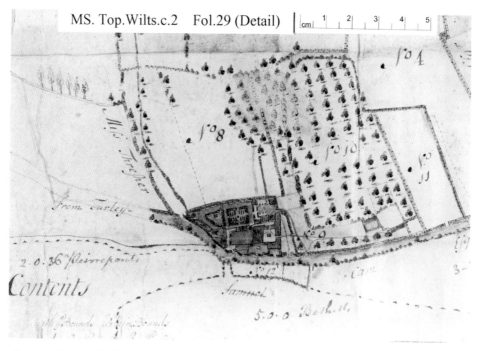

40 *James Sartain's 1777 map of Belcomb shows that the Temple once stood overlooking a public road with no Grotto or Gothick cottage and very little water. An inspired new garden now reaches up almost to the top of the plan.* Bodleian Library, University of Oxford MS. Top. Wilts. C.2, fol.29

strew the Grotto floor. Behind the house, cut into the steep slope was a little courtyard with pavilions at each corner and columns between them. On the axial line from this lost, but clearly once delightful, feature, was a hedged vegetable garden, then another small pavilion in a triangle of topiary hedges. It is not clear whether the little pool was intended as an Arcadian feature or simply a reservoir for Yerbury's cloth making premises, which adjoined the house and lined the road, but in Wood's time it was backed by a stone wall.

To some extent then the present Arcadian perfection has been coaxed into existence since 1800. Only the circular temple, a firm, resounding neo-classical gesture, one much more convincing than Benson's Baroque octagonal temple at Wilbury, can be taken as an early pointer to Arcadian taste in Wiltshire; the rest has grown up around it. Belcomb is a timely reminder of how a garden can be subtly groomed into a new character. The ideal Arcadia that we visit today at Stourhead was once alive with eclectic and most un-Arcadian oddities: a Hermit's Cell, a Chinese Ombrello, a Turkish Tent and a Venetian Seat. All these eclectic gardens of the mid-eighteenth century would have to pass through the neo-classical period around 1790, when what was not a certified Grecian garden building was very liable to be demolished.

One factor of original Belcomb needs to be remembered. Before privacy set in, and the course of the road was altered and a thick belt of trees was planted, that temple must have been clearly visible from the road, a startling advertisement for such a feature. John Wood was as precocious in his attitude to natural landscapes as was William Kent. He would have regretted the planting of those trees. He intended the garden to look out across the Avon to where 'a Cliff, covered with Wood, rises up and terminates the Southern View with a Beauty that renders the Situation of the House agreeable and pleasant'.[12] But he was of Bridgeman's generation; he planned Bath like a Bridgemanesque garden city with an amphitheatre, the King's Circus, linked by Brock Street to a crescent, the Royal Crescent. Bath is the proof that Bridgeman's connected geometric shapes can work to create city theatre. That temple-to-courtyard axis at Belcomb was equally Bridgeman-inspired, but would not in its original layout have been Arcadian, more classical geometry groping towards the villas of Pliny as described in Robert Castell's influential 1728 book, *The Villas of the Ancients Illustrated*.

Wilton's transformation into Arcady was almost contemporary with Belcomb, but earls do not usually take their garden ideas from clothiers. The gardens at Wilton today are memorably beautiful; during the 9th Earl's quite short reign there, from 1733 to 1750, they were even better, touched, if the Rocque map of 1746 is any

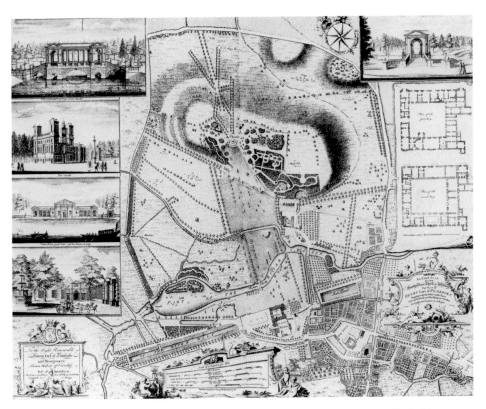

41 *Rocque's 1746 map of the grounds at Wilton in their Arcadian prime, when the Nadder had been dammed to produce a natural lake with islands, while the Wylye still ran in a formal canal and avenues directed the eye to an arch on the hilltop in informal planting.* Bristol University, Special Collections

guide (**41**), with an Arcadian poetry of invention and inspired whimsicality. It is only the fact that Wilton Garden re-invents itself at least once every hundred years that prevents us from ranking the 9th Earl's work alongside that of Henry Hoare at Stourhead. Today the Nadder runs clear, wholesome and unremarkable between confining banks. Earl Henry dammed it up just below the point where the Wylye meets it and the united rivers flow under a road out of the park. The lake thus created stretched back to the Earl's, or Roger Morris', supreme creation, the Palladian Bridge (**42**). This is an architectural improvisation so superior to the Palladio model from which it was drawn that the Empress Catherine the Great of Russia had an exact copy of it built at Tsarskoe Selo, while another two copies were soon built in England at Stowe and Prior Park, Bath.[13] Fully aware of the quality of his creation, the Earl designed that whole lost lake to set it off to perfection. At its far eastern end on the dam that produced it, he built a grandstand, a long pavilion composed using sections of Isaac de Caus' and Nicholas Stone's grotesque carving from the seventeenth-century Grotto House. On this fantasy improvisation visitors could sit, be refreshed and see, away to the west across a natural-seeming lake with wooded islands, the perfect silhouette of the Palladian Bridge. It was a dream landscape, Chinese in its watery outlines, Roman in its object of focus.

In the 9th Earl's day the 'Great Bridge', as Rocque rightly calls it, did not lead tamely to a rough meadow as it does today, but to a level green threaded by wandering streamlets and with the hillside of the old Echo arena beyond. Up on the groves of the hilltop the Earl was planning an eclectic surprise item which John Wood, the antiquary, who had measured the stone circles of prehistoric

42 *The 9th Earl of Pembroke and Roger Morris jointly devised the Palladian Bridge at Wilton in 1737 by using some sections of a triumphal bridge, which Palladio had designed, but never built, to cross the Grand Canal in Venice*

Stanton Drew and then the circles of Stonehenge, would have appreciated. The Earl was preparing a replica of Stonehenge. In the preface to his 1743 book on Avebury another antiquary, William Stukeley, congratulated his 'Lordship' fulsomely on the project:

> A symmetry and harmony of parts, an amazing grandeur in the design, the incredible force of the mechanick powers employ'd in them, the most magnificent effect produc'd, will for ever recommend the works of the Druids, to those of Your Lordship's discerning eye and accurate judgment. We see a convincing demonstration of this, in the fine and costly model of *Stonehenge*, which Your Lordship introduces in the garden at *Wilton*; where, I may be bold to say, it shines amidst the splendours of Inigo Jones' architecture; amidst what he did there in person, and what Your Lordship has since added, so agreeable to the former, as to render the design of that great genius complete.[14]

No illustration survives of this model and the actual stones appear, in the usual Wilton fashion, to have been used as building material for later projects.

To create his Arcadia the 9th Earl had uprooted a large kitchen garden planted obliquely opposite the great South Front. That and a dull formal garden before the long canal east of the house were still drearily present on the bird's eye view of the house and grounds in the 1725 volume of *Vitruvius Britannicus*.[15] In their places the Earl left simple water and lawn, easy of upkeep and in accord with a growing appreciation for a carefully presented natural landscape. What is so interesting is that the Earl, working in the early 1740s, was anticipating that landscape movement usually associated with Lancelot 'Capability' Brown, who at that time was still a gardener in Lord Cobham's employ at Stowe. Brownian landscapes were, in essence, only Arcadian landscapes with few or no eclectic garden buildings. The one fashion elides gently, imperceptibly, into the next. When required Brown would always be ready to design a Greek temple-lodge or a Gothick bath house, but his forte was simplicity and to that he owed his fame.

The long sinuous lake is the signature of this movement in park design. It seems brutal to criticise a park as rewarding as Wilton, but it must have had a wonderful picturesque unity when the 9th Earl's lake reached almost up to the South Front. Both the next two major Wiltshire Arcadias depended upon artificial lakes. Despite its big earth dam, the lake at Stourhead always looked like a natural feature. The lake at Fonthill had to pass first through an initial serpentine phase, as did that at Longleat. The sequences tended to be: first the rectangular canals of London and Wise; these, following royal example in Hyde Park, might be turned into serpentines; then came the standard long, river-like lake of Brown's or Richard Woods' devising; lastly Humphry Repton would come with delicate naturalising touches of tree planting on dams, colour contrasts of foliage and the cloaking of over-regular banks.

When he bought Fonthill House from an old Catholic family, the Cottinghams, in 1745, Alderman Beckford immediately organised a brass band, gave them uniforms and, on occasion, drilled them himself. That gives the mood and character of the Alderman perfectly. He spoke with a marked Jamaican accent, fathered a whole troop of bastard children, was Pitt's right-hand man in the Commons at Westminster, treated George III with a colonial's indifference that left the King speechless, and reshaped his newly-acquired park with predictable, lavish enthusiasm.

His first garden move was the creation of a serpentine by building an earth dam. This produced more problems than it solved because, when he wished to remove the public road from Fonthill House and church, he had to re-route it on the far side of his snaking new lake, then bring it back to the west bank on a five-arched, balustraded bridge. Money was no object to the richest subject of the British crown. His slave-run sugar plantations often brought in £100,000 a year, more than any duke enjoyed. If eclectic garden buildings were the new fashion then the Alderman built a classical portico on the wooded hillside south of the house, and a rotunda, possibly Chinese, above it.[16] For privacy he demolished the medieval church close to his house and rebuilt it as a classical temple in imitation of St Paul's, Covent Garden on the skyline, remote from the village. In 1755, when his multi-winged mansion burnt down, he opened a new quarry of Chilmark stone on the east bank of the lake and built Fonthill Splendens, a magnificent but old-fashioned three-part Palladian palace. Rubble from the quarries helped to create an east bank pleasure garden. Joseph Lane from Tisbury, the next village, who was probably a quarry man, proved to have a talent for grotto building and, as the garden fashion was moving in the 1760s to the Savage Picturesque, the Alderman employed him to build a large Lakeside Grotto under a mound of boulders (**43**). Its central chamber was entered by two twining passages and rewarded visitors with a lyrical water level view back up the lake. Further up in this new woodland a Cold Bath with a smooth ashlar-faced basin was built so that the Alderman could take his dips in private away from the stern eyes of his new, deeply religious, wife Maria, or 'the Begum' as she was known for her domineering ways.

To reach this place of furtive pleasures the Alderman devised two routes. One entailed a long boat trip down from an atmospheric arched and vaulted Boathouse in the north of the lake, a place of shadows and deep swilking waters. The other route involved a descent into a Tunnel Grotto beneath that tiresome public road. Its roof is made of rough stalactitic boulders and on the lake side of the road it emerges in a Hermit's Dell. This has a cave (**44**) where Merlin, or some such magician, is carved in outline, bent over his studies. In its second chamber is the reclining figure of a god, Bacchus according to a foreign visitor, Henri Meister.[17] From the Hermitage it would have been a short walk and a brief crossing to the Alderman's pleasure ground across the lake. Just before he died, of rheumatic fever and hard work, in 1770, the Alderman was having two figures carved, a nymph and a naked god, in the double-arched Quarry Grotto up the hill. These half-

43 *A stream from the petrifying spring trickles down into Alderman Beckford's Lakeside Grotto at Fonthill. His son William employed the Lanes of Tisbury to 'rockify' it with more crystals and niches for flower vases*

44 *Alderman Beckford's Hermitage at Fonthill could be reached by a long rocky passage under the public road. Inside its single chamber are traces of a Merlin relief and another of Bacchus. Above the Hermitage is a Gothick 'Cromlech'*

hewn figures still lie on the quarry floor; they and the multi-caverned park created a marvellous playground for the Alderman's one legitimate child, William, the future Abbey builder. His juvenile writings are full of caves and hidden ways under the earth, places of lustration and mystery. Joseph Lane and his son Josiah went on to a career in grotto building from the beginning at Fonthill[18], but in 1784 the young Beckford brought Josiah back for 'rockifying', a process of turning that Lakeside Grotto into a woodland drawing room, a venue for his celebrated entertainments, with crystals for the walls and niches for flower vases. It was a deliberate recreation of the sylvan revels as painted by Watteau with the trip down the lake as a voyage to Cythera. Arcadia had been created by a man whose adolescent writings described this east bank as a 'Satyr's Range' where Pan and his retinue came to revel in huts by the lakeside.

Miraculously almost everything that the Alderman achieved after the 1755 fire has survived, battered but recognisable and in strictly private grounds.[19] The younger Beckford has become a cult figure, a proto-Byron, almost a proto-Satan, charismatic but fated, amoral but superbly stylish. Because of the private nature of the park, legends have grown up among writers who have never set foot in it. These grottoes built by the Alderman are often attributed to his son, whose gardening was restricted to the hills west of the lake where he planted out an extensive American Garden round the Bitham Lake. Only the Cromlech, a strange heap of twisted stones near the Hermitage, is the son's work. It may be secret and forbidden, but Fonthill rivals Amesbury park for interest and atmosphere. Fortunately anyone can enjoy the Inigo Jones-style triumphal arch, which the Alderman built as a gate lodge over the public road to Tisbury. This, like the nearby Boathouse, is likely to have been designed by John Vardy, a disciple of William Kent.[20] Both Splendens and Fonthill Abbey have been demolished, though a small range of the Abbey survives as a dwelling house in deep woodland. Fonthill is still a place to be relished, an Arcady that has gone Savage Picturesque and Gothick and then has gone dead.

Longleat offers no such nostalgic memories or atmospheric gloom. The 2nd Viscount Weymouth was a bitter, lonely man.[21] He quite probably murdered his wife's lover and then buried him under a floor in Longleat House, but he had none of William Beckford's confidence, talent or style. As recorded in an earlier chapter, it was during the Viscount's long minority that the elaborate formal grounds of Longleat fell into decay. Despite his shunning of general society he did serve as Ranger of Hyde Park and it would have been the serpentine created there for Queen Caroline in 1733 that gave him the impetus to have two sinuous S-curved lakes carved out of the bed of the Leat north of the house. These are both shown on the 1747 estate map by John Ladd (**colour plate 9**).[22] Apart from that Rococo impulse his interests, like those of many social misfits, lay with wild animals. The present celebrated Lions of Longleat occupy the same grounds that the Viscount used, up on the Grove, for his menagerie of leopards, bears, wolves, a vulture, an eagle and a parrot. Household accounts refer to them dismissively as 'ye Live Creaters in ye Grofe'.[23] Longleat has rarely had a normal country house history and, owing to the 2nd Viscount, it missed out on the most interesting and imaginative years in English park design, those of the picturesque Arcadias.

Apart from the serpentine lake, Longleat ignored the new garden fashion. Wilton achieved its Arcadia and then lost everything except that one brilliant bridge. Blessed, however, with an ideal topography, a sudden winding valley, abundantly watered, blessed also with Henry Hoare II, a natural landscape artist with the genial instincts of a showman, Stourhead not only achieved Arcadia, but after a certain regrettable refining process, kept most of it. Today only two threats hang over a garden that rivals anything in Italy or France. The first and obvious threat is the rhododendron; the second is scholarly theory.

Stourhead's owner, The National Trust, does its best with that blast of chemical-coloured blossom that afflicts the grounds each spring, eclipsing the lovely reserve of beech trees, holm oaks, lawn and lake waters with irrelevant municipal park planting. The Trust needs visitors and they react happily to magentas, pinks and acid yellows: eye-watering clashes of artifice. Fortunately, under the wise stewardship of Richard Higgs, the Head Gardener, cautious steps have been taken recently to cut back the encroaching foliage around the garden buildings. Purists like myself can always visit in the dead of winter.

Theory is another, much milder, blight on pleasure. With the very best of intentions Kenneth Woodbridge carried that neo-classicising process of demolishing cheerful but non-classical buildings a stage further.[24] His theory was that the garden had been planted to echo Aeneas' adventures in Virgil's *Aeneid*: his descent into the Underworld, appeals to the gods and quest to found a family home; Rome for Virgil, Stourhead for Henry. It was a solemn notion and appealed for that reason to the serious minded, yet it is contrary to the entire cheerful eclecticism and adventure-park spirit in which Henry Hoare created and enjoyed the gardens at Stourhead. What place has a Turkish Tent, a Chinese Ombrello, a Gothick Greenhouse, a Hermit's Cell or the Bristol High Cross in a garden supposed to symbolise a noble classical epic? How devoted to founding a family home at Stourhead was Henry when he built a little retirement villa for himself in Clapham? If symbolic myth was on his mind how was it that classical scholars visiting Stourhead in Henry's lifetime, men like the Revd Joseph Spence, detected none of it, while William Hoare (no relation), the Bath artist who was painting frescoes of Aurora in the Temple of Apollo, made no mention of his patron's supposedly deep purpose? If the Temple of Flora is where the Sybil begins to lead Aeneas down into Hell, how would the next walk over a high-arched 'Chinese' bridge have symbolised such a descent?

Kenneth Woodbridge probably never took the theory seriously himself.[25] It smacks of an historical 'investigation' on Channel 4. The way to relish Stourhead is to walk its almost sublimely changing circuit in sunshine, starting not from the lower entrance, but from the upper way into the pleasure grounds near the house. Like Alderman Beckford's east bank pleasure grounds, Stourhead landscape has no direct visual connection with its parent house. It is thus the absolute opposite to a seventeenth-century formal garden laid out axially upon a house façade. In 1734, while he was living in Wilbury, Henry persuaded his mother to plant a straight formal avenue of Scots Firs on level ground west of the house. That was his last ever formal planting; Italy would cure him of that and convert him to the Arcadian Picturesque. It is that trick of the Stourhead circuit which creates painterly compositions at every bend and descent that distinguishes it from the Earl of Pembroke's single-vista lake. A true garden detective will spend time in Stourhead House before venturing into the grounds. Painting after painting on the walls, including some quite bad copies, have passages that will then be found living and growing in the garden.

After the formal avenue, now mercifully replanted with limes and with a 1746 obelisk at its far end, the ceremonial circuit dips downhill. Little stone markers appear to direct the visitor to viewpoints where the compositions can be absorbed: the parish church tower below, the Temple of Apollo across the valley or the Pantheon (45), the temple dedicated to Hercules, looming magnificently down by the lake. This is the stretch of pathway through Diana's Woods where

45 *Henry Hoare's garden circuit at Stourhead still creates a series of perfectly composed glimpses, as here with the 1753-4 Pantheon or Temple of Hercules seen from the walk down from the house*

Richard Colt Hoare, Henry's grandson and successor, ruling from 1785 to 1838, pulled down the most playful park buildings, the Venetian Seat, Chinese Alcove and Chinese Ombrello. Colt Hoare wrote that Henry 'overcrowded his gardens with buildings, and unfortunately of different countries, for the Chinese was mixed with the Grecian and the Roman with the Gothic'.[26] Handsome as Henry Flitcroft's Temple of Flora is at the foot of this zigzag descent, it has lost the River God in the little grotto below it and a statue of Neptune rising out of the lake behind a team of sea horses. It is where the lake narrows that the wooden bridge once carried the circuit walk over to the dark wood and the Grotto. Forced now further up the valley, an energetic walker should leave the circuit and go up the valley to find St Peter's Pump, a lively structure of 1474, which Henry rescued when Bristol city council were about to demolish it for road widening in 1768. Most visitors miss it and only motorists seem to reach King Alfred's Tower of 1762, a piece of historicist eclecticism commemorating the King's victory over the Danes and, in an obscure parallel, George III's accession to the throne in 1760. There was always an outer circuit to Stourhead in the eighteenth century for horse riders to gallop around. John Parnell appreciated this feature on his 1768 visit:

> This kind of drive on the brow of a hill dress'd smooth, about the breadth of a race course, is one of the most striking and pleasing of all improvements, affording a charming place for air and exercise any time of the year'.[27]

After King Alfred's Tower, riders would proceed down through the woods to The Convent to take refreshment and view an exhibition of largely spurious historical relics; all very Gothick and gloomy.

Nothing, however, is quite as excitingly gloomy as the Grotto of the Nymph and the River God on the inner, lakeside circuit. It still works its numinous theatre today. The shades of yew, holly and laurel close in, a grim entrance yawns (**colour plate 5**), the sound of water beckons and there, under a vault of rocks in dim light, the springs of the Stour pour out past the statue of the Sleeping Nymph into a deep plunge pool. To the left yet another perfect composition is framed through a jagged arch of rock (**46**), which Joseph Spence recorded in 1765 was 'coverable with a sort of Curtain, when you chuse it', so that the inner darkness could be transformed at the pull of a drape, and plunge pool bathers could be protected from the prying eyes of the visitors on the lake.[28] From the vantage point of the pool, and only at that level, the lake, the Palladian Bridge, the Bristol High Cross, rescued like St Peter's Pump from civic philistines, and Stourton parish church below its wooded hill compose as if in a painting. In addition to that visual virtuosity, ahead, in even deeper shadows, a frighteningly real lead statue of a bearded god (**47**), by John Cheere of 1751, pours out water from his pitcher while beckoning, not to the way out, but back to the lake.

46 *The Temple of Apollo at Stourhead, designed by Henry Flitcroft in 1765, seen through the arch of the Grotto of the Nymph. A curtain could close off the arch to screen bathers in the Cold Bath from boats on the lake*

47 *John Cheere's River God of 1751 points dramatically out from the Grotto at Stourhead to the lake view. The source springs of the Stour should pour out from his urn. Cheere's inspiration was an engraving by Salvator Rosa of the River Tiber*

This is the place to catch the spirit of Henry Hoare. Instead of being subdued by his fabulous creation he would bathe here naked with a group of rollicking visitors whom he had met the night before at the hotel built for them in the village, all to the sound of two French horns, playing in the near perfect acoustics. He described it himself: 'a Souse into that delicious Bath and Grot, fill'd with fresh Magic, is Asiatick Luxury and too much for Mortals'[29], but perfect for rich bankers. It is a reminder that the Age of Reason was not all minuets and powdered wigs, but of gardens with cold baths for bracing tonics. The next building on the circuit, after a small Gothic cottage of around 1785, is a second reminder of the eighteenth century's lusty physicality, the domed Pantheon of 1753-4, Henry Flitcroft's finest park structure and the visual centre of the landscape. Venus and Bacchus, love and wine, stand at its Corinthian-columned entrance to indicate its purpose. Henry Hoare's wife died in 1743 and he lived on unmarried for another forty-two years. This was his pleasure pavilion, its statues were an iconography of overt physicality; after the cold bath he could come to this centrally-heated pleasure dome for – what? On his visit in 1762, Horace Walpole was more intrigued by the heating system, hot air from a stove at the back, than by the statues. Here Henry came to admire his own image, in a temple dedicated to middle-aged virility. Central is Rysbrack's sculpture of the bearded, naked Hercules: glorious cheesecake (**colour plate 10**). The sculptor selected perfect body parts from seven or eight models he found at Broughton's boxing amphitheatre in London and brought them together to make the eighteenth-century superman. Around him are arranged clothed goddesses and another male nude, Meleager the huntsman. Above them are panels of marriage and rape; the walls were originally painted 'a Blossom, (or rather light broken-purple) color'.[30] It was in garden buildings that the eighteenth-century elite escaped from the confines of Palladian symmetry and polite convention. The Pantheon is top lit; there are no windows for prying eyes. It ranks alongside Beckford's Lakeside Grotto and Amesbury's Chinese House on its river bridge: all combine privacy and exotic building.

After the Pantheon everything is bound to be an anti-climax. There was, until Colt Hoare destroyed it in 1814, a Gothic Hermit's or Druid's Cell to balance the classical Grotto on the other side of the lake. It was a late addition to the grounds of 1771 and comprised a series of rocky chambers decorated with the trunks of old trees.[31] Druids run through Wiltshire gardens like a theme, natural to a county which has Stonehenge and Avebury, but here only a few rocky shelters remain. The Temple of Apollo, so prominent in the landscape views, beckons but when reached is never open. In Henry's day it was a prime tourist draw, designed so that, at a point around midday, the sun's rays were reflected in and down upon a cast of the Apollo Belvedere. The National Trust should reinstate the statue and open the temple to visitors.

After the Palladian Bridge and the Bristol High Cross, the Spread Eagle Inn is waiting, as it did in the eighteenth century, to entertain a superior class of visitor. It helps to explain the curious popularity of the lords and gentry, even in modern Britain. Give or take a few notable exceptions, they have enriched the national life, as here at Stourhead.

One example of how the lively aesthetic of Wiltshire's grander Arcadias was distributed out to smaller gardens is Little Durnford on the east bank of the Salisbury Avon, a mile or two above the city. Bishop Richard Pococke, the arch traveller and appraiser of mid–century 'improvements' was there in 1754, finding:

> a great command of water, There are some statues here at the angles of a piece of water. They were given him [Mr Young] by Thomas Earl of Pembroke, and, it is said, were the design of Inigo Jones . . . naked figures in lead, and painted. They relate to some uncommon water diversions, particularly of the bever, the swan &c., and were in the grotto at Wilton.[32]

So yet again here are more spoils from that extraordinarily rich and much valued building. Quite what the beaver and the swan were doing with those 'naked figures' the Bishop does not specify, but lead was usually treated as wax figures are now, with life-like flesh tones. The statues have all gone but the Hermitage, which Pococke saw in a clump of trees 'adorned with Gothic grotesque figures', is now a little pink, thatched cottage of much charm. It has lost its inscription: 'Ie me retire/En tems jespere' and an urn with the inscription: 'If you would rest in peace bury these bones. Here lye interr'd a skeleton found in this place in 1754'.[33] Again we have prehistory, barrows and the Druids. Two burial urns were found at Little Durnford in 1734, so here is yet another manifestation of the county's increasing historical awareness, another angle on the eclectic.

There are, since Wardour Castle lost heart, no other great Arcadias in the county, but there are two truly great Arcadian garden buildings, one at Amesbury yet again: Sir William Chambers' Chinese House, the other an anonymous grotto that Ezekiel and Barnard Dickinson had built at Bowden Park near Lacock. Both are national treasures and both are relatively unknown. What is so impressive about this eclectic spirit of irresponsible imitation that hovers around all these Arcadias is the frequent emergence of an artistic masterpiece from the freedom inherent in this particular building type. A creative inventiveness was released which had been pent up behind conventional Palladian proportions. It took a genius like Inigo Jones or John Wood the Elder to make a Palladian façade sing through its restrictive orders, but an eclectic garden building could often soar through its stylistic release.

Only a perfect photograph or a poem can do justice to Amesbury's Chinese House (**48**). I saw its brightly painted cornices first, flashing among leafless branches as I stalked it through the woods of Vespasian's Camp on the hill above. At water level, as it balances trimly on its little bridge, admiring its own reflections in an Avon backwater, it comes across as a charmed alien, both assured and inappropriate in such a setting; though attendant clumps of bamboo do lend it some exotic support. The Willow Pattern Plate has landed in Wiltshire, yet adopted a strict classical symmetry with tilted gables on each side of its low central roof and a fretwork of surrounding balconies waiting to host alfresco entertainments by the Duchess of Queensberry who commissioned it.

1 Previous page, top *The old farmyard entrance to Avebury Manor. Surprisingly the Jenners, who bought the house in 1907, never replanted the pleached hedges which flanked the path in 1695*

2 Previous page, below *The South Garden at Longford Castle, laid out in 1852, retains its original eight geometrical beds, but they are hidden by a post-1945 move to herbaceous planting*

3 Left *The very early Italian fountain at Wilton, possibly acquired in 1577 when Wilton House was like a college and radiated Renaissance influence. The basin is carved with the arms of the Herberts and the Sidneys for the Countess Mary, wife of the 2nd Earl*

4 Below *Robert Thacker's limited view of 'The Great Parterre at Longleat', of around 1704 gives only glimpses of the Flower Garden on the left, the vegetables on the right. The four main quadrants have none of the patterned parterres shown on later plans.* By permission of the Marquess of Bath, Longleat House, Wiltshire

5   *Looking into the Grotto of the Nymph at Stourhead through its original 1748 entrance before the serpentine passage was added in 1776. The quote from Virgil's Aeneid, Book 1, reads: 'Within, fresh water and seats in the living rock, the home of the nymphs'*

6   *An English attempt in stone at the art of Benvenuto Cellini. Satyrs of about 1550 support the dessert table in Sir William Sharington's Banqueting House tower at Lacock Abbey, a room for viewing the gardens*

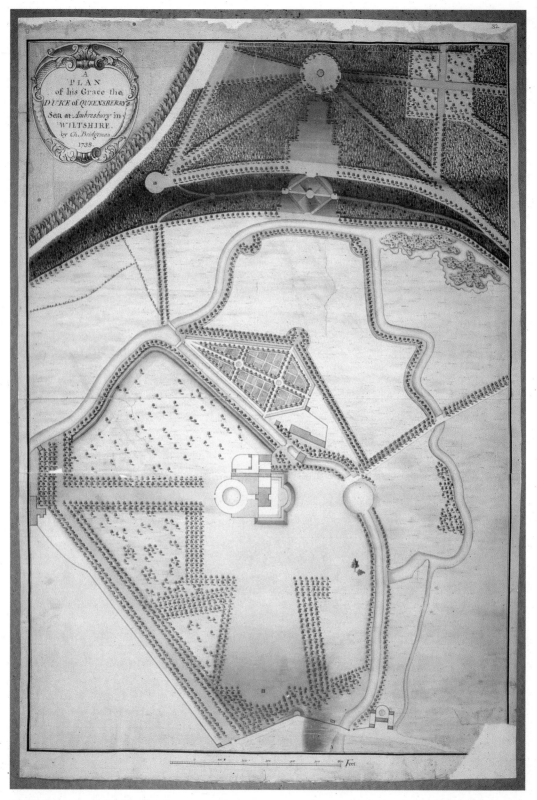

7 *Charles Bridgeman's 1738 plan of the grounds of Amesbury Abbey. A stepped, recessed rectangular clearing in the woods, a Bridgeman trademark, lies above the Diamond in the river bank. Straight avenues and an exedral clearing dominate the grounds to the east.* Bodleian Library, University of Oxford Gough Drawings a.3★, fol.32

8 *An undated plan of around 1700 of the grounds of Old Southbroom House with its gate-piers, formal parterres and castellated wall ending in a domed pavilion.* Wiltshire & Swindon Record Office, 1553/78

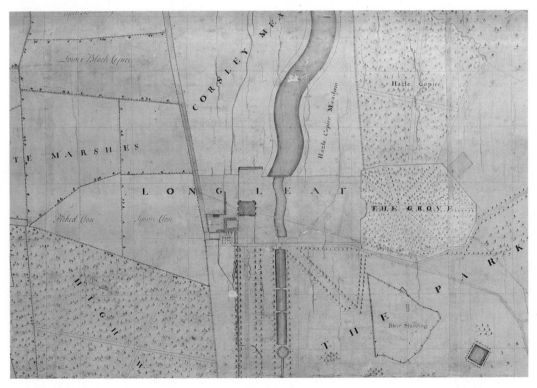

9 *Longleat waits for Brown: the grounds in John Ladd's map of 1747 after their neglect by the 2nd Viscount. His Serpentine remains and the Grove has achieved a separate identity as all the formal gardens have been swept away.* By permission of the Marquess of Bath, Longleat House, Wiltshire

10 Opposite *John Michael Rysbrack carved this statue of Hercules in the Pantheon at Stourhead in 1756 as a tribute to middle-aged virility, probably also to Henry Hoare. While the head is a copy from antiquity, the limbs and body are all modelled on parts of contemporary English boxers and artists*

11 Above, top *The Temple and peninsula on Bowood lake. Capability Brown designed the Temple in 1763 to stand behind the house, and it was not moved to its present ideal site until 1864*

12 Above *The Grotto in the grounds of the Old Castle at Wardour is attributed as usual to the Lanes of Tisbury, but if it is their work then it is to the design of Richard Woods, who intended it in 1764 for a site out in the park*

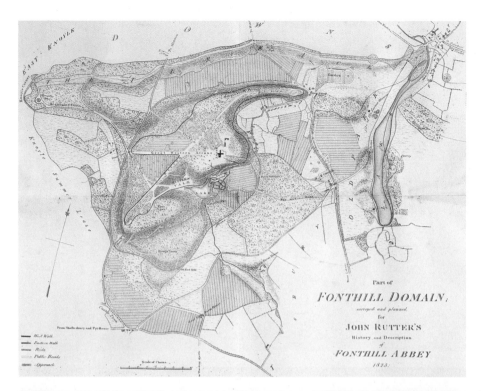

13 Above, top *John Rutter's 1823 map of 'Part of Fonthill Domain'. Alderman Beckford's lake with the grottoes and his son's Satyr's Range is on the far right. William's interest in forestry and the American Garden is evident from the plantations around the central Bitham Lake and the Abbey.* Bristol University, Special Collections

14 Above *The Art Deco work at Biddesden House never loses touch with the neo-Georgian, as here in this decadent 1937 Bacchus-Apollo mosaic by Boris Anrep in the changing room of George Kennedy's 1932 Gazebo*

15 Opposite *Archetypal Victorian garden solutions of steps and balustraded terraces at Castle Combe Manor. The piping youth is a memorial to a cat named Peter*

16 Above *In his* Boke of Iford, *Harold Peto wrote: 'Old buildings or fragments of masonry carry one's mind back to the past in a way that a garden of flowers only cannot do'*

17 Opposite *Looking upstream from the Japanese Tea House at Heale. The Red Bridge was inspired by a 1902* Country Life *article on the Dainichido Gardens at Nikko*

18 *The Half Moon Garden at Avebury Manor, with its buttressed yews, is a conscious early twentieth-century reference to the prehistoric stones nearby*

19 *It takes only twenty years for quite sizeable topiary giants to mature. These in the inner courtyard at South Wraxall Manor are invisible in photographs of 1905 and it is questionable whether A.C. Martin intended them to rival the sixteenth-century range*

20 *Chess pieces in the south-side gardens along the Main Lawn at Hazelbury Manor. These were all planted by Ian Pollard after 1971*

21 *Alison Crowther's Serpent Seat beside the equally curvaceous Rococo pond at Belcombe Court*

22 Above *Anthony Young's rampageous Wild Flower Meadow at Ridley's Cheer*

23 Opposite *This Chinese Ting was shipped entire from China to act as the virtual centrepiece to Julian and Isabel Bannerman's new garden at Seend Manor. The wave-cut beech hedge sets it off in a spirit of cheerful self-mockery*

24 Following page *Gerlad Laing's 'Woman with Wet Hair' stands appropriately in the stream, which runs through the gardens of Chisenbury Priory, where Peter Manser has created a mood of gentle eroticism*

48 *Sir William Chambers is known to have decorated the interior of this Chinese House at Amesbury Abbey to the directions of the Duchess of Queensberry in 1772. Who originally built it in 1750 is less certain*

49 *Sir William Chambers designed the Casina at Wilton around 1758 in his usual strict classical manner. It stands above the Echo recess that featured in the 1630s Wilton Garden conceived by Inigo Jones*

Sir William Chambers, who had designed a perfect neo-classical Casina (**49**) for Wilton back in the late 1750s, is usually put forward as the designer of the Chinese House in 1772, but there are problems. The Revd Richard Woodyeare, touring Wiltshire in 1750 wrote in a letter: 'Ambrosebury. A large body of a man found here, the thigh bone 21 inches. Saw the Duke of Queensberry's: a Chinese House and Bridge and fine canals in the gardens'.[34] Chambers had returned that year from his third voyage to China, but in the autumn was away in Italy. John Harris quotes another early reference by Hanway who visited Amesbury on 14 August 1755 and noticed 'a humble imitation of a Chinese house, which is well shaded and agreeable; but it consists of only one room, and is yet unfinished'.[35] Harris dismisses this 'probably ephemeral affair', urging that by 1772, when Chambers is recorded as decorating the interior with oak leaves and acorns in his usual classical conventionality, the early house was 'doubtless decaying'.[36] Park buildings usually take longer than seventeen years to decay and the case for Chambers' authorship is not convincing. From the hectoring tone of the Duchess' letters to Chambers she seems to have had more to do with the interior decoration than he did.[37] Although we lack a proven designer for an eclectic masterpiece, we do know what the building contained in 1779: one 'Deal Table', a 'brown bason', a sugar dish, one 'small japand tea board' and one small carpet.[38]

The Bowden Park Grotto of the setting sun also lacks a named designer. It stands tucked away behind two great plane trees and a yew to the side of a vast, undulating sheet of perfect lawn in the grounds of James Wyatt's massive, authoritative statement in the Greek Revival, a house that looks to have strayed from Cheltenham. There is something improbable in the idea that the man, Barnard Dickinson, a sugar plantation and slave owner, who paid for such a ruthless house in 1796, could also have inspired the delicate, shadowy charm of the Grotto, but that seems to have been the case. His father Ezekiel left £69,968 in realisable assets on his death in 1788, so Barnard was able to build in wartime when most such projects were suspended.[39]

'Very rocky outside' is the only comment in Pevsner and Cherry's county guide[40], suggesting that neither of them got in through the Gothick-arched French windows, but it is true that a whole catacomb of passageways and Druidic shapes in the brown local sandstone form distracting wings of fern, ivy and gloom on either side. The interior is actually bewildering in its detail: an uneven dome traceried with wavering lines of dark sandstone that half spell out letters and symbols. In its centre is a threatening stalactitic dagger, sheathed in countless crystal rectangles, stabbing downwards. Around it are gathered, in no order, fourteen slightly smaller but still deadly-looking crystal spears. They are not Gothick in their effect, just dangerous.

Initially the walls defy analysis. Rippling reefs of coral dominate, but every inch has shells, spar and other rare corals. Rich triple bands of native English shells start up at random points, swirl frivolously, then end in mid course. Florets of cockle shells with razor shell stamens are everywhere. Huge brain-type corals bulge in corners, pink conches add their Rococo outlines and two frail fans of netted black coral face each other across this astonishing space: oval or octagon, it is never clear, nor meant to be.

Over a buffet alcove five more crystal stalactites jab down; to the left a dark passage twists away out of the shadows, for initially this is an ill-lit interior, details have to be detected from the light of the three doors whose jambs scintillate with inset crystal triangles. At the base of the walls a broad band of ammonite fossils has been set into the floor to confuse the right-angles, a trick Prince Charles' designers have used at Highgrove.[41] The floor itself has tiled rays spreading out from a large central agate, sliced across, and geometrical motifs, one cruciform, star their outer points. The shadows of this complexity are irritating; Mendip mudstones have been cut open to reveal their crystal nests, but a torch is needed to appreciate them. In the Y-tracery overlights of the French windows Regency glass of deep purple, dark green and gold lessens the light from outside. There should be hidden illumination from a concealed skylight.

And then, depending on the state of the sky and the time of day, two hours before sunset comes the impossible transformation scene, with an ambush by the westering sun. As a direct light breaks in, a thousand tiny crystal facets of the place catch into a minute fire. Most rooms light up with candles; Bowden Park's Grotto lights up by the crystals themselves into a chamber of enhanced sunshine, those coloured overlights in the French windows adding an extra drama that may recapture some of 'that strange, necromantic light' the Count Philippe Jacques de Loutherbourg created for his London Eidophusikon presentations and for that 'Demon Temple . . . set apart for tremendous mysteries' that he imposed on Fonthill Splendens to celebrate William Beckford's twenty-first Christmas party in 1782.[42] It is a time trip, an eighteenth-century Rococo recreation that fortunate visitors can still enjoy. While Regency in date, it is wholly Rococo in detail and Arcadian in concept; it has, therefore, to find its place here at the end of a chapter of unusually important and pioneering gardens.

7

Lancelot Brown and Humphry Repton – minimalism and after

Capability Brown's first successful commission in Wiltshire was begun at Bowood in 1761 for the 2nd Earl of Shelburne. It was for a very grand lake, probably the most beautiful Brown ever constructed, in a very grand park. This chapter will, however, open, not with Bowood, but with a small flower garden tucked away in a shallow valley of the Salisbury Plain at Netheravon. It not only preceded Bowood by one year, being designed by Thomas Wright in 1760, but it represents a parallel strain of garden design that always ran counter to Brown's more high profile ventures and which eventually, through the career of Humphry Repton, succeeded and supplanted the Brownian fashion for bold, bare parks of smooth turf, long lakes and trees clumped to exaggerate natural contours. Netheravon anticipated the gardens of the future, the shrubbery pleasure grounds of the early nineteenth century; Bowood was the culmination of an eighteenth-century approach to park styling, essentially an Arcadia, but without the temples.

Netheravon was a hunting lodge of the 3rd Duke of Beaufort, and its garden was for his Duchess. Ten years earlier, in 1750, Wright had designed a garden for her at Badminton, a fantastical Rococo affair of curling pathways, multiple garden buildings and tightly clustered sub-areas.[1] At Netheravon, in the knowledge that his Badminton design had been rejected, Wright produced a modified version of what William Kent had laid out in 1734 for Frederick, Prince of Wales at Carlton House: the Rococo curves pared down to the artfully, almost natural.[2] Wright's plan proposed an irregular lawn circled by a winding path with bushes and trees on the outside.[3] At the south end he included a little temple-seat and at the north a round pool flanked by a greenhouse. But the innovative features were the seven, small, casually shaped flowerbeds scattered in no particular order across the lawn and alongside the paths.

These curved beds, or 'studs', as Joseph Spence called them, looked forward to the subdued intricacies of the villa gardens that Humphry Repton would design when he realised that the fashion for Brown's wide-open landscapes of idealised Nature had peaked. The nineteenth-century Gardenesque would be the next trend, and Wright's Netheravon was an interesting foreshadowing of that. My visit to the garden began as no more than a sentimental pilgrimage to a once significant site where an eccentric genius had worked. The grounds of Netheravon had long been army-occupied and were now the site for a housing development, so there was little chance of finding anything important; but as so often a site visit adds life to a plan.

Netheravon House is a late eighteenth-century brick box. Its north face has an exedra of stables overlooking a dry formal canal and an old dovecote. Wright's garden lay to the south in a deep dell running down to the Avon where the intensity of the effect is theatrical. On the terrace next to the house there would have been just room for the round pool, while at least half of Wright's lawn with its flower 'studs' would have been on a very steep slope that had reverted to downland grass with wild pyramidal orchids. That temple-seat by the pellucid Avon would have been fifty feet lower than the terrace, a dimension not apparent on Wright's plan. No trace of path, pool or temple remained, but it was easy to visualise the enchanted hollow, private and sheltered, that Wright had created and the seductive beauty of its scale. Wright had designed on a small scale whereas Brown always aimed at vast expanses; such a venture would not be forgotten during the years of Brown's grand garden gestures, and his first project in Wiltshire would be very grand indeed.

He had been called in to Bowood in 1757 by the 1st Earl of Shelburne, only six years after launching out as an independent landscape planner and contractor. But the Earl had found his plans hard to understand. He wrote on 2 November 1757 to his eldest son: 'I am persuaded that the man means to present me at some future time, with a well-digested plan for this place and perhaps come to me to explain it. He was very careful in viewing and examining, but was so very reserved as to any hints concerning what would improve the place, that he appeared no more of the Profession which introduced him to me, than would the most unmathematical man in his Majesty's 20th Regiment', which was his son's regiment.[4] He had paid Brown thirty guineas, a fee Brown offered to waive, hoping presumably for a much more profitable commission.

It was not until the 2nd Earl had inherited that Brown was recalled and, in 1761, had his ambitious park proposals accepted. Even then it would be many years before all his planting was carried out, his sizeable earth dam raised and the resultant lake filled. Today daffodils have municipalised his vistas and a lavish children's adventure park has parodied the elegant calm he intended, but Bowood is still very much as Brown designed it.

The family of Petty-Fitzmaurice were descended from a brilliant Irish intellectual and advisor to Charles II. In 1754 they had bought an ill-proportioned and unfinished house. But the 2nd Earl, later made Marquess of Lansdowne for his skill in signing away the American colonies with some dignity, had grand ideas. Even before Brown planned his huge park extensions, Robert Adam was preparing, in an uncoordinated scheme, to build an impressive classical mausoleum for the bones of a family that had no sentimental links to local churches. This was not a commission from either the 1st or the 2nd Earl, but one from the 1st Earl's

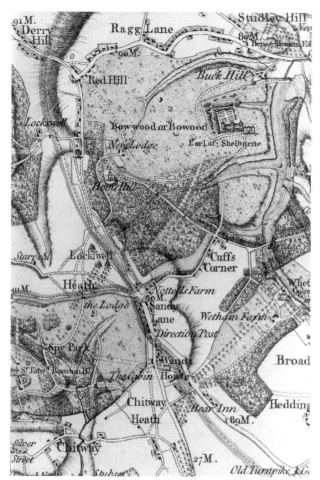

50 *Andrews & Dury's 1773 map illustrates the neighbourly closeness of the parks at Whetham and Bowood. Robert Adam's Mausoleum stands in dense plantations. Brown's lake has filled up, but his circling belt of trees has yet to mature. Spye Park's formal garden is still intact.* Bristol University, Special Collections

widow. She had been left Bowood in the 1st Earl's will and her son had to buy Bowood back from her. In the interval she ordered Robert Adam to produce a mausoleum roughly on the pattern of one in her Irish birthplace, Lixnaw, Co. Kerry.[5] Planned in 1760, it was not completed until 1765.[6]

The 'Plan for the Intended Alterations at Bowood' was drawn up by Brown in 1763.[7] A winding lake was to drown the little hamlet below the house, leaving only a ferryman's cottage to carry the lost right of way (**50**). Sinuous, often broken, woodland was to define the park area and the usual Brown carriage drive would thread those woods. Tree clumps and the Deer Mead Pond were to diversify those central areas of the park. These were often a weakness in Brown's designs as he had no strong feelings for central architectural focus points. One wonders if he ever visited Stourhead. There was, however, to be a temple in a private enclosure behind the house, and according to the contracts his skilled team was to drain and level the ground, create well-surfaced drives and raise the dam.

Entering the park today by the Golden Gates and Charles Barry's Italianate lodge tower, the impact is one of a composed unity; it is like looking at an ideal green

Vernet landscape; the lake, by the fortuitous control of the valley contours, seems natural (**colour plate 11**). But there is no detail of hedge or farm, nothing for the eye to dwell upon except that perfectly sited white Doric temple near the dam. That, however, was not placed there by Brown. It was taken down from the private area in 1864 and then rebuilt where it should have been from the beginning. Brown was not essentially Arcadian minded, he was more a land engineer than a landscape artist. Powell's map of 1763, drawn presumably as a survey guide to what Brown would have to alter, throws a revealing light both on Brown's practical response to the existing features in the park and also on his surprisingly unoriginal functions in that great reshaping. Without taking away Brown's credit for the vision that created the superb new lake, it is apparent that, before he planted a single tree, Bowood Park was already what is now called 'Brownian' in its planting. Round clumps of trees dotted the open park and there was, on a more limited scale than what Brown went on to plant, a circuit belt of trees around the existing park boundaries.

Brown's eight 'Articles'[8], signed with the 2nd Earl on 10 August 1762, promised, by 1766, to make a 'Sunk Fence' around the inner garden, and to 'Level all the Ground between the Kitchen Garden and the Water', sowing it with grass. 'A good and sufficient Head', or dam, was to create the new 'Water . . . making all the Plugs, Grates, and wastes for the discharge of Floods', essentially engineer's work. A 'sham Bridge' carrying a drive was promised, but never materialised; trees and bushes were to be planted 'on the opposite side of the intended Water'; a pond, now lost, was to be made in mid-park and there were to be 'Great Plantations on each side of the Mausoleum', then being built by Adam. Costs were set at £4,300.

Brown and Adam were both relieved of their duties in 1771 and a plan of 1778[9] shows that only slow, though faithful, progress was being made towards Brown's planting. There is no sign on that 1778 plan of the Cascade; indeed Brown had roughed out a drawing for a mill on that strategic site, which would have been a lost opportunity. He seems to have concentrated on handsome empty spaces where carriages could travel fast. The main flaw in a Brownian parkscape, one that Richard Payne Knight would mock savagely but effectively in 1794, came when a carriage stopped and the passengers craved incidents. Brown's tree belts did, however, provide good cover for pheasants and were also perfect for beaters and guns when the time came to shoot the birds.

Around 1785 the Marquess, advised by Charles Hamilton of Painshill, hired the Lanes, Joseph and Josiah, of Tisbury to build a striking Cascade (**51**), twisted round at right-angles to the dam and surrounded by pocket-sized grottoes and the Hermit's Cave with its ammonite roof. That still left a vacancy in the park, which would not be filled until the Doric Temple was moved in 1864 to take up the strategic site which Robert Adam's Mausoleum might have occupied. As a garden building of funereal solemnity the Mausoleum, despite its obscurity, must rank high in the county (**52**); only the Pantheon at Stourhead can outpoint it, but in garden terms it is not easy to place. The building clearly belongs to this chapter, being constructed between 1761

51 *The Cascade at Bowood was not planned by Brown, but it had evolved by 1785 with its scatter of small grottoes by the Lanes of Tisbury. Charles Hamilton of Painshill is supposed to have advised on it*

52 *The way down to the tomb chamber at the back of Robert Adam's Mausoleum at Bowood designed for the dowager Countess of the 1st Earl of Shelburne and completed by 1765*

and 1765, but the rhododendrons and azaleas in the rides around it belong to the next chapter and even to the late twentieth century. A visit during the six weeks of their flowering, when this park within a park is open to the public, is an aesthetic challenge. Treading the grassy walks of the soft greensand soil, a quiet claustrophobia of colour settles upon visitors. Acid yellow azaleas exude a honeyed perfume and clash violently with the prevailing puce, pink, purple, white, aubergine, scarlet, crimson and bronze of the rhododendron jungle.[10] Deep declivities of old quarries punctuate the rides and all the vistas are short. Thick bushes exclude the outside world. Then, as a sobering climax, comes the splendid gloom of the Mausoleum; built of a tawny brown stone, elegant yet heavy within, it tends to silence even small children. The most insensitive cannot escape the historical melancholy of the 1st Earl's white marble sarcophagus, the statue of Memory or the inscription recording the deaths, in August 1944, of both Charles, the 7th Marquess, and his younger brother. Our aristocracy has paid its toll over the years.

Brown visited the Pleydell-Bouveries of Longford Castle in 1761 on the same sweep that brought him the profitable commission to reshape Bowood, but the family was not impressed. Lord Radnor told me that he had found no record of their having paid him even a visiting fee. He did, it seems, advise them to widen the breadth of their exclusively riverine park by siting a large urn and a statue at the end of vistas cut through scrubby woodland. This they did. The urn is by Robert Parsons of Bath; the statue, in a loyal Whig gesture to a supposedly democratic Saxon past, is by J.M. Rysbrack and celebrates King Alfred with a winged angel figure holding a portrait medallion of the King.[11]

Another questing tour for business across the south-west in the early 1760s netted commissions for Brown at Corsham Court for Paul Methuen and at Tottenham Park for Lord Bruce. In neither park was his work notably successful, but both are interesting as being outside his usual design formula. In fairness it should be added that he was preoccupied at Corsham with complex architectural work, adding wings in three different styles, Jacobean, Gothick and neo-Palladian, to the Methuens' existing house.[12] That could account for the poverty of his solutions for the park. He planted 'the great walk', an old fashioned straight avenue to the north and in a contract signed on 6 December 1760 agreed to making:

> a sunke Fence between the house and the Chippenham Road. The draining the ground between the sunke Fence and the line of the garden. To making the Water in the Parks, as also the levelling round it. The levelling round the House, as also in front of the New Building [the east front]. The sunke Fence on the front of the Churchyard. All the planting included, Mr Methuen to find trees and alterations which have been made in the garden. The above articles comes to 1,020 Pounds.[13]

For whatever reason Brown left the park with nothing more than that northern great walk, a roughly round lake much too close to the house for good drainage

53 *The Cold Bath at Corsham is a poetic essay in Jacobean Gothick by Capability Brown with trimmings by John Nash. The plunge pool lies immediately behind the three arches; on the floor above is the changing room*

on a very damp site, and a system of unusually deep ha-ha trenches doubling then, as they do now, for drainage ditches. A sixteenth-century conduit house was left intact, linked to Brown's Gothick Bath House (**53**), a charming two-storey conceit, by a strange sunken area through which the stream from the conduit runs in a stone channel to supply the Bath House and the lake.

Paul Methuen's correspondence with Brown is cold and suspicious. On 17 May 1763 he refused to settle any bills until he had inspected Brown's vouchers.[14] When his son, Paul Cobb Methuen, succeeded in 1795 he immediately called in Humphry Repton to produce a Red Book and correct the Brownian errors. Today, the grounds at Corsham carry the marks of both Brown's and Repton's work.

At Tottenham Park, Brown had to cope with a client, Lord Bruce, later 1st Earl of Ailesbury in the new creation, who was not so much suspicious as unintelligent. But it seems to have been Lord Bruce who propelled Brown into the near impossible task of linking up the old formal avenues around the house, which Lord Burlington had designed in 1721, with the large forest of Savernake a mile away to the north. Between Tottenham and Savernake was a wide stretch of good farmland, which the client was not keen to lose to tree planting. Brown's problem was that Savernake was an old style, star-patterned forest with many straight avenues uniting in a central point unrelated to Tottenham House; Brown disliked geometrical tree planting, even though he had been made to create a straight avenue quite recently at Corsham.

A seventeenth-century star wood of formal rides was usually intended to stand as a separate park feature. There was one at Littlecote, less than a mile from the house, but no attempt was ever made to connect Littlecote house and its 'Great Wood'.[15] It was the same at Melbury in Dorset.[16] Cirencester Park in Gloucestershire was different. There, over the years between 1716 and 1775 Lord Bathurst managed to make one splendid forest park unit out of his Home Park in the east and Oakley Great Park in the west.[17] But that was only achieved by a complex system of interlinking avenues and by filling the gap between the two woods with several imaginatively designed towers, seats and lodges. If Brown knew Cirencester Park then he failed to copy Allen Bathurst's devices for union. When Lord Burlington had been advising on Tottenham Park back in 1730-8 he had urged his brother-in-law to create 'Rooms in the Woods'[18], and had drawn an octagonal pavilion and a banqueting house to lend visual direction. Brown, who had Lord Bruce, the heir and nephew of that brother-in-law, to deal with, made no such provision.

Brown's working methods are conveyed very precisely by the correspondence between Brown and Lord Bruce, and by memoranda written for Lord Bruce by Winckles, the 'Master of the Work' introduced by Brown to Lord Bruce to coordinate the designing and planting.[19] Brown's surveyor, 'Mr Spiers', carried out the survey between April and May 1764[20] and, once the master plan had been drawn up, Winckles would be given a yearly action plan for the contracted works to be agreed by Lord Bruce.[21] Brown would then make a visit and ride the terrain to see if he was satisfied with the improvements. A typical excursion was made on 29 July 1767 with Winckles in subservient attendance:

From then Mr Brown rode with Lord Bruce up Black Fault Bottom and up Durley Common where he made Observation as to the course of the Pales and altering the Clumps in the Park and laying that more open on the Durley Common side which Winckles heard very little of, the Conversation being with his Lordship. Objected to my Orchard being planted behind the Dog Kennel, or any other alteration being made there at least till the Removal of the Park Pale.[22]

On one occasion Lord Bruce's father-in-law, Henry Hoare, rode round the forest with Brown and the two men came to a compromise solution which Hoare tried to explain with a sketchy diagram to his son-in-law 'of what he understands to be Mr Brown's idea for the improvement of the forest so as to make it one great whole'.[23] If Hoare had interpreted correctly, Brown was intending to leave the seventeenth-century star rides in place, but to fill the segments between them with common lands casually clumped with trees. Wandering paths would thread their way through these areas leading to scattered lodges and farms in fields where burgesses of Marlborough had rights to graze their horses and cattle. Lord Bruce, soon to be Earl of Ailesbury, seems to have agreed, merely writing letters to Winckles plaintively demanding: 'a clump near the Salisbury road Mile stone, and if it is to be of fir, it may be fixed upon for my dear youngest son's who thrives exceedingly. But you must remember to make the clump large enough'.[24]

An enormous map of 1786 illustrates the limits of Brown's success.[25] Several 'Bottoms' and 'Lawns' sprawl about between the rides of Savernake; Braden Hook is a central hunting lodge; in fits and starts a typical Brownian carriage route attempts to circle the whole forest. But the main north–south axial line leads not to Tottenham House, but to a corner of its inner gardens, a curious solution. If any one thing works well to link the forest visually with the park it is a tall column, bought second-hand from Battersea.[26] This was erected in 1781, stands in a forest clearing and is visible from the house, but a wide reach of farmland still, in reality, divides forest and park. Thomas Brudenell-Bruce , Earl of Ailesbury in the revived peerage, lived on until 1814 and his heir, the 1st Marquess of Ailesbury, spent far too much money on rebuilding the house to Thomas Cundy's heavy design, calling a halt to any more tree planting.

Whether Brown had been incompetent or unfortunate at Corsham and Tottenham Park, it is not easy to decide, but at least half the skill in laying out a handsome and functional park lies in handling the owner. The other half probably lies in the luck of the topography and, as Fanny Burney reported scornfully, after taking part in George III's royal visit in 1789, Tottenham was 'of great extent and moderate beauty. We drove about the park in garden-chairs; but it is too flat for much diversity of prospect'.[27]

As if despairing of the ungrateful and grudging lords of Wiltshire, Brown gave the county a rest until 1775, when he prepared an impressive scheme[28], for the 8th Lord Arundell at Wardour, which Arundell then ignored, being more intent on building a basilica-chapel for his huge, new, glowering heap of a house. In the intervening years followers of Brown's system of park improvements had been more successful in Wiltshire than Brown himself. Richard Woods, a Catholic surveyor who specialised in work for recusant lords like Arundell had, in 1764, prepared a far more positive scheme for Wardour than that which Brown would draw up in 1775.[29] Woods' map proposed a plethora of eclectic park buildings, fifteen in all, to create a vast Arcadia on a basically Brownian scheme of damming up the infant Nadder to create a chain of crescent-shaped lakes in the great bowl of land that the new Wardour Castle was intended to dominate. Exquisitely detailed elevations of these park buildings were drawn by the hopeful Woods (**54** & **55**)[30], who struggled for years to squeeze from Lord Arundell a little of the money that was being spent on the triumphalist chapel and its altar of semi-precious stone designed by Giacomo Quarenghi, the future architect of Catherine the Great's St Petersburg.

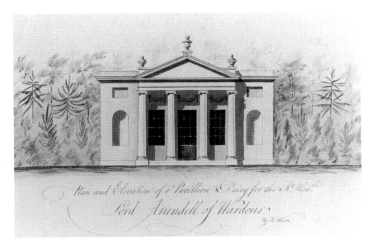

54 *An unexecuted design for a 'Pavillion & Dairy' for Wardour Castle by Richard Woods who had prepared a plan for reshaping the park with eclectic garden buildings in 1764. Wiltshire & Swindon Record Office, 2667/18/21, Folder 1*

55 *Woods designed this spiny Gothick 'Porter's Lodge' for Lord Arundell in the 1760s. An octagonal temple version was built in 1768 in the Lady Grove at Wardour. After falling into decay it was taken down in 1983 and re-erected at Hatfield Priory, Essex. Wiltshire & Swindon Record Office, 2667/18/21, Folder 1*

It is very easy to criticise with hindsight, but the 8th Lord Arundell probably made a basic mistake in abandoning the ruin of the Old Castle down by the lake and building a huge classical house by James Paine on an entirely new site high up on the north side of the bowl of land. The Old Castle had been wrecked after an heroic siege in the Civil War, and for a century afterwards the Arundells had lived on in a modest house near the ruin where an early eighteenth-century print of the time shows the Castle surrounded by a neat, but entirely inappropriate, formal garden of parterres within a balustrade. The Kitchen Garden was up on top of the hill, half a mile from the Old Castle, but out of the frost bowl. Woods moved it over to the New Castle. The wreck of the Castle should make a romantic park feature when viewed from the windows of the New Castle. In fact it is barely visible, lost against the background of hill and trees.

Poor Woods was dismissed in 1772, but by then he had achieved an elegant, shallowly classical Camelia House in a walled Kitchen Garden near the New Castle, which would be completed in all its ponderous pomp in 1776. In addition Woods was allowed to build a Gothic Temple of spiny elegance and an Ice House in the Lady Grove, a pleasure garden adjoining the Kitchen Garden, also a richly rusticated Cold Bath down by the Swan Lake. He had vainly hoped to make the lake into the centre of a Chinese Garden with a dragon boat sailing the waters and a Chinese Temple set on a Chinese Bridge facing the romantic Gothic ruins of the Old Castle. A very tortured Grotto (**colour plate 12**), still standing in the grounds of the Old Castle, is probably that which Woods intended to site near a drive in the middle of the park. As usual in Wiltshire the Grotto is attributed to the Lanes of Tisbury, but it seems too emaciated and linear to be in their style. The Banqueting House on the outer wall of the Old Castle looks as if an estate worker had designed it by improvising around a trained architect's drawing for an octagonal pavilion. It has a clumsy charm and commands a vista of pleasant landscape improvisations. The merit of Wardour Park is its roughness, its quality of 'explorability'. Because Lord Arundell was a Catholic closely involved with his Catholic tenants, there is nothing of the usual Protestant exclusivity about the park. Five rights of way converge on the chapel, whose curious apsidal roofs heave out of the bulky mass of the New Castle. Wardour Park would have pleased Uvedale Price by its rugged rusticity. Price wrote in his 1794 *Essay on the Picturesque*: 'Verdure and smoothness, which are the characteristic beauties of a lawn, are in their nature, allied to monotony'.[31] There has been no manicuring of its fields into lawns, its hedges largely survive and such lakes as exist are, apart from the Swan Lake, chiefly reedy and obscure.

The Dairy (**56**) is reserved to the last because its designer is anonymous, though it is obviously, by its brilliant geometry, a work by John Soane, who was adding transepts to the chapel for the Arundells in 1789-90. It is one of the most original and entirely assured buildings in the whole of Wiltshire, a circle ingeniously lodged within a cube, like some satisfying theorem of interrelated spaces. It should be hunted down where it stands in a back garden behind the chapel close to a

56 *The Dairy at Wardour is so confidently elegant in its geometry that it must have been designed by Sir John Soane when he was adding transepts in 1789 to Quarenghi's Chapel*

battered statue of St Anthony, rescued from the wreck of Fonthill Abbey. Another pleasure at Wardour, one of many available to walkers, is the sunken green way leading down from the New to the Old Castle, passing Ark Farm and the earth dam that holds up the Swan Lake.

The farm, named after the ship, The Ark, that carried the first Catholic settlers to Maryland, has a delightful sheltered garden under the threatening lea of the dam.[32] It was created, post-1951, by Neville Rolfe who moved the three-arched colonnade of alternately blocked rustication, a relic of Woods' Cold Bath, from the front of the farmhouse to the back where it stands as a loggia smothered in roses: Kiftsgate, Rambling Rector and Kathleen Harrap. A cataract tumbles down from the Swan Lake into a new lily pool hedged with iris, candelabra primulas and white aquiligea: a garden within the park and a standing reproach to the casual disorder of grounds which have never quite fulfilled their promise.

The time of the 10th Lord Arundell is outside the range of this chapter, but his hobby was designing Gothic lodges, and while he was not particularly adept, they have a rude attraction and are well worth searching out. Sadly the viewing drive in the woods up above the Old Castle has lost its views as the trees have grown up. As a Catholic I find Wardour Park redolent of Evelyn Waugh's *Sword of Honour* trilogy. This is my favourite part of Wiltshire, accessible but not over-touristed, an ideal England, almost but not quite Arcadian, half genuinely rural, half Valhalla for upper class retirees.

There is no proof that Richard Woods designed for Alderman Beckford at Fonthill when the Fonthill serpentine was widened out into a Brownian-style natural lake; but the two houses are only a few miles apart and Woods must have had plenty of time on his hands as he waited for Lord Arundell to make up his mind. Woods liked his lakes to have the air of being reaches of a long river, and young William Beckford, who often rowed across it, referred to the Fonthill water as 'the river'.[33] Like most Brown-style lakes it was created by an earth dam – the one unlucky exception being the lake at Lydiard Park, home to the feckless and unfortunate St John family, outside Swindon. That was held up by Sir John St John's very solid-looking castellated dam, which unfortunately collapsed in 1911 releasing most of the lake water. Now Lydiard Park has just a chain of muddy ponds pleasantly overgrown like a Wiltshire bayou, the haunt of joggers and addictive duck feeders. Lydiard House faces inwards to a lovely open glade of mature trees with some fine cedars, but that is not what the eighteenth-century St Johns intended. There is the long line of a ha-ha hidden among the trees – clear proof that guests in the reception rooms of the house were meant to look out over the ha-ha to open country in the front, and down long avenues to the right-hand side. The avenues are to be replanted and work should begin soon on the restoration of the battlemented dam and the reinstatement of the lake. This will be Swindon's eighteenth-century response to the recreation of the formal seventeenth-century Privy Garden at Hampton Court: the reinstatement of an entire Capability Brown-style lake and ideal parkscape.

While considering the gardens of this interval between Brown's major engagements in the county it is worth mentioning Henry Penruddocke Wyndham's ambitious town garden at Wyndham House in the grounds of St Edmund's College in Salisbury. It has long since been built over, but from a pre-1780 plan of it, drawn by Richard Woods, it seems to have been similar to Thomas Wright's flower garden at Netheravon.[34] The house faced a large circular lawn and the walk around it had bushes or flowers on the inner side with trees on the outer punctuated with 'pedestals and figures'. An octagonal basin, a survivor perhaps from an earlier layout, centred the lawn. A small summerhouse is drawn 'if required' in the top right-hand corner. To the left of this principal lawn is a long oval with three tree clumps. Several park benches are marked suggesting that the garden might have been intended as an inner city park to be used by privileged members of Salisbury's middle classes. In his *Beauties of Wiltshire*, John Britton mentions 'a little Gothic porch', taken down when James Wyatt was carrying out his notorious restoration of the cathedral, and re-erected in this garden where 'the addition of a pointed roof, and the appearance of the ivy, which has already begun to creep along the niches, render this a very pleasing object, when viewed either from the house, or from the road'.[35] Mr Wyndham, who must have had Gothic leanings, also put up an urn to the memory 'of a bloody battle, fought between Cynric, King of the West Saxons and the Britons in 552'.[36]

Bradford-on-Avon has been luckier with its town gardens, many of this period still surviving. Westbury House has a surprisingly grand, correctly detailed Palladian Garden House two storeys high with a portico of four Tuscan columns. Bradford Hall has a three-storey Gazebo, the so-called 'Dovecote', designed to keep an eye on workers in the neighbouring cloth factory; also two garden alcoves, one Tuscan, one Doric. The most charming of the town's gardens is the smallest. St Margaret's Place is a stone-paved walk of eight houses, their gardens lying behind exedral recesses on the other side of the walk. That belonging to Number 5 is a miniature Rococo layout, cramming a Palladian Seat, the trace of a Gothic Arcade, a roofless Gazebo and a classical central ornament, all onto a lawn 20 feet square. The town was prosperous in the mid-eighteenth century and its golden stone carved easily.

In 1775 Lancelot Brown made a happy return to Wiltshire, the county of his earlier difficulties. At Longleat he was allowed to do very much as he pleased, taking a broad view of the state into which the grounds had lapsed (**57**), suggesting radical solutions, draining, ditching and smoothing the turf, softening some banks of the 2nd Viscount's Serpentine and initiating the planting of thousands of trees. As it stands today, Longleat Park is much as Brown broad-brushed it out, even

57 *In this aerial photograph of Longleat one bank of the Leat retains its 1683 outline and there are clear traces of the multiple enclosures which the Brompton Park partners laid up the hill, leading to the Grove. Capability Brown enlarged the serpentine lake and its banks were later softened by Humphry Repton.* Crown copyright, NMR

though very few of the trees which he advised to be planted have survived two and a half centuries of storm. Tree ring analysis of the Long Standing after the great storm of 1987 showed that most of the trees had been planted between 1861 and 1879. Brown's contracts with the 3rd Viscount Weymouth were dated 1757, 1758, 1759 and 1763.[37]

After being incarcerated for many years in a Horningsham cottage with his father and Watson, his father's servant, the new 3rd Viscount, who reigned from 1751 to 1796, had a taste for major park improvements and lordly living. In 1789, as a reward for his high aristocratic profile, he was made Marquess of Bath. Brown played some part in raising that profile. Brown's principal changes were to the south-west of the park around High Wood. The Leat was subject to occasional catastrophic flooding, so Brown created a new walled Kitchen Garden and general service area down in the corner of the park, conveniently near the labourers of Horningsham village. By the terms of the third article of his third 1759 contract, he made a scenic drive from the walled garden to the house through High Wood with 'Shrubs, trees of various Sorts and Turf'. He did not propose his favourite device of a fast scenic carriage drive all around the park. Longleat's unusual topography would have made that perilous. What Brown offered, at a cost of £6,131.15.0, was his expertise and his trained team of labourers providing well-drained green turf on easy curves of land sloping down to natural-looking lakes and ponds, six in all, in a rather bare valley. By the seventh article of his first 1757 contract he had proposed extensive tree planting of 'Trees of different sorts, Lord Weymouth to find Trees' on that visually strategic ridge east of the house from the Grove to Park Hill – the Long Standing. This was where that oddly moveable landscape feature, Heaven's Gate, a viewpoint back to the house, shifted over the years in a southerly direction to its present place.[38]

That £6,000 had given the Viscount some financial distress and it was not until 1772 that he had recovered and begun beech planting in a fine frenzy of improvements, stung perhaps by Horace Walpole's disparaging 'the water is not well contrived, the ponds do not unite well and the cascades have not water enough'.[39] In 1772, 45,500 trees were planted in Aucombe Bottom and Wind Hill; 91,258 more were planted between 4 October 1773 and 9 April 1774. That was the year when the Long Standing as we see it today began to take shape with 200 ash, 200 Scotch fir, 200 chestnut, 300 birch and 300 beech with 500 more beech the next year. High Wood received 7,000 oaks, 7,000 ash and 200 beech between 1778 and 1779. By 1796, the year of the 1st Marquess' death, there were few bare slopes left in the Longleat valley; and as usual where Brown's heavy feet had trodden, no Arcadian park buildings, just trees, grass and water.

That should have been Humphry Repton's opportunity. For much of his gardening career he spent his time tidying up, or more often hoping to tidy up, after Brown. As a garden designer Repton was more reputation and communication than realisation. His Red Books, with their moveable slides showing how a park could be improved, were brilliant devices, working on the upper class mind-set in the same way that make-over programmes work on television today. They suggested the need for change, then offered easy ways to effect it. But Repton never mastered Brown's technical know-how on soil and drainage. He had vision but no back-up team of skilled labourers to realise that vision. Brown was formidable as well as affable; Repton was ingratiating, mild and easily cast aside once his brain had been picked at the price of £45, the standard charge for one of his Red Books.

At New Park, or Roundway House as it soon became known, just outside Devizes, he produced an unusually lively Red Book, but little else.[40] That was in 1794. At Longleat in 1804 he did much the same.[41] His Red Book would have transformed the park, but his practical efforts were largely confined to the Shearwater, a fishing lake away from the house. He did visit Bowood to advise on a greenhouse in August 1797, but only for one day.[42] His true sweeping up operation was at Corsham where, as mentioned earlier, Brown had left the grounds in a most unsatisfactory condition.

The Corsham Red Book has been lost, but Repton's first reaction was to urge that the Brownian lake should be filled in and a long lake created in the gully leading away to the east of the house. In a letter with a sketch, dated 28 January 1797, addressed to the Methuens' steward, Clutterbuck, Repton laid down exact measurements for the height and width of the new earth dam, which the contractor, Mr Dudley Clarke, was to construct.[43] Repton's principal concern was that the dam should be wide enough to be extensively planted up and screened with trees. In the event Clarke laid down his own procedures and dimensions[44], ignoring Repton, but the new lake works excellently when viewed from the east front, backed by the trees which Repton was so anxious to plant, and centred by John Nash's Boathouse.

It is not clear what else Repton did at Corsham. I suspect, but cannot prove, that he was responsible for that curious sunken area crossed by a curved rill that lies between the Conduit House and Brown's Bath House, this last altered later by Nash. Whatever planting the dell received originally has been lost, but it has that air of a villa garden's minor feature that suggests Repton. Easily the most dramatic and enjoyable garden device at Corsham dates back no further than 1967. Lord Methuen employed Ernest Tew to add some late Gothic roof vaulting which was being demolished at the Hall in Bradford-on-Avon to the rear of Brown and Nash's Bath House. As a result it is possible to mount a steep dark passage at the back of the bath and then turn sharp right via the Bradford Porch with its rich vaulting to emerge suddenly into a secret garden full of light and further revelations. A right-hand door leads to that rill garden, the Conduit House and the Arboretum; a turn to the left leads to the topiary garden, the Kissing Gate and the Venetian Garden Room. Best of all, with a glance backwards and with luck, one of Corsham's many peacocks will be perched self-consciously on Tew's tiled roof. This is how a garden should work, pregnant with possibilities and insisting upon choices.

Repton's time at Corsham did not end happily. As Brown had discovered earlier, the Methuens paid close attention to accounts, and Paul Cobb Methuen had to tell Repton: 'Your account is perfectly correct except in the particular of £10.10.0 November 24th which I have a receipt for. This I have deducted in the draft which is for £143.4.0.' However, he added, 'Corsham is no doubt considerably improved in your hands & we are much pleased with what you have done there'.[45] Repton was terribly embarrassed, produced elaborate excuses and was still trying to win himself back into the good graces of the family as late as 1803. He genuinely valued his few days in the polite, relaxed company of the gentry and aristocracy more than his fees, but was, nevertheless, careful to exact every penny in expenses. His real function at sites such as Corsham appears to have been that of middle man, guarding the family he was serving from being overcharged by contractors.

The watercolours of Repton's incomplete Red Book for New Park, Roundway, the text for which does not survive, were trendily un-Brownian in that, on the map of the grounds (**58**), he proposed a picturesque pathway for walkers instead of the predictable Brownian carriage ride around the park perimeter. As usual it is necessary to walk the park in order to understand Repton's decisions. A mildly desirable ribbon development of modern housing has colonised New Park's drive and a classical lodge of 1840 was built on the London Road, not at Repton's chosen site in the Kitchen Garden wood. James Wyatt's eleven-bay Grecian villa was demolished in 1954, but a surprisingly civilised new Roundway has been contrived with a few classical flourishes out of the old stable quadrangle. It is here that Repton's problem becomes apparent – there is no view. Yet 1794, the year of his visit, was a time when Richard Payne Knight, Uvedale Price and the Picturesque aficionados were dominant; there had

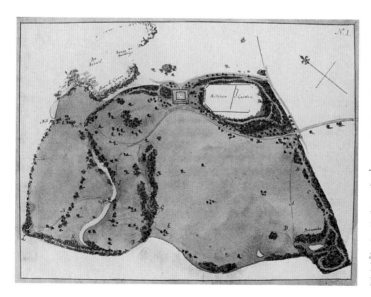

58 *Humphry Repton's 1794 proposals for reshaping the grounds of New Park, Roundway are clear from this map in his Red Book for James Sutton. A picturesque route would lead out west over a sinuous new lake and a walkers' circuit would thread the steep central grove.* Gloucestershire Record Office, D/1571, E396

to be views; but James Sutton's new villa stared out south across a flat field. Today that field boasts the second biggest oriental plane and copper beech and the sixth biggest noble fir in Wiltshire, also three tremendous cedars and a rare fern leaf beech. In Repton's day it was blank open parkland.

His solution was to create a shady winding walk in the woods around the walled Kitchen Garden, an excitingly visual drive out to Conscience Lane in the west, and a long circuit walk around the park plateau itself with picturesque possibilities at every turn. This path can still, with difficulty, be followed. Walkers were to set off initially down a steep valley along that west drive. One of Repton's before and after slides shows how the view north could be widened by cutting down a few pine trees to reveal a distant winding road. By painting a brick cottage white and adding a few white columns to a Gate Lodge on Conscience Lane two other views to the west could be given focus. More daringly Repton proposed, in before and after views (**59 & 60**), that a new Grotto-Cave should be dug out from the steep wooded cliff that rises to the east of the valley bottom.

At that point walkers could rest before climbing the cliff itself up a stepped path to regain the top of the plateau. Dense undergrowth makes the cliff impassable today. Once up on high again walkers could enjoy all the views westwards that the house could not command, and to enhance the foreground Repton proposed damming a small mill stream to create a Richard Woods-style river-lake, dramatically bridged by the visual drive to Conscience Lane. At the far south-eastern corner of the path, a little wood offered shade and a maze of paths. The effects would have been Picturesque, but not Arcadian. Only that Lodge could, at a pinch, be described as a garden building; otherwise it was Nature, Nature, all the way. Sadly only the western drive was ever laid down. New Park never achieved a lake, a grotto or even, as far as can be seen, steps up that cliff.

The ineffectuality of Repton's Red Book for Longleat is even more to be regretted. While the Roundway Red Book proves that he was keeping abreast of the Picturesque movement and Romanticism, the Longleat book reveals him moving into Victorian eclecticism in building styles with an easy confidence, designing a Boathouse and Fishing Pavilion in the manner of the 1520s, and a viewing pavilion for the 'Hill above the Pheasantry' and a 'Park Gate' in perfect imitation of the Jacobethan style that Jeffry Wyatville had been producing in his designs for the new service buildings at Longleat from 1800. The date of the Red Book is 1804, so there is a possibility that the two men were working together closely, even though Repton's text is critical of Wyatville's flouting of the correct architectural hierarchies between the parent house and its projected service ranges.

A lovely dreamy air of rough meadows, picnic parties, shepherds, sheep and happy children sailing their boats exudes from Repton's illustrations. He is bringing people back into the landscape, what he calls 'inhabitancy'. There is no trace of a formal garden; Longleat House is shown standing directly in the fields, but Repton is trying to correct the emptiness of the Brown landscape by siting boldly designed buildings at strategic points. His Jacobethan viewing pavilion

59 *At the point on New Park's drive where Repton proposed the walkers' route should branch away, he wanted to create a Grotto-Cave where they could rest. Here he has drawn workers digging one out of the bank.* Gloucestershire Record Office, D/1571, E396

60 *When the slide is pulled back, this is how Repton envisaged the scheme with a couple resting in the new Grotto, the scrubby trees cleared away and a vista revealed with deer on the slopes of Roundway Down. Steps at the side lead up the cliff to a viewpoint. Nothing came of this scene.* Gloucestershire Record Office, D/1571, E396

would, if it had been built, have dominated views up from the house to the Grove on the hill across the Leat, while his Fishing Lodge ingeniously combined a flat for the boatman's family up a spiral staircase above the gentry's refreshment rooms. For all his often syrupy concern for visible snatches of warm human activity in his parks, Repton retained that Regency arrogance towards the needs of the lower orders. The Park Gate Lodge which one view proposes has two rooms plus a little entrance hall. One room is the 'living room', the other combines the function of 'back kitchen' and 'bedroom', but the outside walls are richly panelled and ornate. The design may look Victorian in its confident eclecticism, but the social outlook that inspired it was still that of the ill-named Age of Reason, the eighteenth century.

Repton knew exactly where, in Wiltshire, he should have been employed in order to advise at the cutting edge of a great Picturesque scheme.[46] In 1799 he had written to the infamous William Beckford offering his services as Beckford began to create on the western heights of Fonthill park (**colour plate 13**) a vast American Garden as a worthy setting for the extraordinary Abbey (**61**) that James Wyatt was building for him on the hilltop. Beckford wrote back refusing politely, saying that it was impossible 'not to be flattered with an offer to contribute to the Ornament of my place from an Artist of your Eminence and Celebrity', but that he, Beckford, was managing nicely by himself.[47] That was no more than the truth. Beckford's American Garden on the west side of Fonthill lake and the Alpine Garden, which his old tutor, the Revd John Lettice, was laying out around the quarries on the east side of the lake, were Wiltshire's grandest Picturesque projects. Lettice's Alpine Garden was intimate and gently fey. After prettifying in 1784 his father's Savage Picturesque Lakeside Grotto and the Cold Bath half way up the wood, Beckford had tired of that Satyr's Range, his childhood playground, and handed it all over to Lettice, who was now acting as tutor to Beckford's two daughters. One result was a Fairies' Lawn, in a ravine carved out long before as a cart road to the quarries; today it is dark and oppressively wooded, quite un-fairylike. There was also a Rose Lawn, Bowling Green, Root House, precipice walk, and an urn to the memory of Beckford's guru, Alexander Cozens. The girls' pleasure pavilion, called the Paliaro, was a thatched wooden hut supported by six unbarked firs as columns and intended to evoke an Italian shepherd's hut. This had gone by 1832. In its prime all the paths of the Alpine Garden were planted around with flowers. It was a feature of Fonthill's Picturesque planting that before wild Nature took over along any route there should be first a choice planting of azaleas, rhododendrons and perennials. True wildness was not required.

That Paliaro also was typical of Fonthill's new generation of garden buildings. The Alderman Beckford temples and savage grottoes were out. In their place were more delicate ephemeral structures. Beckford never attempted to complete his father's triangular tower on Beacon Hill to the west of the lake; instead he had a Moss House and a Norwegian Hut built, structures that could melt into the greenery. His great Western Avenue, a broad carriage road, swooped over a public

61 *An illustration of how a quite modest garden pavilion can grow into a house, and a house into an architectural monster. The East Transept on the right was the last, 1812, and most gargantuan, section of Fonthill Abbey.* Bristol University, Special Collections

road on a bridge to bend north along a high terrace through which the Fonthill-Hindon road still burrows in a tunnel. But none of its surfacing was harsh gravel. Instead Beckford's woodsmen had devised a gentle, yielding, 'elastic body of various kinds of ever-green moss, low ground-fern . . . wild thyme and numerous sweet-smelling ground-flowers; the whole matted and interlaced together by a network of wild strawberries'.[48]

There was an exquisitely precious note to Beckford's gardening. John Rutter writes that 'the Carolina rose profusely studded the walls with its gorgeous blossoms – the allspice of the same region shed its exquisite perfume over the whole length of the gardens, and the arbutus luxuriated in groups as lofty and as branching as the Portugal Laurel'.[49] When one of Beckford's keenest admirers, William Venn Lansdown, made a pilgrimage to fallen Fonthill Abbey in 1844, he found the shrubbery that his hero had planted around the little Bitham Lake still flowering profusely, and speculated airily that, under the waters of the lake where Beckford had bathed in the company of a handsome Albanian servant, 'lay the fairy palace of the Naiads, the guardians of this terrestrial Paradise'.[50] There is always something self-congratulatory and intense about the refined perceptions of Repton, Beckford and Venn Lansdown. Only the elite with the finest minds could share the purest experiences. William Wordsworth must bear much of the blame for this mind-set.

Not all the gardening at Fonthill went into the wide fringes of the Nine Mile Walk and the Great Western Avenue. There was a little Herb Garden, under the particular charge of Beckford's dwarf attendant, Pierre de Grailly, in an enclosure quite close to the Abbey walls, and one illustration of the Abbey's cloister shows a fountain in the centre surrounded by pots of flowers and a striped awning covering a walk around the walls, set out with tables and chairs like a Parisian restaurant.[51] Surprisingly Beckford seems not to have shared the Gardenesque passion for big greenhouses. Perhaps a conservatory would have looked out of place up against the walls of a Gothic abbey. What he did spend a small fortune on was the south-facing complex of a garden servicing area on the hillside between Fonthill Bishop and Fonthill Gifford. This, the working hub of the estate, was completed in 1797:

> The Hot Walls, Pineries, Conservatories, quantity of glazed Frame-work, the Gardener's House, importation of soil for this extensive spot of many acres, with its plantation and nurseries, and an extensive inclosure of handsome brick-wall round the whole, have altogether concurred to render this work almost as unrivalled in magnitude and convenience, as it must have been in matter of expense.[52]

And while the Abbey has been reduced to the Lancaster Tower, isolated in the middle of a dull woodland, the greater part of its service complex, adapted and altered, but still extensive, remains unnoticed in all the occasional flurries of interest that surround the frequent Beckford exhibitions and Beckford centenaries.

8

An uncertainty of direction –
nineteenth-century gardens

This is the chapter of stylistic chaos, often a delightful chaos, as it will include one of the five most enjoyable and atmospheric gardens in the county at Devizes Castle, but a chaos nevertheless. The Gardenesque represented a nervous breakdown in the advance of English garden design. Suddenly there was too much choice, too much technological expertise in horticultural science, too many historic styles from which to borrow, too many flowers, shrubs and trees pouring in from a world empire. Those eclectic Arcadias like Stourhead had been symptoms of approaching nervousness with their range of potential borrowing: Grecian, Turkish, Chinese, Moorish, Druidic. Then came the trauma of Capability Brown's technology with his trained teams of workers creating handsome simplifications of landscape in the interests of economy, sport and speed. Repton followed – the great communicator and populariser. He told the gentry that they could all make over their grounds with trellis, arches, urns, fountains, greenhouses and conservatories fragrant with the flowers and fruits of the world.

Happily, all styles linger on in gardens after their sell-by date. Lot 2 in the sale particulars of May 1812 for the relatively new, seven-bay 1773 Southbroom House on the fringes of Devizes, lists just such a fortunate surviving garden. In the grounds of an older mansion of the Drew family, along with 'Garden, Orchard, two water mills' and 'Three Mill Ponds, offering constant delight to those who partake of the Enjoyment of Fishing', was a 'Wilderness':

> In the latter is a Hermitage, neatly fitted up, most delightfully situate in a commanding Spot in the centre of about Three Acres of Wood, formed originally by Nature and subsequently improved by Art, till it has attained Perfection as a Wilderness, with Serpentine Walks winding in a variety of Directions through this enchanting Maze. In the centre are Running Streams wearing the appearance of Cascades; the murmuring of which, together with the indistinct View of the

Meandering Streams below, and the variety of Delights with which this little Paradise abounds, has for many Years been the object of sojournment and admiration to the neighbouring Gentry, and who were allowed the *privilege* Two Days in a Week, by the late Possessor. A most inviting Sport is here presented for the Erection of a Sporting Cottage as the surrounding neighbourhood is admirably adapted to give facility to the Views of those who delight in Field Sports.[1]

This is a perfect instance of a watery Arcadia being touted, not so much for its umbrageous charms as for a pheasant shoot and for fishing waters. Amazingly something of Arcadia lingers on around Drews Pond on the outer suburbs of Devizes, but only just. The superior housing estates are advancing, but down the hill and in the woods springs still break out, stone walls create an illusion of privacy and there is an island in the largest of the mill ponds.

Bishopstrow has been much luckier. The old house, a mullion-windowed wing of which remains next to the mill house and cottages, had a long oval pleasure garden, split down its length by a high stone wall dividing the orchard from the walks beside the mill stream of the Wylye River. When William Temple decided to build a new house of refined Regency elegance on the other side of the Warminster-Salisbury main road, he valued his old garden so much that he built a tunnel under the road to preserve the connection. That tunnel today is part of the magic. I have to be careful not to over-praise this garden because I visited Bishopstrow under a brilliantly clear November sky when the garden was sensationally golden with the turn of leaf in a very late autumn; so the conditions could not have been more flattering. Temple's new house of 1817 is now a hotel, which retains its hidden garden deliciously unkempt and tousled as an extra for its paying guests, scything a circuit path for them through the grass. A Palladian arch of writhing vermiculated rustication has the date 1815 and WT set over each entrance to the tunnel, and after its shadows the dazzle of yellow leaf and sunshine in the happy confusion of this late Arcadia is overwhelming.

Arcadian charms are not easy to define. Somewhere, in the contrast between highly sophisticated and allusive garden buildings scattered apparently at random around rough lawns and fine trees, they create a climate of consistent aesthetic surprise. Moving around them, the perspectives bring buildings and trees together in changing compositions so that a visitor is caught visualising capriccios inadvertently. From the tunnel exit at Bishopstrow a monopteric Doric Temple (**62**), a vast cedar, dark laurels, brilliant deciduous trees and an octagonal Moorish Kiosk are all working together. For a few minutes it is possible to appreciate what Henry Hoare's eclectic Stourhead must have been like before Colt Hoare purged it of Chinese, Turkish and Venetian garden buildings.

The scythed path leads down past a Gothic door in the garden wall, and from that point onwards the wide, clear canal of the millstream takes over, edged by terraced lawn. A carriage bridge carries a drive across the water, but all the garden

62 *Whoever designed this garden temple for Bishopstrow got the proportions of the dome wrong. It stands in a riverine Regency Arcadia across the road from William Temple's new Bishopstrow House of 1817*

is on this north side of the stream. Kiosk, temple and cedar change places again on the walk towards the mill. Hidden completely in ivy is a Vine House, struggling to survive. The stone wall hides most of the old orchard to the left and on the right the divided millstream falls in a cataract down brick steps. Ahead, at the garden's end, a Venetian Seat, another reminder of lost Stourhead, crumbles away by the waterside. Across the stream there was once a Spa and a Cold Bath; now only water voles bathe.

The path turns back through the orchard with yews blocking out the road on the right hand and the temple in its laurels becomes again the visual focus. One rare treasure remains to be searched out. Down the side lane to the highly sketch-worthy range of mill buildings there is a footpath to Bishopstrow church. To carry this across the garden's canal William Temple must have called in Coalbrookdale or some notably superior iron foundry to make him possibly the most airily beautiful small bridge in Britain. It leaps the canal in an effortless curve and by some quality of the metal even the iron footpath is unrusted after two hundred years. Each alternate support to the handrail is topped by an iron acorn and a wavy classical motif runs along the sides of its iron arch. This is industrial design uncorrupted by nineteenth-century utilitarianism. The extra pleasure was having Bishopstrow all to myself except for an old man working in the mill house garden across the water.

The garden of the Old Parsonage at Bremhill was a very different pleasure. If Southbroom and Bishopstrow are hangover gardens, then Bremhill was a deliberate throwback to the 1740s when the third-rate poet William Shenstone was laying out a poetic-picturesque two-mile circuit around his gentleman's farmhouse, The Leasowes, in north Worcestershire.[2] At Bremhill, within sight of Calne and Bowood, a fourth-rate poet, the Revd William Lisle Bowles, was creating in the 1820s another poetic-picturesque circuit around his parsonage house.[3] But the Bowles circuit was barely three hundred yards in length and in 1820 the Picturesque movement was no longer at the cutting edge of garden fashion. However, Bowles did correspond with Coleridge when he was living in Calne and Bowles entertained quite a galaxy of minor celebrities like Sir Humphry Davy and Madame de Staël. Unlike The Leasowes, Bremhill had no waterfall, only west-facing views of the Marlborough downs and, a mile away, the Gothic ruins of Stanley Abbey for antiquarian plunder.

Bowles wrote an account of his garden in laboured prose in his 1828 *The Parochial History of Bremhill*, with a London publisher and an engraving of his much pinnacled, Gothic-parapetted parsonage. A few fragments from the paths he describes survive, pieces of Gothic carving from Stanley Abbey and a little pool.[4] The most interesting relic of his antiquarian interests is a miniature Druidic cave, a fake prehistoric remain. Bowles was excited by Druids and wrote much nonsense on the subject. For instance: 'The temple at Avebury being in form the same as the mystic emblem of the Deity in the Zodiac of Hermes, and this very Hermes, or Thoth, being Tant, or Mercury the chief and greatest Deity of the British Celts, let us enquire from whom is this Thoth derived?' and so on, all quite spurious.[5]

Today his garden trail begins conventionally with a long straight terrace backed by the churchyard wall. The terrace ends where Bowles had placed an urn, with an inscription in Latin to the memory of his dead brother. Below this, according to that published account, was 'a small piece of water, originally a square pond'. From this the walk 'leads into a darker shade, and descending some steps, placed to give a picturesque appearance to the bank, you enter a kind of cave, with a dripping rill'.[6] The rill still drips and some worn rocks of the cave can be distinguished with the eye of faith. In this damp area are five irregular blocks of the dark local sandstone (**63**), the same rock that was used by the Lanes of Tisbury for grottoes by the waterfall at Bowood. There may well be a reference to Avebury here, indeed Bowles writes of Avebury as 'probably the most magnificent monument of the kind in the world'.[7] So here, as late as 1830, Bowles was reviving the Druid cults that John Wood the Elder of Bath wrote about in his 1742 *Essay towards a description of Bath*, and in the same fluent nonsense.[8] The editor of *The Poetical Works of Bowles*, published in 1855, described him as the 'Father of modern poetry'.[9] He should have described him as the aged grandchild of eighteenth-century poetry. An example of his trite heroic couplets, taken from a garden seat facing the churchyard at Bremhill reads:

> *There lie the village dead, and there too I —*
> *When yonder dial points the hour, shall lie.*
> *Stranger, in peace pursue thy onward road*
> BUT NE'ER FORGET THY LONG AND LAST ABODE![10]

63 *Describing the garden of his Parsonage at Bremhill in 1828, the Revd William Lisle Bowles wrote: 'you enter a kind of cave, with a dripping rill'. This is all that is left of his Druidic evocations*

Thomas Gray's *An Elegy Wrote in a Country Church Yard* has much to answer for; but even today the garden of Bremhill Old Parsonage offers a valuable lesson on the intellectual predispositions of an initiate of the Picturesque movement: how much significance could be read into how little if the will was there. The Bremhill circuit ends on a terrace below the house at an obelisk with the curious inscription of 'Anno Pacis/1814/WLB', while England was still at war with France.

These then, Southbroom, Bishopstrow and Bremhill, are garden echoes of eighteenth-century thinking. To capture the very different horticultural tone of the new, nineteenth century, three more gardens evoke that mood: Grittleton has a park of experimental technology, Devizes Castle one of historicist romance and Longford has grounds shaped to rigid patterns of Victorian conventionality.

There is something Dickensian about Grittleton, the house and its estate, its origins and its development. Joseph Neeld, a London barrister, a bachelor and a man with no experience of country life, was left in 1827 with an enormous fortune, £900,000, a multi-millionaire in twenty-first century terms, by a miserly great uncle. Following the traditional way of spending great wealth and creating an appropriate social position, he bought an estate in the eastern shadows of ducal Badminton. Estate villages like Alderton, Grittleton, Sevington and Leigh Delamere, all visible from the M4 motorway, retain many Neeld farms and cottages while at its centre, around the core of a small Jacobean manor house at Grittleton, Neeld slowly, first with James Thomson as his architect[11], then with

Henry Clutton, raised a hippopotamus among Wiltshire houses, neither Italianate nor neo–Norman, nor neo–Jacobean, but a Neeldian amalgam of all three. Clutton's are the dainty Jacobean gables sitting absurdly on Thomson's Norman lower floors.

Compared with its immense façades the grounds of Grittleton have always been an anti-climax. A conservatory that could hold an entire orange grove now easily contains a swimming pool which overlooks a sunken formal garden with geometric beds.[12] Further out in the landscape is a sentimental statue group to match other such sculptures with which Neeld filled his new house. There is little else to see close to the house, but on the perimeter lies Grittleton's main interest, its semaphore towers, a unique complex of lodges and estate houses all visually connected by Neeld's impractical system.[13] Semaphore towers had been common to France and England during the Napoleonic wars, but they depended on constant alertness from a team of watchful soldiers working in shifts and doing nothing else but scanning the towers on each side of them in a chain. Francis Goodwin had included a Grecian Telegraph Lodge in his 1835 *Rural Architecture* and this may have given Neeld the idea of communicating across his considerable estate by semaphore arms. There are towers on Fosse Lodge, Foscote Lodge where Neeld's estate agent lived (**64**), Sevington and the estate stables at West Foscote. Sevington has the most

64 *One of the semaphore towers that Joseph Neeld constructed at Grittleton in the 1830s to link the parts of his estate, lodges and stables, to the main house*

remarkable tower, a replica of the medieval bell tower on Leigh Delamere church. Controlling them all should have been the tall neo-Norman structure which Thomson had designed to crown the house. Henry Clutton replaced this with the present vaguely Italian stump. Unless the lodge keepers' wives kept their eyes constantly on the skyline, the semaphore arms could have flapped in vain for hours and there are no reports of Neeld's neighbours hurrying to copy him. In 1856 he died childless. His marriage to Lady Caroline Ashley-Cooper, a sister of the devoutly evangelical Earl of Shaftesbury, had collapsed after four days when Lady Caroline found Neeld's love child, Anne Maria, living happily in the house.[14] The estate passed to Neeld's brother John whose six sons all died without a male heir, so, in a satisfying moral twist, one of Anne Maria's children finally inherited. The house now functions appropriately as a school of lively charm, not even remotely Dotheboys; the Dickensian parallels have ended, but neither the gardens nor the grounds can be described as an advertisement for Victorian garden technology.

For most of the Middle Ages the Castle at Devizes was a key royal stronghold, one good reason for the relative calm and loyalty of Wiltshire as a county.[15] But by 1648 its walls had been very thoroughly slighted by order of Cromwell and it was not until the nineteenth century that a castle reared up again on the site high above that most rewardingly English of market towns, with its textured and stylistically conflicting façades, twin Norman churches, brewery and market place.

My approach to the Castle garden, hopeful and unheralded, was like a delightful parody of a medieval romance. The massive twin-towered gateway had a door of solid beams; beyond it the driveway swung left above a deep, dry moat of green lawns with the Castle's wildly fanciful towers rising up from the steep hillside and motte. At a point where the tunnel of an abandoned railway line burst out of the hill, the drive swung back right, climbing sharply to reach the front door of the Castle complex, which is now in divided ownership.[16] Before I could even ring one of the doorbells, one of the two owners, Annie Kemp, looked down from the battlements, some thirty feet above, and invited me to step in by the sally-port. She was, I found, standing on the edge of the nineteenth-century rampart garden. So began one of my most memorable Wiltshire visits.

Where the garden at Devizes Castle is concerned I have to warn readers that I am unable to be impartial. While it is not the greatest, the most beautiful nor the most stylistically significant garden in Wiltshire, it is the one I like the most. The reason for my prejudice is that this enchanted enclosure, deep sunken below the theatrical towers and outrageous enrichments of the Castle is neo-Norman in its details, and my D.Phil thesis at Oxford was written on the neo-Norman, that oddball style of heightened, sometimes faintly absurd, Romanesque revival that ran parallel with the Gothic Revival in this country. With all its faults I love the style and Devizes has the most atmospheric neo-Norman garden of any I have ever visited.[17]

Approaching up steps from the north my first glimpse was through a solid Norman arch in an embattled wall, capped by those rounded casket motifs which are the hallmark of many buildings by Henry Edmund Goodridge of Bath, the architect who built Beckford's Tower up on Lansdown. But the most remarkable structure, the Fernery (**65**), a glazed neo-Norman arcade not unlike the bridge of a Romanesque ocean liner, which can be seen through the arch, is by G.A. Randall, not Goodridge, an addition of 1860-80 to the main building of 1838. The garden scene that opens up, or more exactly, sinks down as this sally-port gateway is passed, is so exhilaratingly complex and multi-textured as to defy definition. For a start the sad wreck of Randall's wonderful neo-Norman Conservatory lies in heaps of broken wood. The 1888 sale particulars describe it as 'a handsome building of octagonal form, about 35ft in diameter, paved with Minton tiles, and heated and ventilated in the best manner, and filled with a choice collection of Exotic Plants'.[18] All the fragments (**66**) have been lovingly guarded by Annie Kemp in the hope that some benefactor will swoop down and finance its restoration. The Fernery beyond it is safe from anything but an earthquake or a collapse in the railway tunnel that pierces the Castle hill, a relic of the abandoned 1857-62 branch line that once linked this richly bucolic provincial town to the outside world.[19]

65 *G.A. Randall's neo-Norman Fernery of the 1860s at Devizes Castle stands above the wreck of his equally neo-Norman Conservatory. Behind it is an eighteenth-century windmill topped up and tricked out with Henry Edmund Goodridge's neo-Norman detail*

66 *The sally-port gateway to the battlement walk of Devizes Castle. In front lie the sad remains of its neo-Norman Conservatory, still waiting for a restoration project*

Goodridge's improbable towers were England's under-praised and rarely noticed answer to Bavaria's Neuschwanstein Schloss, and below them is this deep hollow, with lawns, the stubs of walls and specimen trees ranging from copper beech to Wellingtonia and Scots Pine, all unexpectedly at home in this otherworldly and entirely private walled dell. Before going down into it, the glory of the garden is its terrace walk along the ramparts; all the views are inward because trees cut out Devizes town. The walk is deeply shaded and lined on the outside by Goodridge's battlements, which are studded at frequent intervals by that uncertain architect's deviant inventions: niches, recesses, gateways, each one inset with a sharp triangular gable, beset with huge ferns and liberally carved with cable mouldings, billet mouldings and the usual Norman zigzag enrichments, all larger and richer than their authentic models.

Lastly, however, down steep steps, is a real Norman arch taken during a restoration of St John's church in the town, deliciously decayed with chinless heads as label stops.[20] Further steps lead up to the stub of a medieval south tower, but the main way now leads down into the hollow, a vegetable garden, a nineteenth-century ice house, the remains of the twelfth-century hall and the nightmare complexities of Goodridge and Randall. There are token flowers and there are lawns, but it is the sense of safe enclosure that remains foremost in the memory.

The man who raised this palace of the loveably absurd was Valentine Leach, a local and clearly very successful tradesman. He died in 1842, a mere four years after the place had been built on the old royal foundations. His son, Robert Valentine Leach returned home in 1860 to rescue the fabric, working on it with G.A. Randall for the next twenty years. Most of the garden's liveliest features date to Randall, not Goodridge.[21] What is important about the garden, apart from its dilapidated beauty, is the way it conflicts with so much standard, trim-bedded Victorian garden design. Possibly that shattered Orangery could be described as 'Gardenesque', but the grounds as a whole seem to have been conceived in the spirit of Tennyson's Arthurian poems, under, one suspects, the influence too of the romantic novels of Disraeli and Sir Walter Scott. It would make a splendid setting for a film of *Ivanhoe*, standing in for genuinely Norman Conisbrough.

If only Victorian garden designers could always have worked at this pitch of imaginative sensibility, producing stage sets for the *Idylls of the King*. Longford Castle is no more medieval than is Devizes Castle, having been built during the time of Elizabethan rather than Victorian romanticism, but Longford has not been so lucky in its garden. The Robert Thacker prints of the 1680s show it handsomely set behind walled formal gardens with wild Metaphysical conceits on its approach drive; then there was an obscurely chronicled but obviously delightful eighteenth-century Arcadian interlude, of which a little survives. But in 1852 a plan was made, after the 3rd Earl of Radnor had moved to Coleshill following the death in 1851 of his wife Judith, for an archetypically conventional Victorian bedding scheme of quite unsuitable municipal vintage.[22] The plan is unsigned, for six geometrically patterned bedding plots, extended in execution to eight, each centred on an urn.[23] The garden was maintained every year with low plants in line with the 1852 designs until 1940.[24] After the war the present Earl's father went herbaceous while still keeping to the 1852 layout (**colour plate 2**). As a result the long rectangle below the balustraded south terrace looks pleasantly untidy with phlox, dahlias, heliopsis, rudbeckia and rather too much tall mullein taking their seasonal turn to add colour and subsequent messy decay. But if ever a house deserved a gracious Edwardian setting of tall, immaculate yew hedges, garden rooms and hidden pavilions it was Longford. It is not a house for open bedding, however thoughtfully handled. It is worth dwelling on the Longford solution as it was, and still is, so general in the county: balustrade, steps, urns, eggs of yew; regimented, uninteresting and unflattering to a house. While it will irritate some gardeners to say so, flowers are only of secondary importance when making a frame for a beautiful house, and often an undesirable distraction.

The best feature of the 1852 layout at Longford is the exedra at its far end where statuary from that mysterious lost Arcadia has been assembled. The Tempietto is by William Privet; it dates from 1769 and shelters a lovely lead statue of Flora by John Cheere. The composition centres upon a row of six tall herms: Antinous, Hermes, Bacchus, Young Faunus, Old Faunus and Pan. These have rare quality and the lecherous selection of subjects is more suggestive of the eighteenth rather than the nineteenth century. Dark red floribunda roses back them and behind them a mature copper beech saves the whole garden from its oppressive horizontal emphasis. Twice a year the ground beneath the tree is radiant with white cyclamen.

Hidden away in the Wilderness behind the miniature golf course is a shell-hooded Seat very much in the Jacobethan style of studded stonework, as on the entrance front of the Castle, which was remodelled by Anthony Salvin. The shapely three-arched bridge that swings out over the Avon from the castle and does so much to add a French Loire-side accent to it all, is by Gambier Parry of 1914. We can invariably trust the Edwardians to be sure-footed in their garden buildings.

The trouble with this standard Victorian pattern of garden designing is that everything can be seen at once. It is meant to impress, as seventeenth-century gardens also were, with grandeur, wealth and authority. There is no room for surprise or for charm. One urn or stone basin is very like another. Balustrades are entirely predictable as punctuation. Possibly it is unfair to claim that wealth and authority were key aims in these 'Italianate' gardens of the mid-nineteenth century. So many of the patrons who laid them out were Italophiles who had spent their honeymoons in Italy, as John Christian Boode and his wife Clementina of Lucknam Park had, for a whole year. Italy obsessed the Victorians and they tended to take for their gardens and parks the worst two features they could have chosen: an open parkscape in the Brown manner cut through, as at Lucknam, with one straight avenue; then, tucked away on the garden side of the house, a balustraded area with the predictable bedding. At Lucknam amends were made in the shape of a brilliantly spatial Italianate North Lodge.[25]

Nothing becomes one of these pattern Victorian gardens so much as the loss of its parent house. In the haunted grounds of Fonthill there is a forlorn and intensely atmospheric garden that once fronted the fifth, or was it the sixth, Fonthill House? Even Pevsner and Cherry are confused about the attribution[26], but it was Italianate with a tall Osborne House-style belvedere tower. The Morrisons built it, with J.B. Papworth, T.H. Wyatt and David Brandon all contributing to the design. Country houses in that delectable but oddly fated valley have short life spans: 1846 to 1921 in this case. But the Wyatt and Brandon garden, a wide three-part terrace with steps down to a second semicircular terrace, balustraded as usual, has not only survived but, by a happy quirk of nostalgia, been kept up, not with flowers but with well cut lawns, an oasis of order on the wooded hillside.[27] Two richly ornate groups of statuary, the Four Seasons and the Fair Elements, cousins to that couple at Grittleton, preside over a moving emptiness. They came from the 1855 International Exhibition in Paris and are styled in the enthusiastic French manner with garlanded, hyperactive nymphs. Anyone disappointed by the relics of Beckford's Abbey higher up the hill should find these garden ghosts rather more satisfying; but they are on private land.

Even lordly Wilton fell to the 'Italian' formula, though what is essentially 'Italian' about the pattern is hard to define. Even Wilton's Gothic parish church went Italianate with T.H. Wyatt and David Brandon's wonderfully authoritative basilica, rising alien but assured on the main street. Unfortunately there is nothing in Wilton House's 'Italian' Garden of this quality (**67**). It lies west of the House facing that unexpectedly relaxed and almost suburban west front with an absolute galaxy of the finest stonework and garden building clustered around Westmacott's commonplace beds of roses. In its centre is that superb marble fountain which

67 *An unusual view of Wilton House in almost suburban mood with Westmacott's 1826 Italian Garden in the foreground and some original details of one of Inigo Jones' viewing towers just visible on the right*

featured in an earlier chapter on sixteenth- and seventeenth-century Wilton. Looking down on the beds are those marble reliefs by Nicholas Stone of nereids and mermen, survivors of the great Grotto House of 1635; and down one long path is the Holbein Porch. Yet with all this inspiring competition Westmacott's pavilion is unremarkable.

There is something about this Italianate response: the quartering of beds, the central feature, the small round basins of water, that dulls the gardener's imagination; they all seem to respond to the enclosure with pink floribundas and forget-me-nots. This is probably an unjust generalisation, but that is how the memory recalls the indistinguishable Italianates of Trafalgar House, Lackham, Hartham Park and Frankleigh.[28] It would even have been better, with these houses, to have left them with the Capability Brown treatment and let the field grass come sweeping up to their drawing room windows. There should be something more to a garden than a terrace to keep smokers' feet dry when they step out for 'a breath of fresh air'. The puzzling thing about these mid-Victorian Italianates is how little they owe to Italy. Iford Manor has a true Italian garden, a terraced hillside of invention and inspired artifice. But Iford is Edwardian in date. It belongs to the next chapter, to 1899; but if Harold Peto could catch the Italian spirit of variety and surprise, why did the mid-Victorian garden shapers, men like Joseph Paxton, Charles Barry and W.A. Nesfield, reduce it to an arid formula?

There had to be exceptions. I had seen the gardens of Cowbridge House, near Malmesbury, in old photographs at Devizes Museum. They were heavily balustraded it is true, but had an impressive variety of levels and trees. On a hopeful visit I found that the branch line railway to Malmesbury had got there first, slicing through the Avon valley; and the Lucent Technologies office and works complex had got there second. I was only a poor third. There was, however, one strange relic. In a wood of sweet chestnuts and cedars behind the house, on the edge of a tarmac car park, a Chinese pavilion (**68**) of angular charm built of wood and brick nogging had somehow survived.

Castle Combe Manor, which has been taken over by an intensely American-oriented hotel rather than a technological company, has been much better served. At some time around 1884, when St Peter's church at Biddestone was demolished and its pinnacles removed to enliven Castle Combe, Mr Lowndes, the owner, was creating a modestly satisfying Italian hillside garden behind the Manor. A *Country Life* article of 5 May 1900 writes of Mr Lowndes as if he were almost dead. He is 'unmarried', it remarks pointedly, 'but his heir is a prominent member of the Cabinet', which suggests that he was old and past marrying age in 1900, so 1884 was probably the rough date of his garden making.

It is not a typical Edwardian layout of garden rooms opening one into another through dark hedge walls, but an 'Italian' garden appropriate to a steep hillside. This means that the water meadows of the By-Brook, which could so easily have been shaped into a formal sequence of pools and waterfalls, have been left as a

68 *This Chinese pavilion of wood and brick noggin in one corner of a car park is all that survives of a grand Victorian Italianate garden at Cowbridge, near Malmesbury*

69 *The Fern House at Castle Combe Manor, now roofless, is a Flamboyant Gothic structure of the 1880s in an otherwise Italianate hillside garden*

plain green setting for the Manor, the drive from the village curving impressively through them, past a tumbling weir and over an elegant bridge, giving visitors an excellent introduction to the nondescript but picturesque ranges of seventeenth- and nineteenth-century building. A statue of a thoughtful nude youth playing upon a pipe, inscribed as a memorial to a cat called Peter (**colour plate 15**), is made prominent by the simplicity of the setting, and there is a small round pond with a fountain.

The wooded valley slopes lie immediately behind the house, climbed by a long flight of balustraded stone steps. Above this, the hillside has been carved into a scallop slope of clipped box hedges topped by and focused upon what was Lowndes' Fern House (**69**), now a roofless arbour of vaguely Flamboyant Gothic with a pool on one wing and a seat in the middle. There is another nude youth playing a pipe, giving this formal area a Wildean air. To the left a long yew walk leads away through the steep woods, to the right there is another garden with a bridge across a public bridleway. Separate garden rooms may not yet be emerging, but they are not far away. Castle Combe Manor is only just pre-Sir Reginald Blomfield in its planning. If we had its exact date it would be surprising to find it any more than ten years earlier than Blomfield's 1892 *The Formal Garden in England*. Castle Combe edges towards the historicist with its pinnacle-snatching, but Mr Lowndes had not grasped, despite living in a village as paintable and antique as Castle Combe, the potential in copying native garden forms.

General Pitt-Rivers probably had seen the value in imitating earlier garden designs, but would not have been interested in exploiting them. The estate which he inherited in 1880, when he was fifty-three, was enormous – 31,000 acres over the two counties of Wiltshire and Dorset. Around Rushmore House the park was suitably large, pleasant rolling and forested country, the truest remaining relic of Cranborne Chase, but not rich in park features. The General was instinctively an Arts and Crafts enthusiast, and built in that style the North and South Lodges; these are picturesque, half-timbered structures, a mile and a half apart on the park's long axis. Rushmore is not manorial and the General was persuaded to build a chapel or Jubilee Room as he preferred to call it, in the most remote part of the park, across the drive from the North Lodge and in a roughly similar style. Rushmore House, which he had inherited from the 6th Lord Rivers, was late Georgian classical in style, and that may have been why the General built in 1890, quite out of character, a substantial circular Corinthian Temple of Vesta just north of the house to celebrate the birth of a boy-child to his eldest son.[29] That now overlooks a cricket field, Rushmore having been taken over by Sandroyd School with its remarkable score of distinguished old boys, including Antony Eden, Michael Ramsay, Randolph Churchill, Ranulph Fiennes and Antony Armstrong-Jones.

Such a tally seems appropriate as the general was himself a new age man, Darwinian, free-thinking, scientific and too sociologically alert to the problems of his time to be concerned with evoking the historicist past. To understand his mind and the way he had slotted himself into his contemporary late Victorian world, it helps to have read G.B. Shaw's *Heartbreak House* and E.M. Forster's *A Room with a View*. The General died in 1900, aged seventy-three, so he was not technically an Edwardian, and that is fitting. There is something, 'after us the Deluge', about Edwardian society, a premonition of doom, a clock ticking, dancing on the deck of the Titanic, and that was not remotely the way the General lived or saw the future.

He was a high-minded, confident Victorian who had given up on God, but not on the Empire or on his fellow man. An expert on guns and gunnery, he had retired from the army with the rank of Lieutenant General in 1882, having already succeeded to the Pitt-Rivers wealth and estate. So many of his remote relatives had died, leaving him the heir, that it is tempting to envisage him going around with his guns, cunningly assassinating them like the D'Asgoigne character played in the 'Kind Hearts and Coronets' film by Alec Guiness. As a convinced atheist Pitt-Rivers was, needless to say, far too moral for that. His true profession was that of an archaeologist with strong anthropological leanings and he pioneered scientific methods of excavating prehistoric sites, working tirelessly with a team of labourers to dig the barrows and earthworks of the area. What he unearthed he exhibited in a new museum set up improbably in the village of Farnham, just down the road from his seat, Rushmore Park at Tollard Royal.

Farnham could never be described as a readily accessible museum site, and it was in part to attract new visitors to the area and to his new hotel at Farnham that the General began to create his intensely idealistic and unlikely leisure garden on the wooded hillside above Tollard Royal. These, the Larmer Tree Gardens, must be the eeriest, remotest and saddest of pleasure grounds in that long succession which goes back in the county at least as far as Stourhead. They were re-opened by Michael Pitt-Rivers, great-grandson of their creator, in 1999 after they had closed in 1966. It might be wise to go quickly to visit them as they may not remain open for long.[30]

The Gardens are a relic of that hopeful time in the last twenty years of the nineteenth century when the working classes had been given the vote by Parliament and mobility by the bicycle. Horses and cyclists shared together the dusty roads and, before the Labour Party began to seem a threat, the ruling classes were anxious to educate and civilise their potential new masters. General Pitt-Rivers began to lay out the Gardens in the early 1880s with the shrewd addition of 100 cycle racks. With an eighteen-hole golf course next door the gardens were a success. Major celebrations were held on Whit Monday, August Bank Holiday and the first Wednesday in September. Thomas Hardy paid a visit in 1895 when twelve thousand 'Vauxhall Lights' lit up the grounds and the Green was full of dancing couples. 'Quite the prettiest sight I ever saw in my life', he exclaimed, and promptly wrote a poem. He was staying for a week at Rushmore with the General and Mrs Pitt-Rivers for the September festival at the Gardens. Hardy led off the folk dancing, mainly polka mazurkas and schottisches, on the Green, with Mrs Grove, the General's daughter. There was a full moon and fine weather, but Hardy suffered a stiff leg and never danced again.[31]

The earliest building was a classical temple (1880) above the Dell. Then, with cast-offs from the Wembley Exhibition, an Indian mood set in, with ornate

70 *Magnificently restored by Michael Pitt-Rivers in 1998, the Singing Temple at the Larmer Tree Gardens above Tollard Royal was built by General Pitt-Rivers in 1895 to entertain and educate the masses*

wooden picnic pavilions designed to overlook the Green and whatever was going on in the 1895 Singing Temple (**70**), a big classical proscenium arch and open-air stage for plays and concerts. A band made up of sixteen of the General's employees played on Sundays dressed in the costumes of old-time Cranborne Chase Keepers.[32] Entrance was free and crockery and cutlery for picnics were free also. It was Merrie England actually functioning.

The revival of the gardens by Michael Pitt-Rivers was a generous, optimistic gesture. The laurels that divided the grounds into six quarters were cut back; most of the Indian pavilions were repaired; the old Larmer Treee, a wych elm where King John used to rendezvous with his huntsmen at a point where two counties and three parishes meet, had gone, so Pitt-Rivers ceremoniously planted a new one, and shortly after died.

When I made my visit a notice over the half-timbered Lodge described the gardens as 'Timeless, relaxed, Captivating': all true, but even the ticket office was closed and just one old couple was wandering the green lawns. Sir Joseph Boehm's 1883 statue of 'The Hunter of Early Days', overlooking the green and exemplifying the General's anthropological leanings, has been moved to safety, but the effect of the pavilions around the green is eerily impressive. All around are shining laurel bushes and rough woodlands. The Singing Temple dominates with a beautiful new backcloth, a pastiche of a Claude Arcadia. Only the pierrots and playlets are missing. Around the woodland circle are the 1897 Lower Indian Room, the Vista of 1882, thatched and cosy down a laurel avenue, the General's Room (1899), a grand Indian royal box, and the 1880 Temple with a special Cranborne classical order, the bucrania all furnished with stag's antlers.[33] The Dell is full of hydrangeas and bronze storks stand in its pool. It is peaceful, pine scented and idyllic; the question is, do we deserve it?

Until we have all read and absorbed the message of Forster's *Howards End*, joined the Green Party and, in a clinching gesture, turned vegetarian, the answer must be that we do not deserve it nor sincerely want it. The memory of the Larmer Tree Gardens should lie uneasily at the back of the mind through all the self-indulgent aristocratic refinements of the gardens of the next chapter. It was the simple Eden garden of the Arts and Crafts movement, of honest labour in an ultimately classless society, the peasant aesthetics of William Morris, olde England curiously married to a new Empire. It seems appropriate, that after stepping out at the Larmer Tree Gardens on the arm of a lady, Thomas Hardy never danced again.

9

The extended reign of King Edward VII – 1880-1923

If Queen Victoria had pined away for sorrow in the 1880s and if her son Edward had cut back on cigars and high living to attain a ripe old age, then the 'Edwardian Garden' would have occupied its true time phase rather than that compressed between the actual dates, 1901-11, of Edward VII's reign.

The Arts and Crafts movement represented a patriotic maturity, a stepping back to confident Englishness after the wild eclecticism of the High Victorian period. In garden design the imitation of Italian, French and Dutch historic styles was phased out. Historicist pride in the Elizabethan-Jacobean past became the garden fashion, with a tendency to consider the garden as an extension to the living spaces of a house rather than an exhibition area for the display of horticultural expertise.

Two men, William Robinson and Reginald Blomfield, and their two books: Robinson's *The English Flower Garden* (1883) and Blomfield's *The Formal Garden in England* (1892), championed two opposing views as to how gardens should be created. Robinson argued intensely, angrily even, for relaxed, natural-seeming flowers and flowering bushes. Blomfield believed that architects should plan gardens as openly artificial and ordered areas, distinct from wild Nature. William Kent may have believed, back in the eighteenth century, that garden designers should jump fences and see all Nature as a garden; Blomfield, with William Morris behind him, would turn those fences into solid walls and thick hedges to keep Nature at a distance.

It was a rewarding and necessary conflict of ideas, with Blomfield victorious overall, but some valuable concessions made to Robinson's camp. Edwardian gardens are easily recognised. There is a formula – take walls of dark yew hedges, spires of topiary, stately flights of steps, with garden houses in convincing vernacular forms, and rectangular waters; then confine flowers, preferably to one tremendous herbaceous border as geometrical in impact as the hedges, but subtly graded in tints, and there is a lordly whole, but composed of several separate parts for privacy, pleasure and conversation.

The emphasis in such layouts varies from county to county, which makes the research and the writing of the Edwardian chapter the most exciting in each county garden volume. Gloucestershire was very room-conscious with distinct divisions of wall or hedge between each area. Dorset owners, in the same period, often designed gardens as frames to the beguiling seventeenth-century façades of their manor houses. Wiltshire, if one is honest, was not so inventively blessed in architecture and its garden planners seem to have responded with wide open arms to the county's smooth chalk contours. There has also been in Wiltshire an adolescent delight in towering topiary eggs. Perhaps Wiltshire's open skies cry out for vertical gestures. Surely the tallest leylandia hedge in Britain must be that four-storey monster which conceals an entire office block from the garden of Malmesbury House in the close at Salisbury.

Outwards and upwards has been the theme of Wiltshire's Edwardians. On Bowood's double terraces (**71**), by Robert Smirke of 1818 and then George Kennedy of 1851, the 1900 planting of yews has gone comically wrong. They lean, wind-warped, like drunken old men, over Lady Mary Keen's tastefully tinted flower beds of 1996; while Geiss' metal stags of 1852 turn their antlered heads away in shame. Keevil Manor has not been so exposed to westerlies and on its quite small lawn the Twelve Apostles (**72**) have grown and grown, like leeks in Yorkshire. These topiary eggs at Keevil are eggs in cups; a thirty-rung ladder barely services their tops and they bully and subdue their pleasant, gabled vernacular parent house. Its porch-cum-garden house and outer gateway, both with delicately carved seating niches of 1611, look steadfastly outwards, away from the giants who have taken over their east lawn.

It is probable that the Apostles were planted quite recently in historic terms, by Sir John Wallington, who died in 1910. Edwardian topiary grows with deceptive speed as back issues of *Country Life* will testify. On the entrance front of South Wraxall Manor today, the wonderfully eccentric topiary shapes on the terrace fight for a visitor's attention with the architecture of the house, but in 1905 they were paltry saplings, four feet high. At Westwood Manor the alteration of garden emphasis over seventy-five years is even more striking. There is virtually nothing now in the principal north garden, but large geometrical bushes, concentrated in its western half. They force the eye down sharp green vistas into its empty, tall-hedged eastern half. Most memorably the modest ranges of the manor house itself have, jostling up against them, a carefully clipped yew house of two apparent storeys. This lumpish toy commands not just the north garden, but also the entrance court. Yet the *Country Life* issue for 14 August 1926 shows not a single geometric bush and no vestige of the topiary house. They must all have been the whimsical creations of the retired diplomat, Mr Edgar Lister. He had recently bought Westwood, and indeed wrote the *Country Life* article himself with no description of the gardens. His beloved needlework fills the photographs of the interiors with fussy detail, in odd contrast to the discipline of lawn and topiary that he must have planned outside. Two ranges of the clothier, Thomas Horton's 1515–30 occupancy and a Jacobean gateway on the third side of Westwood's entrance court, had created the perfect opportunity for planting an authentic knot garden overlooked by Horton's first-floor oriel

71 *The yew bushes, planted in 1900 on Sir Robert Smirke's top terrace of 1818 at Bowood, have all bowed deferentially to the wind. Bowood's demolished parent house stood in the gap on the right looking down the terrace of Robert Adam's Orangery*

72 *Wiltshire is a county of outsize topiary. Here the Twelve Apostles are gathered menacingly on the lawns of Keevil Manor. The porch was built in 1611 to double as a little garden house with carved seating niches*

window. But now the yew house and more yews columns have taken over the fourth side. They permit views into the barn Court with its low-branched mulberry proffering fruits and its sea of white cyclamen, but a rare opportunity to recreate the true visuals of 1530-1620 has not been taken. The National Trust, Westwood's present owner, could never fell its yew house; visitors demand their money's worth of memorable gimmicks.

Unless the Larmer Tree Gardens, which were begun as early as 1880, are described as Edwardian on account of their laurel-defined six quarters, which are very like garden rooms, the Edwardian garden style seems to have been introduced to the county by Harold Peto, some time in the 1890s.

There is, however, uncertainty over which of Harold Peto's gardens in Wiltshire came first: Hartham Park, north of Corsham, or his own garden at Iford Manor, near Bradford-on-Avon. Peto bought Iford from the Rooke family in 1899, while 1903 is the date usually suggested for his work at Hartham. But Sir John Poynder Dickson Poynder succeeded to the Hartham house and estates in 1888, and it is unlikely that he waited fifteen years before beginning ambitious changes in the gardens under Peto's direction. Certainly the additions to the existing James Wyatt house of 1790, which Sir John entrusted to MacVicar Anderson, were begun immediately in 1888, so Hartham, if he was planning there at the same time, would have been Peto's introduction to the county. He had been a successful architect, working in partnership with Ernest George, and this shows at Hartham as does his recent love affair with Italy.

Peto designed two dramatic new garden areas for Hartham, both self-contained but neither related to the house nor to the views out from it. He allowed two modest, balustraded garden areas, one to the entrance front, one to the south front, both conventional in the Gardenesque Italianate manner, with rose beds and yew balls, to remain undisturbed. Then, above this South Garden, up steps to a much higher contour, he had a replica of the Warwick Vase carved from a single block of stone taken from the Box quarries, and used this as the visual hinge to project out at right-angles a long South Terrace lined with herbaceous borders, confined by massive yew 'ranges'. This leads to Peto's favourite cliché from Alma-Tadema's paintings: an exedral stone seat with two white marble urns from Verona. Alma-Tadema always painted half-naked lovelies reclining on such seats, usually looking down to a sea coast. Conscious that the Wiltshire landscape, though pleasant, was without focus, Peto designed a round Rose Garden with a central lion column. This is now lost; there are just cows in a meadow, and the only way back to the house is via the Terrace again: not an imaginative solution.

Peto's second feature was a walled Water Garden where a long lily canal, flanked by paving and some flowers, led to a steeply roofed Italian Loggia and the T-stroke of a second canal, the two forming together a sizeable pond for carp. Where the canals met Peto designed a balustraded bridge on a shallow curve, creating an ingenious foreground of its gracious curve crossing the geometric canal to front the Loggia. To the right were rose beds and a simple classical alcove. All this was, again, completely out of sight of the house, though now an attractively ramshackle royal tennis court bulks unexpectedly to the side, like an old canal warehouse.

Far more intrusive is a modern addition, so philistine in concept as to be a garden drama in itself. A bare, graceless, stone house has been built in the middle of the walled garden and across the site of the long canal, confronting the Loggia and reducing the lily canal to an eighth of its original length. A pretty late Gothic pavilion survives in one corner. Hartham Park House is now a conference centre; Wyatt's stables stand as a telling rebuke to what happens now around it; of that Rose Garden I could see little sign, but the carp are alive and well fed.

Peto can be assessed with more justice at Iford, a steep hillside garden backed with fine woodlands above the River Frome. The clothier's tall, handsome Palladian house, which Peto bought in 1899, remains little changed, but its gardens are engagingly self-indulgent and Peto-created.[1] Two distinct axes give coherence to an otherwise confusingly crowded three-acre triangle of stony garden events. The north–south axis climbs by enchanting fits and starts from the Loggia and Exedra Pool at the side of the house, where visitors will enter.[2] It mounts a flight of steps to a lower terrace, then jumps a little lawn to a round lily pond and passes through the east–west axis of the Great Terrace at a column cluster. At that point most visitors will desert the south–north climb for the level east–west terrace with its multiple garden buildings. But the north axis does continue, very steeply, into the billowing woodlands via rustic steps to the eye-catching column in the trees that Peto raised, during the 1914-18 Great War, to the memory of Edward VII, the 'Peacemaker'.

If the Great Terrace (**73**) is followed to the left and west it runs fifty feet above the house, balustraded and boldly dramatised by classical columns and a pergola to tall twin columns by the Italian Loggia of the Casita (**74**) and another of Peto's favourite exedral seats overlooking, a trifle anti-climactically, a little orchard. All Iford's best views are out to the south-west over the Frome valley, the bridge with its whimsical statue of Britannia and a striking bronze statue of the Dying Gaul on the wall of the private experimental garden across the lane. A mere half of the Great Terrace has been covered, but already the bewildering richness of Peto's invention and his collection of antique stone fragments will have become apparent. A very Lutyensesque rill runs behind The Casita to a watery grot beside a token Japanese Garden. Another coy, curvaceous rill twists its way down to the Exedra Pool at the entrance. Tiny pools hide among fern, well-worn statues, and crumbling marble columns catch the eye and the sound of water, not in any great Tivoli-style flow, but in trickles and gurgles, is always in the ear in this western half of the grounds. Iford's garden diverts brilliantly, visitors edge their way along from one capital, wellhead, antique sarcophagus or statue to another. Peto was a sensitive, intelligent designer and he feared that he might have made his garden somewhat museum-like. There is no point in retrospective flattery. That is precisely what he did. Iford is not an ordinary Peto garden, it is a hillside where picturesque beauty balances uneasily with historic artefacts.

73 *If Harold Peto had not been an architect and garden designer he would have kept an antique shop. Here his Great Terrace, laid out after 1899 at his own house, Iford Manor, is gloriously cluttered with Italian sculpture and sarcophagi*

74 *The Casita at the west end of Iford's Great Terrace is an ingenious and almost convincing recreation of an Italo-Byzantine garden house. Peto kept his topiary under strict control, unlike most Wiltshire gardeners*

Peto had travelled widely, in Italy of course, but also in Egypt, Greece and France; and if only he could have brought himself to part with his purchases he could have set up in trade as an antique dealer (**colour plate 16**).[3] Nothing that he bought was of the first rank[4], but he had all of John Ruskin's feeling for the textures of warm stone and delicately coloured veins of rare marble. To experience this very late Victorian aesthetic obsession to the full it is necessary to go back to the The Cloisters (**2**) at the far eastern end of the Great Terrace, passing on the way a native English Summerhouse of the eighteenth century, which Peto brought across the lane from the private walled garden. Peto was a Roman Catholic and he built the The Cloisters, where candles still burn in devotion, partly as a Christian chapel, partly as a place where he could relish his marbles.

Time and the moist English climate of this wooded valley have not been kind to Peto's stones. He began in 1916 to explain his obsession in *The Boke of Iford*, but never finished writing it. Peto projects himself as a human bower bird, first weaving a nest then decorating it, as a Malaysian bower bird does, with valued items. A bower bird loves shiny, black artefacts, the shells of black beetles; Harold Peto loved chunks of marble, the rarer the better. Greek Cipollino, Brescia Africano, pink Verona marble and Parian were his pleasure, and one he was anxious to share. A modern visitor should try to empathise with that Victorian aesthetic, but it is not easy. In The Cloisters, immediately to the right of the entrance is a table top which *The Boke* describes as 'a most remarkable panel of Brescia Universelle . . . an extremely rare marble which comes from the Soudan . . . Lord Lansdown has two slabs of it mounted as sideboards, mine', Peto gloats endearingly, 'is the third, and there were only four in the block'.[5] He claims that it 'contains the most astonishing varieties of greens that I know and with beautiful bits of Jasper'.[6]

Visitors will make their own judgements, but to me the Jasper has gone almost black and the 'greens' are like dying lichens. It requires an effort of the imagination to see it clean, subtle and gleaming under Peto's caressing hand; but for a living experience of a lost aesthetic outlook, to see things as Browning and Ruskin would have seen them, Iford cannot be matched. One word of warning – Iford, facing west of south, needs sunshine. Avoid it on an average English summer's day of cloud; visit when the Great Terrace bakes in heat and The Cloisters and The Casita offer a grateful shade. Iford is not quite Wiltshire; it has an uneasily mixed nationality.

If visitors have the opportunity to look inside the experimental garden across the lane on one of its rare open days, they should take it, as the owners and their Head Gardener, Leon Butler, have created a remarkable twentieth-century conceit. A chequerboard of box has been grown on a quite steeply sloping hard landscape of cement squares into which Mrs Cartwright-Hignett's four-line poem on the uses of Time has been set in pebbles: 'Time is our chequer board of dark and bright, with peace, turmoil, grieving and delight. And in the end there is no more time to tell, so to make amends, love and use time well'. It concludes with the initials of both the poetess and her gardeners.

Heale, in the Avon valley's most garden-rich stretch, at Woodford above Salisbury, was Harold Peto's third and last Wiltshire garden design. At Heale House, where he was working for Louis Greville, who had bought the place in 1894, Peto's career meshes with that of Detmar Jellings Blow, a better architect than garden designer. Blow added wings in a convincing Artisan Mannerist classicism of the mid-seventeenth century to Heale after 1894. Peto laid out three attractive, but typically slightly self-conscious gardens between 1901 and 1906 at the front and the back of the house. Meanwhile, less than a mile up the Avon, Blow was rebuilding Wilsford House for Lord Glenconner; and, at the same time, designing Little Ridge on the east side of the lake at Fonthill for the Morrisons. At both his two houses Blow designed the gardens. If the various commissions are considered competitively, then Peto comes out ahead of Blow, but Louis Greville, a brother of Lord Warwick, was a more inventive gardener than either of the two professionals.

Peto had given him a long downward sloping front garden that begins in a suburban manner with a yew hedge, a little front gate and an opening Top Terrace. This has Peto's usual exedral seats, one at each end.[7] The garden, therefore, begins where most end. A York stone-flagged path leads straight down to the front door between mop-headed acacias which have replaced Peto's laburnums. Lawns, clipped box beds and twin fishponds flank the path, an inappropriately suburban approach to a country house. Around the back the Avon, crystal clear, fast flowing, but only a foot or two deep, has inspired Peto to design a delightfully grandiloquent gesture: a balustraded Boat Terrace with steps down, as if some gilded pinnace with trumpeters and well-dressed ladies in crinolines were expected to come sailing down that casual stream. It is unlikely to have been much used, but irises and roses make free with it.

Louis Greville, who had been a Secretary at the British embassy in Tokyo, had an even more fanciful notion. *Country Life* had featured an article, one of three, by Mrs Hugh Fraser, on 'Gardens in Japan'.[8] Illustrated in her enthusiastic account were the Red Lacquer Bridge at Nikko and a tea house in the same Dainichido Gardens. Inspired, Greville brought over four expert Japanese gardeners, and soon Peto's very English layout of Boat Terrace, Long Border and Sundial Garden were outfaced by a river composition which is breathtaking at all seasons, but edges on an alien sublime in springtime when the magnolias are out and few leaves are on the trees. The Upper, or Drowning Carrier stream of the Avon's water meadow system winds first under a replica of the Red Lacquer Bridge (**colour plate 17**).[9] Behind it are the magnolias, one white, one pink and then Heale's master stroke: an eight tatami mat Tea House (**75**) of elegantly understated wood and thatch. Under this the Avon rushes cheerfully then hurries on past a convoluted Tea Garden of divided streams, twining paths and little flat bridges.

This last area has never quite recovered from wartime neglect. Its planting of iris, skunk cabbage and gunnera lacks the precision of an authentic Japanese garden and the two stone lanterns look lost, despite support from bamboo, willow and Japanese

75 *The Avon runs out with a musical chuckle from under Heale House's Japanese eight tatami mat Tea House. Louis Greville had served in the Tokyo embassy and brought Japanese craftsmen over in 1913 to shake up Peto's Italian garden*

Maple. But this is carping. Greville achieved the impossible: he equalled the oriental charm of Amesbury's Chinese House three miles up-river. After the Tea House the Tunnel Garden across the lawn seems tame, though it is in fact a successful later improvisation on a Peto rose garden of 1910. The four round box bushes in the centre around a pool are Peto survivors. The apple tree tunnels, which create its distinctive vistas, are plantings of 1965. That Long Pergola above it with its seat is planted alternately with laburnums and wisterias; roses clematis and sweet peas are interposed. There is another huge wisteria up on Peto's Top Terrace. Wisteria is a very Edwardian climber, Art Nouveau in its outlines.

What gave Heale garden its special air of the improbable on my two visits, in spring 2003, were the overflying warplanes, Tornadoes loaded down with missiles, roaring and circling again and again overhead as they practised for Iraq. Below them this river garden of inventions exuded an open and relaxed air of leisured wealth and exotic borrowings from the other side of the world. With its foreign notes and military thunderings, Heale is the most essentially Wiltshire of gardens. This has never been a shrinking, remote and rural county but, from prehistoric times, an embattled crossroads of a shire, influenced readily by the world outside.

After Heale, Detmar Blow's Wilsford House garden and Little Ridge garden at Fonthill were uninspired. Little Ridge was demolished in 1972 with its garden, which was a quartered square below a bastion terrace.[10] An angel sundial centred the square and in one corner a pretty vernacular summerhouse, arched and open, was built in 1906. Wilsford garden was as bland as Wilsford House. Curious pains were taken to save the mature creepers from the building that preceded it, as if Blow knew that his dull elevations would need to be cloaked. When it became the home of the committedly effete Stephen Tennant, Siegfried Sassoon's lover, he sensibly allowed the grounds to run decadently wild. That era has passed and order has returned. Hatch House garden was described at length in chapter four. Blow restored it sensitively in 1908[11], and planted topiary hedges in the spirit of its surviving three-hundred-year-old yew hedge north of the house.

There is this distinct cluster of Peto and Blow gardens in Wiltshire's deep south. Even though Peto himself lived in mid-Wiltshire near Bradford-on-Avon, he was not drawn to the heavier soils and level lands of the north. But at least five Edwardian gardens are in north Wiltshire and one other, at Avebury Manor, lies in the county's mid-point.

Avebury Manor's gardens are inspired, imaginative and visually memorable. Its maze of sarsen-walled enclosures has been described in an earlier chapter, based upon the plan of 1695 drawn up after Sir Richard Holford bought the property in 1692. Nothing of much significance was done to the gardens between that time and 1902 when Colonel Leopold Jenner and his wife, Nora, took a short lease, becoming thereby the envy of their like-minded friends in the 'ex-Foreign Office' circle of garden fanciers. Most members of this group – Edgar Lister at Westwood Manor, Louis Greville at Heale, Colonel Cooper at Cold Ashton and Jenner's brother, Sir Walter, at Lytes Cary Manor – had to start in their hobby homes with very little in the way of Elizabethan garden structures to work on. The Jenners, in contrast, had hit upon a quaintly charming house of about 1557 still surrounded by an authentic early garden frame. As soon as they had tested Avebury out, the Jenners bought the Manor and its estate in 1907 and, for the next twenty years, advised by Gilbert Jenkins, gardened with a brilliant mixture of wise restraint and poetic panache that would have surprised the original Tudor gardeners.

The Jenners built that small garden house tucked away in the New Stables corner of the east, or entrance, garden. They also articulated a route around the corner of the house into what was the Cherry, or old entrance, Court, and set up two pineapple-topped piers to mark the original entrance into the Cherry Court from the south. My visit was made on a radiant March day when a great simplicity of colour reigned – pale green lawns, dark green yews, grey walls. It is in the next enclosure, the Half-Moon Garden (**colour plate 18**), that the Jenners continued that Wiltshire garden tradition of prehistoric reference. The curved wall was Sir Richard Holford's, but it was the Jenners and Jenkins who planted and trained an overwhelming arc of yew buttresses along that curved wall and its raised path. Avebury's prehistoric stones never make a complete circle. Time has fractured them. But they still present massive arcs of masonry, and the Jenners' yew buttresses were a clear reference to those threatening sarsen stones poised over their deep ditch.

This is not a cosy garden. The curved path leads straight into a dark, spirit-crushing corridor of yew hedges, the Italian Walk so called, but entirely un-Italian in its remorseless vistas. It leads grimly around the Orchard to the Lion Walk and so back to the Manor. There in a cramped area between the west library wing of the house and the curved wall, is yet another of Wiltshire's characteristic topiary gardens grown into mad, extravagant geometry. The confinement of the Topiary Garden makes it far more claustrophobic than Keevil's Twelve Apostles and there is a battery of thrusting, angular castle walls of precisely clipped yew. It would be interesting to make a psychological study of the effect that trimming these monsters each year has upon the clipper. Certainly the mere sight of them affects a visitor; they are deeply impressive, like living robots, but they are not welcoming, only assertive.

Of the five north Wiltshire Edwardians, three – Great Chalfield Manor, Hazelbury and South Wraxall Manor – have to be ranked as five stars. So it is something of a relief to turn from over-worked praise to The Courts at Holt, an interesting half-failure among Wiltshire gardens, and one that throws valuable light upon the predicaments which must often face the National Trust when generous owners offer properties that it does not really want.

Until 1888 the house at the centre of The Courts was a mill owner's residence and most of the western half of the grounds was lumbered with the leats, chimneys and water wheels of a cloth weaving factory. William Davis pulled all this down, using the rubble to fill two mill ponds. After a period of neglect the architect, Sir George Hastings, bought the property in 1900, built the Ionic Temple, also a conservatory in stylish Regency pastiche and a loggia which links house and garden quite effectively. The house, not open to the public, has a bucolic charm that Nikolaus Pevsner instinctively hated: 'an instructive example', he wrote, 'of what a vulgar mind can do with promising elements'.[12] Hastings also brought in a jumble of garden ornaments from the Ranelagh Club in London, and he must be blamed for the garden's central failure.

His seven-and-a-half acres, with mature trees east and west, desperately needed a sense of enclosure from the village houses, and then perhaps a chain of hedged or walled revelations threaded around water features from the old factory's sources of supply. The way in should be from the west through woodland and orchard, not from the east where most of the features can be taken in at once: Pillar Garden, Temple Borders, Lily Pond, and House Lawns. A pleached lime walk has been planted to try to conceal these, but it leads visitors illogically to a front door they cannot enter and to notices asking them not to peer rudely in at windows which they must brush past.

The rill in the Temple Borders is unimaginatively handled, the Pillars, once used for cloth drying, make up an anorexic Stonehenge and the Dye Pool is confronted with the ugly backside of the Ionic Temple. Round the west side of the house a pretty water feature fills an awkward corner with iris, japonica, fig and wisteria. Then comes one good surprise view of a lawn orchestrated by bulbous topiary shapes and hedged exedras; but to the north the back gardens of village houses intrude. In the Orchard 150,000 *Scilla Siberica* shimmer magically for two weeks of the year and a young arboretum is well planted with narcissi. A radical reshaping by a gardener of genius is required. Nothing here needs to be reverently preserved, only imaginatively re-animated, the water features in particular.

Charlton Park is happily very private; the Jacobean house is a condominium, well guarded. Its grounds claim one Edwardian note because in their eighteenth-century walled garden Lady Suffolk drove long herbaceous borders backed with yew hedges down to a lily pond fronting two Georgian gardeners' cottages.[13] These last were linked by a greenhouse, but Lady Suffolk added a convex colonnade to mask the potting sheds and draped it with wisteria.

Now for the major Edwardian gardens of the north, most cheerful and open of which must be Great Chalfield Manor. Robert Fuller, a successful electrical engineer, bought that loveably dilapidated medieval house, with its wide moats, terraces and jewel-like All Saints Church, in 1905. He paid Alfred Parsons, a watercolourist and member of the Newbury architectural practice, Parsons and Partridge, a fee of fifty guineas a year for three years to create a garden worthy of the carefully restored house; the construction to cost £250, the plants £100.[14] Fuller's son and grandson have, with the help of the National Trust, kept the gardens at a peak of Parsons' perfection. A pleasant field walk over from the Trust's neighbouring garden at The Courts, Holt, should put the respective worth of the two into sharp perspective.

The best point of entry is between All Saints and the house. This brings Parsons' lordly area stunningly into view with a long wide lawn dominated by two

76 *The stone paved Rose Court at Great Chalfield Manor is a more intimate corner of the wide terraced gardens that Alfred Parsons was paid to create, at a fee of fifty guineas a year for three years, after Robert Fuller bought the old house in 1905*

superb yew houses like Tudor garden lodges topped with a jelly mould of green turrets. Within they are dense enough to be rainproof, garden rooms in themselves. A quatrefoil pond is set between them and there are no other distractions except for an entirely arthritic, multi-crutched mulberry tree. Ahead a Tudoresque stone garden pavilion beckons and the path to it lies along a terrace of small semi-circular bastions, some old, some Edwardian, all smothered in roses. On my June visit the whole upper garden was heavily perfumed by them.

This terrace walk is the Hadrian's Wall between sophistication and the wild, the dry land of smooth lawn and a water world of rough meadow, old orchard and woods studded with rare native flowers, which caution urges should not be named. The way down to this truly Wild Garden passes the Summerhouse, which is two-storeyed, one for outlook, one for quiet. It is Edwardian, not medieval. Below it a shallow reach of Chalfield's brimming moats teems with breeding fish that splatter and splash dramatically as you approach. A peony walk leads down to the trees, a village house or two, and the main moat. A lower terrace walk runs between this and a faster running stream. Chalfield is criss-crossed with springs, small paths and tiny slab bridges; a weir runs noisily down among the trees and beyond them there is no parkland, only pastoral fields. But up to the right the mood changes back to the intimate domestic, in a south-facing court (**76**) with half-timbered range on the left and medieval turrets on the right. Roses still held the dominance on my visit, but the most exotic perfume was from a pineapple broom brought over from Morocco in 1968. The paving stones demanded careful treading as their intersticies teemed with wild strawberries. It is the natural point for entry directly into the screens passage of the Great Hall, imaginatively restored with whimsical faces and masks by Sir Harold Brakspear for Robert Fuller.

Before leaving this bemusing and memorable survival of Edwardian good sense the church deserves to be visited, for botanical reasons if for nothing else, to enjoy Andrew Taylor's stained glass in the south aisle: a 1999 evocation of the wild flowers from that magical, half civilised lower section of the grounds. Seven species at least can be picked out in the light blues and greens below a paler sky alive with swallows. In Wiltshire one keeps finding the perfectly covetable garden: Amesbury, Heale, Iford; then comes Great Chalfield with a new perfection to put all the others down in rank. Alfred Parsons could have given Harold Peto lessons in how gardens should respond to an existing house and topography.

So, for that matter, could A.C. Martin, another architect, who restored South Wraxall Manor and its gardens for Richardson Cox between 1900 and 1902. Dorset has a wealth of sixteenth- and seventeenth-century manor houses, Wiltshire is rich in domestic architecture of the Wars of the Roses like Great Chalfield and South Wraxall, surprisingly open, half-defended manor houses of the lesser gentry,

77 *Grotesque topiary forms screen the gatehouse and south front of South Wraxall Manor. A.C. Martin laid out the gardens as he restored the house in 1900-2 for Richardson Cox. The geometrical island and sundial are 1968 intrusions to a circular swimming pool*

armed rather against wandering groups of paid-off soldiery than serious armies. Great Chalfield had the advantage of a terraced, sloping site; at South Wraxall, Martin had to garden on level ground less generously watered, but with courts and ranges of picturesque richness, the buildings, for the most part, of Robert Long, who was MP for the county in 1433.

Consequently South Wraxall Manor's gardens have nothing like Great Chalfield's unity, but rather four separate gardens strung along an architectural trail. The entrance front has been handled entirely as Richard Payne Knight would have approved and Capability Brown would have scorned. Martin threw all his efforts into a first impact. Ahead, up the drive, is the gatehouse with its oriel window, to the left are hedges and trees screening the outer garden completely, all the attention goes to the right where the front garden (**77**) has been taken over by genial triffids. Did Martin play chess? It seems likely as most of his topiary army stand like huge pawns ands monster bishops. Others sway drunkenly in the Bowood style, several have been topped by peacock clippings that have bulged and lost their definition; but they dominate the front range of the Manor. In the far corner of this populated space an octagonal summerhouse hides at the end of a pleached plane avenue, spying out over the lane. Central to the pleasant nondescript rose beds is a circular pool with a geometrical island and sundial at its centre, shaped like Laura Place in Bath. This is a 1968 alteration to the original circular swimming pool. Through the gatehouse arch into the original entrance courtyard of the Manor the topiary and the architecture fight much more fiercely (**colour plate 19**). The topiary blocks try to conceal the splendid eight-light window, double transomed, to Sir Walter Long's late seventeenth-century dining room and largely succeed. Early *Country Life* photographs show far more flowers and creepers.[15] Did Martin realise quite what his little yew saplings would do visually to the courtyard a hundred years later?

Out to the north there was, in 1905, a conventional herbaceous border walk to the Croquet Lawn; its delphiniums, poppies, larkspur, phlox, foxglove, helianthus and dahlias sound pre-Gertrude Jekyll. In one corner of the Croquet Lawn another triffid has almost concealed a little seat, which no one would wish to sit on. There are scant outward views; the gardens are open in the Wiltshire style, but the topography leaves them inward looking. The fourth garden is the one hidden from the entrance drive on its left-hand side and it is wilder, more ragged, far less topiaried than the others but probably only a shadow of its original 1902 planting. Rose beds flanked by grass walks lead to another pool, rectangular like a moat this time, with a causeway to a square green island on which stands a young goddess. This Moat Garden is screened on its perimeter by yews, bays, willows, copper beech and weeping pears. Overlooking the island Martin placed a borrowing from Peto, yet another of those Alma-Tadema-style exedral seats for half-clothed dancing girls.

Last and most awesome of all the Edwardians comes Hazelbury, begun before the First World War by Sir Humphrey Elgar-Jennings, but still being worked upon and extended until 1994. It is Edwardian in concept, but wholly Gloucestershire Edwardian, not Wiltshire at all in anything but its scale: a huge Cotswold garden pitched on the last southern outliers of the limestone edge. Its early history and its maps were considered in the chapter to which they belonged, but technically, by date, most of present day Hazelbury should be reserved until the last chapter of this book. However, Hazelbury's lordly air and gracious, distinctly dated manners insist on an Edwardian placing.

The mystery of Hazelbury, which it is hoped this account will help to resolve, is that it is so little known nationally when it has to be ranked among the great gardens, not just of England, but of Europe. There is also the mystery of who was principally responsible for its conception and projection. It could have been Sir Humphrey with his architect, the Ballets Russes-sounding Ivan Ivanovitch, a connection which might explain the imperial, quite un-English scale of the garden; or was it Mr George Kidston, who bought Hazelbury in 1919 and spent, with the help of his architect Harold Brakspear, £450,000 on an archaeological revamping of the house? Someone with that much money to spend might easily have had grand garden ideas. He employed eighteen gardeners, which sounds impressive at such a late date.

Between 1943 and 1971 Hazelbury was a girls' school and much can decay in a garden in twenty-eight years. Then came the Pollard years when many of the apparently Edwardian features were realised. Ian and Barbara Pollard have moved now to Malmesbury Abbey House, and the vigorous invention which Ian is putting into the creation of new gardens there indicates that much of the present Hazelbury was his work. He did, however, have only four gardeners to George Kidston's eighteen; but much of the un-Edwardian elements in the gardens, notably Avebury reborn (**1**), with seven immense Scottish megaliths in a deep amphitheatre circled by dolmens of juniper, are by Ian Pollard of 1985, as was a yew henge, now uprooted.[16]

A campaign or route march needs to be planned and followed rigorously if Hazelbury's gardens are to be taken in during one of those precious rare days when the present fortunate owners open the grounds for charity or amateur dramatics. In this account the Tudor and Jacobean elements of the garden will be taken for granted. A sharp right turn after entering between armorial gate piers will lead, behind the steward's house, to a very large rock garden, jewelled with the usual plants, but not firmly shaped around large enough rocks to be truly memorable. Up and behind this is the Pollard Laburnum Walk, stunning, like all such single flowering creations, for a fortnight each year. Its scale is splendid and it leads on into great beech hedges that guard the Main Lawn, and the double rampart of sequential gardens, from a right of way and the outside world. Why the Edwardians did not plant beech with its varying colours rather than funereal yew can probably be explained by their fixation with Italy, but it is to be regretted, as this outer avenue of Hazelbury is one of the most spatially atmospheric parts of the garden.

78 *Daedalus crafts his wings for Icarus on the Main Lawn at Hazelbury Manor. The double rows of topiary behind him were shaped during Ian Pollard's residence in the late twentieth century*

Slightly below it and immediately flanking the Main Lawn is a row of garden rooms. All these features are of Ian Pollard's creation and repeated on the far, north side of the Lawn. One garden room is an old Orchard, one is the Chess Set Garden in topiary (**colour plate 20**), one is plausibly sub-tropical, another has flowerbeds arranged reverently around a curious, shapeless stone: a very Pollard touch. Half way along this sequence are two matching garden houses, fifteenth century in aspect, but probably Kidston creations and derived from earlier fragments. They work excellently, ushering a visitor out into the Main Lawn itself. This alone should have made Hazelbury famous. It is the size of a football pitch. While I was at its further eastern end enjoying a 2002 sculpture by Tim Chalk of Daedalus (**78**) in a half circle of bronze bollards that recount the flight and fall of his son Icarus, a rehearsal of *Romeo and Juliet* was taking place at the other end and Romeo was dying to the applause of a sizeable ad hoc audience. Yet so vast is the Main Lawn that the sounds came over no more intrusively than birdsong. The actors were using for their tiring rooms a set of yew houses at the west end of the Lawn. At my east end there was sufficient break in the enclosing trees to allow a vivid flash of rapeseed blossom growing in the big open fields outside. Hazelbury, like Great Chalfield and South Wraxall, is all ambitious garden with no real park.

On the north side of the Lawn the garden rooms set off again within the treble beech walls and at their eastern end offer glimpses of the generally retiring and undistinguished complex of the parent house. It is not possible to circumnavigate this village-like rambling structure so a firm decision must be made now to abandon what the 1626 'Map of the Lordship of Colerne' calls the 'Orcha Ground' and make for the 'Botto Gro' and the 'Northe Ground' on the other side of the house.[17] One of the weaknesses of this garden is the siting of the house – so far back from the edge of the valley that none of the impressive views down the Avon to Bath can be enjoyed. To remedy this, Ian Pollard built a high viewing mound, which has yet to be assimilated into the grounds and, indeed, may never be enclosed under the present more moderate regime.[18] Tony Venison reports that in one Pollard experiment hay bales were rotted down on a slope and wild flowers planted in the richer soil to pick out the head and the eye of a dragon in red and gold.[19] A seat was prepared from which this spectacle could be enjoyed, but whether it was successful is not recorded; certainly with such projects we are moving far out from the Edwardian garden image and into the Modern.

The precise garden enclosures and apparent Archery Walk on the west side of the house were described in an earlier chapter. It only remains to mention the recent planting in a sector, which is genuinely Tudor, not imitation Edwardian Tudor, in its layout. The top terrace up against the wall and the actual site of the archery contests is planted on one side with juniper skyrocket and on the other with roses, lavender and clematis, the usual combination, also an impressive show of aquilegia. One terrace down is the Wild Garden and the Mulberry Lawn.

A last suggestion should be made for walkers unable to visit these remarkable grounds on an open day. A network of public field paths surrounds the gardens. There is a real charm in legitimate garden stalking and the public right of way from the B3109 runs along the beech hedges that guard the Main Lawn on the south-east side. Anyone following it can look over a low wall through the Laburnum Walk and then take in, at various gaps, much of the sensational topiary of the Chess Set Garden and the twin garden houses. Nearer the house any number of tantalising glimpses of the forecourt garden and that regimented Kitchen Garden are available, again from public paths. All that is needed is a large-scale Ordnance Survey map; Hazelbury is quite one of the most rewarding gardens in the county as its high walls and defensive bastions conceal only the inner grounds. But the best walking time is when the trees are leafless.

10

The county's greatest garden age –
the later twentieth century

There is very little Art Deco work in Wiltshire gardens and virtually no trace of the continental Modern Movement that is present just across the county border in Somerset at Pen Pits, Penslewood.[1] Hazelbury's garden history may explain this: Edwardian design being followed until, in the 1970s and 1980s, it merged into a playful Celtic mysticism, with dragon's eyes being framed in wild flowers and massive 'prehistoric' stone circles raised as garden toys. Wiltshire, or south Wiltshire at least, can seem an oppressively old landscape, with burial mounds of the dead on skylines, defensive earthworks on hilltops, ancient roadways criss-crossing the maps, and Stonehenge and Avebury as tremendous relics of lost worship. This presence of the past probably accounts for a persistent vein in the county's twentieth-century gardens of airy spirituality, symbolism, numinous insights, philosophical perceptions and a tiresome whimsicality as the garden designers groped for a new style neither Arcadian classical nor yew-hedged aristocratic.

One theme of this chapter will be that the vice of the county's many, and often impressive, layouts was simply whimsy. It pervades the *Shell Guide* to the county in the series that John Betjeman edited and Robert Byron ostensibly wrote. But the guiding hand behind that text is clearly that of Edith Olivier.[2] She lived in the Day (Dairy) House in that corner of the park at Wilton where the newly combined Nadder and Wylye escape from lordly control and pass on through water meadows to Salisbury and the Avon. Edith was Rex Whistler's guru and Whistler was a potentially great artist enfeebled by charming whimsicality.[3] Eventually she surfaced as Mayor of Wilton; but long before that she had been at the centre of a group of lively, laughing, inventive, gay pranksters, London weekenders for the most part, carrying the manners of Chelsea out to Siegfried Sassoon's Heytesbury, Stephen Tennant's Wilsford, the Day House itself if, like Rex, they were especially favoured, but most of all to Ashcombe, the remotest house in Wiltshire.

It was Edith Olivier who directed the society photographer and theatre designer, Cecil Beaton, to Ashcombe, deep in its forest valley, miles from anywhere except

Tollard Royal and Berwick St Leonard. He fell in love with it at first sight, took two seven-year leases on the place, restored and decorated the buildings and gardened with, inevitably, artful whimsy. He filled the Laundry House (a whimsical name for the dower house of Robert Barber's vanished, 1686, Ashcombe Manor House) with distinguished but unserious guests. Salvador Dali was lured there on one occasion, Augustus John and his wife Dorelia came often, Rex, of course, was a frequent guest, Lord Berners, Christopher Sykes, and Oliver Messel advised, perversely, on interior decoration. H.G. Wells came in a pin-stripe suit and a Homburg hat, Tilly Losch dressed as a Meissen shepherdess, Alfred Beit arrived in an aeroplane, but landed at Ferne, not attempting a parachute jump, Ottoline Morrell from Garsington came in rows of pearls and a picture hat; the Stavordales and the Weymouths represented county society, Lord David Cecil represented Oxford, John Sutro staged a revue where everyone could pretend to be everyone else. In a party where all came dressed as their opposites, Lady Castlerosse arrived as a nun, Tom Mitford was just quietly himself, and Edith? Cecil Beaton kept her exclusively to himself. Edith was too precious to share; she did not flourish in company.

In 1949, when he had not been able to renew his leases any further, Beaton wrote a nostalgic memoir to his lost house that recaptures movingly his first frustrated visit, ordered out by the keeper of the valley's pheasants, but captivated by the potential of the stables to serve as Orangery and Studio, by the haunted quality of the elegant little 'Laundry' in lilac coloured brick and by the ilex grove in the deserted garden.[4] Once he had moved in he planted thousands of daffodils, but the chalk soil was grudging; the wild snowdrops in the woods flourished with no care, supplying local gypsies with an episodic income. A little formal garden with massively squared stones was a success and the courtyard between the Laundry and the stables took on the air of an Austrian Baroque garden with the handsome stable arch, the parade of round-headed windows and their rich Gibbs surrounds. The effect with grass, seats and some limited flower planting was neo-Georgian even though the elements were genuinely William and Mary. This was because Beaton had a gift for playful visual undercutting, as in his contemporary state photographs of the Queen in gently camp pomp. Most of Beaton's photographs of Ashcombe gardens have, for instance, in their foreground, the bare bottoms of Castor and Pollux (**79**), two more than life size statues of elegantly nude young men; they at least seem at home.

To appreciate Beaton's ingenuity and charisma in drawing so many to such an inaccessible house and garden, a personal visit to Ashcombe is a must. There is nothing else in Wiltshire quite like it, not even in the county's 'empty quarter' beyond Ludgershall. First seen from the lip of the downs after the long climb up from Berwick St Leonard, the place looks like a second Eden. Instead of bare fields, the deep valley is total forest, ash trees for the most part, with just one clearing to the side of the house where a side valley joins the main one. A drive with warning notices leads precipitously downwards. When I visited, the American pop and film star Madonna and her husband had bought the house;

79 *Cecil Beaton brought Castor and Pollux in to Ashcombe to add a characteristic note of naughty challenge to the lawns in his fifteen-year tenancy of this house, isolated in a deep downland hollow.* Beaton Archives/ Sotheby's

privacy not party-going was the mood, but a public right of way led down into the forest and I took it.

Cecil Beaton mentions the pheasants as an obsession of his landlord, but nothing was a preparation for their numbers. The entire ash wood was one vast chicken run of the birds, metal cylinders containing their food were scattered around and from every third bush a scrawny brown bird erupted like a fussy rocket. The valley was seedily over-pheasanted, but in the middle of disillusionment the survival of much of the Barbers' seventeenth-century formal garden was a pleasant surprise. Beaton had bought a detailed eighteenth-century topographical oil painting of the estate and much of its detail had survived the overgrowth of trees and birds.[5] The Laundry, still lilac brick, was poised at the top of Robert Barber's long, slanting axial drive, its supporting walls intact. The big Kitchen Garden to the side had gone to grass, but shrewder tenants than Beaton had not wasted their money on flowers but gone Edwardian and planted the line of gardens, along the Grotto, with Irish yews and they had flourished. There was no trace of the Barber garden temple up the hill to the west. After a long steep climb up through woodland I regained the lip of the downs and left Ashcombe entirely disenchanted. Why anyone should wish to live in the middle of a thick, featureless woodland is a mystery, but a revelation of character.

Bryan Guinness did far more for Biddesden House in the 'empty quarter' than Beaton did for Ashcombe, but then Guinness was the owner, not the leaseholder, and he was comfortably rich. The early eighteenth-century gardens of Biddesden were described in an earlier chapter. Mr Guinness' contribution to house and grounds was not 'Moderne' angularity, but neo-Georgian whimsicality. The initial shaft of light-hearted wit came when Dora Carrington of the celebrated Lytton Strachey circle painted a *trompe l'œil* in one of the blocked Georgian windows of Biddesden's ground floor. It showed a cook, a cat and a canary. This was so much enjoyed that Guinness brought in, not Rex Whistler himself, but Roland Pym who painted in much the same slick, figurative style. He filled these blocked windows with Jane Austen characters: a lady playing a harp, another reading a letter and, in the third, a charming flirtation scene, all painted in 1935. There is some evidence that these were inspired by Margaret Irvine's book, *Still she wished for company*, about a lonely little girl who looks into the windows of an old house and sees its one time inhabitants still alive.[6]

Up on the hill to the west of the house George Kennedy had built in 1932 a Gazebo (**80**) to double as a changing room for a moat-like swimming pool. With its green copper dome, big bay window and little classical pediment this could not

80 *George Kennedy built this lively Gazebo and changing room for Bryan Guinness on the hill above Biddesden in 1932. The thatched garden wall, visible to the right, is as old as the house, and dates from 1711*

be described as Modern, but at least it was asymmetrical. When in 1937 Boris Anrep decorated the tower room with aggressively angular mosaic figures of the Muses – Cleo, Erato and Thalia – and a Bacchus-Apollo (**colour plate 14**) in challengingly unharmonious but brilliant colours, a more distinctively Art Deco note was sounded. Pym's nereid astride a sea horse in the central room was more acceptably pretty. Stephen Tomlin's 1935 statue of a naked girl set among hollyhocks at the top of the walled Kitchen Garden expressed the fluent simplifications of the period. All in all the concentration of art and function was impressively fashionable. On the hot August day of my visit the pool was alive with young people and the 1930s illusion was perfect.

Then came the war, 1939-45, from which the Art Deco with all its vigorous patterning and ornament never recovered; because after the war came twenty-five years of comparative national poverty when the country staggered from one financial crisis to another and both architecture and garden design were hijacked by the cult of enforced simplicity. This was simply a case of making the best of a bad job. If money was scarce then ornament and richness of detail could be declared vulgar, even immoral, by opinion shapers in the media. It is a generalisation to describe the time from 1940 to 1970 as the Wilderness Years in Wiltshire's and the nation's gardens, but there is much truth in that sweeping description. Then, after 1972, prosperity set in. Quietly the country's park and garden owners became wealthy again and the last thirty years of the century, as Britain became the fourth largest economy in the world, were a time when lively gardens, some amusing, some embarrassing, some beautiful, and one or two genuinely great, were laid out in the county. There are so many that teams have to be made to clarify the profusion: Gardens of the New Rococo, Statue Gardens, Gardens of the Whimsical Contrivance and Great Gardens.

All these four teams are, however, based on what can be described as a New Floral Competence, or Getrude Jekyll Updated. From the 1970s onwards a breed of skilled and sensitive plantsmen and plantswomen arose to meet the demands of this revived economy. They were garden designers who could coax scent, colour, seclusion and variety out of the most unpromising topography. Antony Young's post-1987 creation at Ridley's Cheer, Mountain Bower, a notorious frost hollow with shallow, grudging soil on a limestone base, is typical of these Gardens of the Effortless Competence, evolved from much leaf mould, an exact awareness of any plant's potential and the collection of seed from travels about the world, chiefly south-east Asia.

Ridley's Cheer is not easy to describe. It cossets its parent house rather than encloses it in any formality; and like most such gardens it has no commanding garden building. There is a semi-formal box punctuation in the terrace outside the French windows, a punctuation continued in the blue-themed Potager on the far side of the Great Lawn. But then the planting takes over, scented for preference and principally of roses. A list, however, of favourites such as Ghislaine de Feligonde, Paul's Himlayan, *Rosa Longicuspis* and *Rosa Banksiae* 'Lutea', convey little to the average reader. Only the experience of them, rioting over arch, beside steps and over walls, is completely captivating. This is the essential late twentieth-century garden.

The same absolute competence carries the new Arboretum and the Wild Flower Meadow beyond it (**colour plate 22**). These are the lovely clichés of our present garden age. To add that *Acer cappadocicum*, *Acer oliverianum*, Chinese box, Norway maples, *Quercus libani* and *Liquidambar Orientalis* are flourishing among many other exotics in the Arboretum may confuse the mind, but is at least a hint of the variety that Antony Young, working like John Evelyn in his 'Elaboratorie', but in Antony's case after personal travels and personal collection, has persuaded to tolerate Wiltshire's not always welcoming soil.

In the quite limited span of the last thirty years, chronology is not of much significance. Upon this ground base of informed competence it is the gardens of influence that need to be focused upon and Shute, while not in any way the most popular or the most visited, is unquestionably the most internationally acclaimed and prestigious of all Wiltshire's late twentieth-century gardens. Between 1970 and 1988 three people created it: Geoffrey Jellicoe, knighted in 1979 for his work on gardens, and the owners of the garden, Michael and Lady Anne Tree. Jellicoe has been given most of the credit because he spun around Shute and its waters the gnomic, pretentious critical jargon, part mystical, part philosophical, in which late twentieth-century intellectuals loved to lose their wits. And Shute is, for all its slight flowers, so memorably beautiful yet elusive in its charm that Jellicoe's word spinning has been accepted. A garden so mysterious in its appeal can carry this analysis of poetic obscurity.

My belief is that, just as poets occasionally, in a corpus of pleasant mediocrity, come across dazzling moments of inspiration: Wordsworth for instance, on Westminster Bridge, Marvell on his frustratingly coy mistress, so good gardeners like Jellicoe sometimes hit upon a topography that exactly suits their particular talent, in Jellicoe's case the handling of water; at which point they produce a garden of genius provided they are backed by sympathetic owners and planters, like the Trees.

The generous source springs of the Nadder River rise in the grounds of Shute House, an impressively austere villa of about 1730 in the manner of Colen Campbell. When the Trees moved there from Mereworth Castle in 1968 they called their friend Jellicoe in to advise them on an existing garden of great potential for a Jellicoe treatment. West of the house was a roughly square Kitchen Garden and a straight canal pointing to a primeval spring bubbling up into a pool in the woods. Before reaching that pool the canal bent south into an irregularly-shaped water, with a smaller natural pool east of it in the woods to receive the Nadder waters that then ran south-east into open country overlooked by the lawns of Shute House. For the next twenty years the Jellicoe-Tree team changed little but trimmed and adjusted the existing waters by poetic strokes of artifice with statues, topiary figures, small bridges, flowers and musical cataracts. After an hour walking their paths and contrived confrontations all other gardens will seem crude and heavy-handed. Shute is very, very precious. You enter at your peril; it could turn you into a garden snob.

Jellicoe revelled in the belief of the Greek philosopher Heraclitus (who eventually jumped into the crater of Mount Etna) that all things are in flux. First he dramatised the source pool with a seat that faced two ways: one into the classical Canal, dignified by busts of Ovid, Virgil and Lucretius, the other into woodland where the primeval source pool and the irregular arms of water all pressed the Romantic inspiration. His ingenious invention to devise a classical water course was to lead a straight Rill down through six flower beds, under little stone bridges and over four cataracts, or chutes, to join the main flow of the infant Nadder which had wound its way deviously down by the Romantic route through the woods. Thus, in obscure Jelliconian symbolism, classical and Romantic thought united to vitalise the outside world in a Bog Garden. That was Jellicoe's basic concept, faithfully realised by Michael and Anne Tree, and this is how it comes across to a wary, but admiring visitor today when some of its features are already a little past their prime.

Shute House itself stands alongside the village lane. It is reserved, symmetrical, unforthcoming, almost, the word has to be used, Scottish, so it may well be by Campbell. On its garden front wide lawns slope down to a foreground field with ponds and a backdrop of pleasant, hilly Wiltshire. A cedar is prominent. Round the

81 *Looking down the Rill that Sir Geoffrey Jellicoe devised for Shute House during its 1970-88 occupancy by Michael and Lady Anne Tree. It is one of the most memorable modern gardens in England. The cascades play a harmonic chord*

side of the house the garden mood livens up somewhat. An apple tree arch leads into a paved sitting out area under which the Rill (**81**), the garden's classical strand, emerges to hurry down through six richly flowering beds to the celebrated four chutes, the bubble fountains and a final statue, all in a rigidly straight line. By varying the fall of water with different numbers of copper V's set in concrete the chutes are supposed to sound treble, alto, tenor and bass to produce a harmonic chord. Everyone loves the notion, but I suspect the Emperor is tone deaf. The bubble fountains, an idea borrowed from Shalimar gardens in Kashmir, are a lively delight worked by gravity.

Straight ahead from the sitting out area is the Philosopher's Grove, a triangle of ilex. To the left is a conventional six-square Potager, the squares lined with box, the vegetables, apples and fruit attractively combined. But to the right is the Canal, a key feature. It can only be appreciated from the two-way seat at the far end, but the green walk along its side follows islets of lilies, *Zantedeschia aethiopoca*.[7] In the *Fagus sylvatica* hedge across the green weedy Canal (**82**), balconies have been cut to give glimpses of the orderly Potager, the civilized world, which you are leaving behind to experience the primitive.

From the two-way seat the busts of the classical poets of orderly gardens could be seen originally set over two Grottoes, ungenerously scaled; most visitors think they are drains. The busts of Ovid, Virgil and Lucretius, which have no Romantic equivalents, have now been replaced by other statuary of no iconographic significance. Looking the other way there is the source spring, clear watered, but green with mosses. Now the downhill path follows casual Romantic waters, Lady Anne's planting and a stone nymph, until the Laurel Tunnel projects visitors into the Temple Garden. This is meant to inspire awe with sinister topiary figures, a topiary spire and a topiary Temple arch, but they have not grown properly. Escape is across deliberately difficult stepping stones to the foot of the classical Rill, which here joins its harmonious waters with the rough Romantic stream. The Bog Garden brims with gunnera, iris, peonies, four kinds of geranium, ominous rocks and a carved figure from Zimbabwe. At this point the allegory fails because the waters flow on into four ponds, two of them dug out for Jellicoe. They are supposed to represent placid reflection upon infinity, but they just look like ordinary small ponds. Capability Brown would have been bolder. Lady Anne's planting, as much as Geoffrey Jellicoe's intellectual allegories, was the making of Shute's undoubted beauty.[8] Try to visit it before it overgrows, as gardens have a habit of doing.

With money flowing in from a revitalised economy, most of Wiltshire's new garden projectors turned to the Rococo notion of a garden set about with eclectic cultural areas to divert and surprise. Seend Manor, for instance, is transforming, under the guidance of Julian and Isabel Bannerman, its vast walled former Kitchen Garden into four quadrants, divided by fifteen-foot pleached hedges of hornbeam.[9] England comes first (**83**) with a cottage ornée for goblins in one corner and Noisette roses planted up teakwood obelisks in beds of Regale lilies around a

82 *The Canal was in place at Shute before Jellicoe began to reshape the grounds. He created the balconies that give glimpses into the Philosopher's Grove and set up busts to Ovid, Virgil and Lucretius. This is the classical as opposed to the Romantic theme at Shute*

83 *Julian and Isabel Bannerman have created this cottage ornée for goblins in one corner of the vast walled garden at Seend Manor. Four quadrants represent England, Africa, China and Italy. New prosperity is producing a garden renaissance in Britain*

gazebo of teak draped with New Dawn, Awakening and Cecile Brunner roses. The African quadrant has an obelisk with four sphinxes in a bed of gunnera. Grandest of all is a Chinese quadrant. A double-tiered Chinese pavilion or 'Ting' (**colour plate 23**) towers out above a waving dragon-backed beech hedge and catches the eye from every point of Africa and England. Lastly Italy has a long swimming pool, a Doric Loggia, vast terracotta pots and a changing room reconstituted from a Williamane garden pavilion.[10] The garden's floor of multi-coloured paving stones and Welsh river pebbles set endways is impressive, but judgement on the whole lively complex must attend on maturity. On my visit the trained Italian ivy was still going up in circles on the walls. What could be fully appreciated was the visual impact of a brilliant new ha-ha in the main garden in front of the house, opening up a stunning view of the ramparts of the downs seen across a broad valley.

A wonderfully Pooterish compression of the Rococo garden, like something out of Dickens, has been devised in the small back garden of number 32 off the A365 west of Melksham: the Outdoor Studio.[11] Here the Howards, Alvin and Judith, have squeezed nine Rococo divertissements into a quarter of an acre reviving that irreverent, exploratory English feeling for diversity that made the 'English Garden' copied all over western Europe. Formal French parterres face a Chinese Water Garden (**84**) where a stream from a small pot flows under a red willow pattern bridge. A dovecote modelled on a Batty Langley garden temple design stands opposite a Roman fountain inscribed 'Et in Arcadia Ego'. Next comes a garden turned into a chapel and a lock keeper's tea house rescued from the Kennet and Avon canal. A rose-trimmed swing out of Fragonard awaits Charlotte, the Howards' daughter, beside a lantern-hung tea tent and a Grotto for garden rubbish. Finally a climb up the Tudor-style Tree House gives a consciously contrived view of the sunset and a view down on to a rose garden with an armillary sphere. Without a scrap of condescension I admired it as proof of what lively spirits can make of the most unpromising garden areas.

In the same happy mood of positive Rococo invention but with a wealth of often exquisite detail, Paul and Caroline Weiland have, over the last twelve years, created new gardens at Belcombe Court. An earlier chapter traced how, somewhere in the early nineteenth century, John Wood's quite formal templar layout had been softened and made into a convincing 1750s Rococo pastiche. The Weilands, together with Arnie Maynard and other landscape designers, have improvised imaginatively around this enchanting core. Below the original circular temple, fragments of the Fishing Pavilion, once sited close to the Avon, have been rebuilt with a little avenue of wisteria and summer flowers leading to its door. It has undoubted charm, but is perhaps a trifle too formal for such a relaxed site.

What has been a stroke of inspired patronage is the new interior to the nineteenth-century pseudo-Jacobean Summerhouse just above the main house. After four months of patient work by Edmir Blott this has become a Shell Grotto to rank with the finest in England. One side wall has a great maze of shell paths to bemuse and perplex the eye. Other darker or lighter trails of shell winding

84 *Alvin and Judith Howard have contrived to squeeze eight or nine themed gardens into the back of a modest suburban house on the Bath Road out of Melksham*

through the massed scallops, cockles, mussels and exotics spell out the initials of the Weiland family. But it is the triangular pedimented space that can only be described as an artwork of the first rank. Cream, silver, violet and purple shells work together in an abstract colour symphony of subtle shading, The three-dimensional, rough corrugations of the shells themselves fight against mere prettiness to create something sculptural that catches the western light to extraordinary effect.

Much else lies ahead: a crunching grove of hazelnut bushes, a greenhouse overwhelmingly ablaze with solid banks of mixed bouganvillea, a Boule Court densely shaded from any 'Provençal' sun by hanging maple branches. Then the six green, wave-like terraces of the walled hill garden rise up from a long, brash bed of *lobelia cordenalis* and Bishop of Llandaff dahlias. To one side of this hot terrace stands a stainless steel water topiary fountain, its gleaming flow picking up the matching shapes of the real topiary around it. Above the green terraces lies the Bathing Pavilion, a long wooden structure of green oak beams, more rustic English cow byre than Italianate. This, with changing rooms and dining area, commands the pool itself which brims over perpetually at its lower edge giving the clear impression that the water, while actually recycled, continues downhill in the grassy waves of terrace. Cursed with a level site, the Bannermans' swimming area at Seend Manor can never match this vibrant invention.

Sunlight pours into this south-facing slope, and if the impertinent hoots of passing trains are a reminder of the real world this is, nevertheless, a garden of

85 *Alison Crowther's giant nutmegs scatter the lawns of Belcombe Court where the Weilands have transformed and enlivened the gardens over the last few years under the imaginative direction of Peter Bazeley and other designers*

86 *The grounds of moated Cole Park have been given by Lady Weinberg the ruthlessly angular formal gardens which they might have had in the late seventeenth century, and that Kip and Knyff would then have drawn in 1709. They work superbly*

disparate areas which all, except the Fishing Pavilion, work in accord with the small wings, courtyards and chapel-like barn of the house complex. The Weilands have created a surprise party feeling with unexpected carved extras lying about the grounds: huge wooden nutmegs (**85**) bigger than footballs stand in the grass, and there is a sinuous snake-like wooden seat (**colour plate 21**) looking ready to slither back into the serpentine pond.[12] If it were not that so much of Belcombe was there before its recent renaissance it would be right to call it Wiltshire's third 'great' modern garden. As at Shute, garden designer and patron have met in inspired partnership.

At Cole Park, however, that stern classical box in the dim fields outside Malmesbury, gardener and patron were one and the same. The well known designer Lady Weinberg bought Cole Park eighteen years ago. The display of Kip and Knyff engravings in her front hall shows that she not knows only her garden history, but has applied her knowledge with firm but sophisticated discipline. Cole Park has been 'Kipped', with gardens that the authors of *Britannia Illustrata* would have praised.

As you motor up Cole Park's long, hedgeless approach drive, the Weinberg planting takes over quite abruptly. Young chestnut trees, planted far too closely together by ordinary standards, create a dense green tunnel. This bears to the right and a wide, stone-walled moat of murky fawn-coloured water is crossed, no overgrown toy but a true defensive feature, and there, behind tightly shading chestnut growth around a gravel forecourt, is the house: a Tudor core, and a 1775 classical front. Brick pavilions, of the seventeenth century but much altered, fill the front angles of the forecourt.

Twenty years ago when I was listing the place for the Department of the Environment, there were a few fine trees and little else in the grounds.[13] This time I walked them in an unremitting July downpour. Gardens which can survive such weather are good indeed. Cole Park weathered the weather triumphantly. The square of lawn on the garden front within the moated rectangle would, in a Kip, be lined with alternate spires of conifer and box. Here the area is regimented, which is the correct verb to use, with young *Cerberus*, whitethorn trees, their neat tubular crowns clipped two or three times a year. They will be allowed to rise to the level of the first storey windows and then stopped. There are no flowers, and except in the exuberant, though still disciplined, Kitchen Garden, Cole Park does not encourage them: grass, tree-geometries and paths at right-angles are the order of the day.

To the south side a tall rectangle of beeches is growing (**86**), whether this will enclose a rectangular canal or an inlaid marble table has yet to be decided. A long straight walk between high yew hedges takes over the direction and leads to the new brick walls of the Kitchen Garden where the sheer fertility of the soil contrives to soften the rigidity of the design. Entrance is between a row of quince trees on the short side of the rectangle; down the long sides plum trees dangle their heavy burdens. The cross walks are lined with high climbing raspberries, blackberries and loganberries; tall spiked heads of the wilder kind of artichokes tower up aggressively, and there are many wicker spires that support beans and sweet peas while encouraging a firm growth of rosemary at their base.

The far end of this walled garden is occupied by a long greenhouse on a metal frame of ogee arches, a heavily perfumed space of lilies and orchids. Out on the other side the trees break open to reveal a wider reach of the moat with black swans, more elegant, if that is possible, than their white sisters, and a few orange tree-ducks, not elegant at all. The springs of this area require a whole chain of ponds to take the waters of the moat out and down to the winding Avon. As a last ruthless feature the bridge back across the moat, a steep, slippery wooden arch, has no handrail. As my reward for not falling in I was given coffee fragrant with crushed cardamoms, as in some Bedouin tent; usually I get offered instant. Cole Park kitchen, like its garden, has style. Another plus was that I do not recall a single herbaceous border: Kip's views do not feature them.

Lady Weinberg's garden stands in a class of its own. No one else dares do a Kip, but statue gardens group interestingly together because, more than any other garden, they lay their owners' psyches devastatingly bare. Biddestone, Chisenbury and Cantax are all of the first rank, but are refreshingly unalike and all, courageously, are open on occasions to the public.

Biddestone Manor begins predictably. A seventeenth-century, gabled Cotswold vernacular house in a winsome clutter of stone barns, it confronts the main road with a quartered square of lavender and roses, in the middle of which four fountain jets play on a naked young man who turns out to be a mini version of Michelangelo's 'David'. Round the back of the house a large, disturbingly open, wooden-fenced garden slowly improves, but still cries out for the confinements that Lady Weinberg gave Cole Park. If a vista does not please, it should be closed off. A willow pattern island in a lakelet should improve with time as may a bushy woodland area and a round maze of prunus, beech and berberis, designed by Jane Fernley-Whittingstall. Then a huge upturned elm tree stump, a lily pond and the dramatic metal head of a stallion by Nick Fidian-Green compose wildly together, giving notice that the garden is about to step up its assault on a quiet visitor's sensibility.

Across a wide, flower-edged lawn lies the great double wall of Biddestone, a tall dark double row of yews with a narrow corridor between them and several entrances at its sides or lower end. These alternative entrances are a mistake as the whole point of this dramatic corridor is to approach an ominous, black metal statue of a phallic figure, some monstrous heathen image, planted at one end with a tall lime tree rising behind it like a canopy. Enter half way up and the drama is halved. There is a brick moon gate at the house-side end of this sinister corridor and, overhung with wisteria, it makes an amusing surprise way in. One expects some homely Gertrude Jekyll flowerbeds and then steps into the scenario for a human sacrifice.

Garden sculptures are very revealing, very helpful as memory markers, but sometimes, as here at Biddestone, controversial. As if the black phallic idol were not aggressive enough, in the middle of the next lawn, shamelessly exposed, is a second black metal sex object, this time a couple locked in intercourse (**87**), but athletically

87 *A sculpture of athletic lovers in the grounds of Biddestone Manor, a garden unusually rich in varied statuary*

suspended horizontally above the grass. The verdict has to be: well, it is a private garden, no one asked us to come in and it does make a talking point. Roman gardens had such statues as standard features.

Two charmingly relaxed and intimate small gardens cosy up to the house walls at this point, both sunken, one with a black metal cheetah by a Japanese maple. In this dramatic area two further enclosed gardens perceptibly and perhaps deliberately lower Biddestone's psychic temperature. With a Potager of sensational sweet peas and a sun-trap swimming pool garden against a stone barn wall, the circuit concludes.

Biddestone was of the north as are its Scandinavian owners. Chisenbury Priory is of the deep south. It lies in a valley a mile or two upstream from Netheravon at a point where a slow moving leat has been cut down through a leafy fold of land. A self-consciously smart, urban-style brick front of 1767 has been added to the seventeenth-century core and Peter Manser has worked hard to give it the herbaceous borders and burst of sky blue campanula that such an unrevealing front deserves. The rear elevation is more mellow, but what now catches the eye is a vast downhill sweep of perfect grass, impelling the visitor leat-wards down a winding dark green pergola smothered in blue clematis. Very little of the slow leat is actually visible in another herbaceous richness where yellow loosestrife and lilies take over from the blues and a tiny flint bridge leads across into an old orchard and an ingenuity of lawns and statues.

Gerald Laing has clearly been the Mansers' favourite sculptor and, while there is nothing as outrageously sensual at the sexual set-pieces of Biddestone, Laing's mood has been gently erotic. 'A Woman Waiting' enlivens the Bowling Alley, which extends on a curve between espaliered apple trees and a lovely thatched chalk wall. 'Woman with Wet Hair' (**colour plate 24**) stands, appropriately, in the leat near a large willow, and this odd little stream has been lured at intervals into tiny waterfalls and then coaxed to spit pleasantly out of the mouth of a Laing bronze fish. Chisenbury garden is subtly but efficiently directional; it creates a circuit while seeming quite random. After the spouting fish a wonderful nest of enclosed gardens closes in on the visitor: Stone Garden, White Garden, Blue Garden, visual impact after visual impact, all in the best tradition of the Edwardian garden, but very recent in creation.

At the Stone Garden the walls and the pavement with an eating out area from the house make a complete mood change from the soft textures and colours bushing around the leat. A statue of a girl, not by Gerald Laing, stands in a fountain and, while I was there in mid-July, evening primroses were flourishing wholesomely. Next came the White Garden with peonies and the athletic, sweet-scented Kiftsgate rose sprawling over a cypress bower. Though 'White', the effect here was dark and enclosing, but release comes in the third step, the Blue Garden, larkspur dominated by four firm, formal beds and four stunning pyramids of sweet peas. The paths are brick, old man or lad's love was plentiful, but the left-hand pier of two unusually sited brick garden piers brings an end to this inspired sequence, quite one of the richest and most enjoyable garden events in the county.

The rest is pleasant but less intense. The leat winds on, deepening and crossed by an iron bridge. It divides the Orchard from the White Garden where grasses and trees grow around an enormous apple made of granite. This challenges the curiosity, but then fails to satisfy it. Was Eden in Peter Manser's mind when he set it here?

Cantax House, the last of the statued trio, is a village street garden in the heart of National Trust Lacock yet far from bland in its mood. This was the house where Lacock's doctor lived. Now, between its simple Queen Anne front and the little stone stables, where the doctor kept his pony and trap, Deborah van der Beek, the sculptress, has planted an ambitious complex of garden rooms on a narrow strip of ground alongside the village street, cut through by a slow moving, murky brown tributary of the Avon.

At first entry it all appears conventional until a sideways glance down the high beech hedge bedded out with catmint reveals an aggressive black nude standing guard on the lawn over three golden apples. It is Paris, in *ciment fondu*, about to award Venus the prize and start the Trojan War. Behind him the lawn dips down to trees overhanging the brook and a set of stepping stones planted deliberately low so that only an eighth of an inch separates the foot from the water level. Geoffrey Jellicoe plays the same game at Shute. A look upstream will reveal a perfectly adequate bridge to the garden enclosures on the other bank.

These are no stately Edwardian affairs. A rough 1990s maze of multiple planted hedges takes over, centred on a ragged yew dome with windows cut out in it to

88 *Three Angry Men, a sculpture in cedar wood by Anthony Griffiths, looks down on the abandoned tennis court at Cantax House where Deborah van der Beek has dedicated a complex new formal layout to such display*

spy into the garden rooms on all its four sides. In addition the dome sits on a cross axis from a seat in the wall along the village street down to a big, ex-tennis, lawn. This lawn, though simple compared with the coloured delights of the rooms, is irresistible as the axis dips down into its mysterious spaces. Two huge wooden cable drums, like outsize cotton reels, lie on the lawn, toys discarded by giant children. In the rough grass and cow parsley beyond Anthony Griffiths' cedar wood sculpture, 'Three Angry Men' (**88**), all nude, big-buttocked and split by sudden natural wounds in the wood, dominates the space, the ultimate discussion piece. Up to the side a white Rambling Rector rose has climbed a large apple tree beside the stables, and the overwhelmingly picturesque houses of Lacock are visible over the wall.

Back at the yew dome, one of the four rooms is a Potager of sweet peas, foxgloves and broad beans; a second is a plain lawn dazzlingly hedged in with red hot pokers blazing away in a green gloom. The third and fourth are less memorable, planned with old-fashioned flowers around geometrical figures in the lawns. But there are more statues across the stream. Crossing, this time sedately by the bridge, a white torso of a headless woman catches the eye, sinisterly sited in the brown water and yet another garden room, the seventh of this entertaining layout, is visible behind the studio. This back garden is an entirely separate world. The rear of the house is as wild and unexpected in its angles and extensions as the front was reserved and predictable. A raised bed of dianthus is set to scent the kitchen windows, huge poppies that seem to be made of rough brown paper dominate the borders and there are seats to overlook an unexpectedly grand flight of steps to lead stickleback fishers down to the stream. I have mentioned only the less disturbing statues, and Deborah's 'Jubilant Artemis', set on a plinth in that yew dome, is an eye-opener to rank with the many-breasted mother of Asia in the gardens at the Villa d'Este at Tivoli. Cantax House garden does not hide the fact that it is a sales pitch, so the statues may vary, though the ingenuity of the layout will remain.

The gardens at Wiltshire's agricultural college at Lackham Park have been conceived in the same vein of multiple interlocking areas as the last three sculpture gardens, but those who know the superbly complex topiary gardens at the Dorset agricultural college at Kingston Maurward will find Lackham disappointing. The students have designed several themed areas including a somewhat brashly coloured seventeenth-century parterre, and there is an interesting sensory garden. But the new layouts are limp on containing features and a Rupert House with cut-out figures of Bill the Badger and the rest undercuts the otherwise serious approach.

Longleat is so vast and so tourist oriented that it seems to force its way into almost every chapter of this book. While many of its gardens and grounds are noble, something of its twentieth-century standards may be judged by a notice on its rose garden in front of the Orangery. This announces that 'The Maze of Love', designed by Graham Burgess in 1993, was laid out with 5,000 box plants, 1,300 rose plants, including the suggestive 'First Kiss', 'Adam', 'Eve' and

89 *The grounds of Longleat in all their new diversity. Moving from top right diagonally are the world's longest Maze, the Railway Station, the Orangery and Maze of Love next to the Boat Dock. The Sun Maze and Lunar Labyrinth are beside the lake.* English Heritage, NMR

'Seduction' roses. 'As you walk through the maze', the notice reads, 'you are expected to kiss your partner each time you pass under a heart shaped arch'. There are other mazes in the pleasure grounds: the longest hedge maze in the world when it was planted in 1975 and, nearer the house, the Sun Maze and Lunar Labyrinth (**89**) designed by Randoll Coate for the present Lord Bath.

A certain emotional continuity in the Thynne family is suggested by an epitaph in the neighbouring pets' graveyard: to a Pekinese, 'My Pansy with a sooty face', who died 'Sunday, June 4th 1937 aged 5 years'. Her owner, Lady Bath, wrote:

> *And when I stand alone and grey*
> *Outside the forest, Lord I pray*
> *That I may hear her little bark*
> *To lead me through the unknown dark.*

There are more verses in the same style of uninhibited sentimentality and perhaps, in the end, there is something engagingly open about the Thynnes' handling of their property. They catch the spirit of the age and we probably deserve them. They obviously give the public what the public wants.

Much the same can be said about the new gardens at Malmesbury Abbey House, which should perhaps have been included along with the twentieth-century Rococo ventures. But they are a new enterprise by Ian Pollard, who did so much

175

90 *Most astonishing and dazzlingly effective in its lime avenue context is the Ieoh Ming Pei pyramidal Millennium Pavilion at Oare House. The butler has just brought lunch, in his car, for the party eating there in total transparency*

to enliven Hazelbury from its Edwardian dream-time, and they are so raw and recent that they cannot be judged fairly, though they are already a tourist draw.[14] The enormous ruined arches of the Abbey lower impressively over them and yew hedges record the foundations of its Lady Chapel. A 'Saxon Arch' (actually Norman) links one garden room to another and there is a large circular Herb Garden with a green loggia. Down in the lower garden the Avon, a murky stream, does nothing to raise the tone, and one strange cascade tumbles down out of thin air from new rockwork. Time will tell how it will settle down. Just now it is a standing proof that flowers alone do not make a garden.

Oare House, a neat, townish brick box of 1740, built for a London wine merchant, Harry Deacon, has a garden that makes an appropriate conclusion to this unusually rich chapter, because it demonstrates exactly what does make a garden; and that is a great garden building. There is no warning from the village street of what lies ahead, though a mature lime avenue leads away handsomely on the other side of the lane from the house. Between 1921 and 1925 Clough Williams-Ellis added wings to the house and gardens to the south. *Country Life* photographs of the time show how he miscalculated.[15] The walled garden leading up to his diminutive Palladian Loggia has been overwhelmed by the double avenue of pleached lime trees, which he planted. Behind the Loggia are a big Potager and a Croquet Lawn enriched by billowing hedges. Tucked into Williams-Ellis' south wing is a sun-trap garden with two wooden sheep.

All this is commonplace. Then comes one of England's greatest garden strokes, to rank with William Kent's Worcester Lodge at Badminton and James Gibbs' Gothic Temple at Stowe. A wide lawn, too wide for its central kneeling figure of a blackamoor and its herbaceous borders, swoops down to urn-topped gate-piers, rich ironwork, topiary and the Miami hints of a pale blue swimming pool. All this is subdued to mere stage scenery by what happens beyond.

The downs rise quite sharply and the lime woods have been cut open in a broad avenue with individual trees seemingly manicured on a grand scale into pyramidal shapes. At the top of the avenue, perhaps half a mile distant or slightly more, the skyline is pierced by Ieoh Ming Pei's needle-sharp pyramid of glass and steel (**90**); much steeper than his pyramid at the Louvre and its metal girders more angular. It has none of the repetitive network that calms the Paris pyramid. In addition it is more transparent, with clear storeys, a stage of steps and then the dining room, complete on the blazing hot July day when I saw it, with a butler serving lunch to guests and distantly visible from the lime avenue. It was commissioned by Mrs Henry Keswick as a 'folly' to celebrate the Millennium.

To describe the pyramid as beautiful is unhelpful. It is demanding; it does not rest easily on the downland turf. Tall as a three-storey house, it is challengingly modern, not remotely gardenesque, classical or even comfortable, but a geometric pagoda that asks the eye to unravel its logic. It is a great garden achievement. Oare House gardens are rarely open to the public, but a side lane to the south offers glimpses of the Pei building looking like a glorious Chinese space vehicle.

As an aesthetic conservative I find it heartening that my country can still produce landowners rich enough and artistically committed enough to raise such a building, and set the precision of it against the broad, solid roll of the Marlborough Downs. Wilton House be warned! The primacy of Inigo Jones and the 9th Earl's Palladian Bridge is at risk. A Chinese American has created another Wiltshire garden building of equal panache.

Gazetteer

The following is a list of gardens of significant historic importance, which are covered in this book and are open to the public.

Abbreviations

NT	National Trust
EH	English Heritage
P	Privately owned, but regularly open
NGS	Privately owned but open occasionally as part of the National Gardens Scheme
H	Hotel
LA	Local Authority
AC	Agricultural College

Abbey House Gardens, Malmesbury (P)

Avebury Manor (NT)

Biddestone Manor House (NGS)

Bishopstrow House (H)

Bolehyde Manor (NGS)

Bowood Park (P)

Cantax House, Lacock (NGS)

Castle Combe Manor House (H)

Charlton Park, Malmesbury (P)

Chisenbury Priory, Enford (NGS)

Corsham Court (P)

The Courts, Holt (NT)

Fonthill House, Tisbury (NGS)

Great Chalfield Manor (NT)

Hazelbury Manor (NGS)

Heale House, Woodford (P)

Iford Manor (P)

Lackham Park (AC)

Lacock Abbey (NT)

Larmer Tree Gardens (P)

Little Durnford Manor (NGS)

Longleat, Warminster (P)

Lucknam Park, Colerne (H)

Lydiard Park, Lydiard Tregoze (LA)

The Moot, Downton (LA)

Newhouse, Whiteparish (P)

Oare House, Pewsey (NGS)

Outdoor Studio, Melksham (NGS)

Ridley's Cheer, Mountain Bower (NGS)

Seend Manor (NGS)

Sheldon Manor (P)

Stourhead (NT)

Wardour Old Castle (EH)

Westwood Manor (NT)

Wilton House (P)

Notes

1 Gardens of the English medieval vernacular

1. Quoted in Alison Weir, *Eleanor of Aquitaine. By the Wrath of God, Queen of England*, 2000, p.218. Hoveden died about 1201 so he was a contemporary writer.
2. T.B. James & A.M. Robinson, *Clarendon Palace*, 1988, p.58.
3. T.B. James, *The Palaces of Medieval England 1050-1550*, 1990, pp.154-72.
4. For a reproduction of this map see J.J. Hammond, 'Clarendon Park', *Wiltshire Notes and Queries*, vol.8 (March, 1914), pp.1-7; opposite p.1.
5. 'Story of Sheldon Manor', *Wiltshire Gardens Trust Journal*, vol.27 (Spring, 1993), p.4.
6. Eleanor Gibbs, *Sheldon Manor* (Great Sheldon, 1993), p.9.
7. Wiltshire & Swindon Record Office, 184/4. All subsequent references to documents in the Record Office will be abbreviated to WSRO.
8. William Stukeley, *Abury, a Temple of the British Druids*, 2 vols, 1743, 2, p.15.
9. *Ibid.*, 2, p.13.
10. *Avebury Manor* (National Trust leaflet, 1997), p.5.
11. These accompany the map.
12. Pevsner-Cherry, *Wiltshire*, 1975, p.125.
13. WSRO, 318/2 and 2780/25 respectively.
14. See *Country Life*, 20 February 1926.

2 John Aubrey and the lady gardeners

1. The Herberts had been made Wardens of Clarendon Forest for the course of two generations; see *Wiltshire Notes and Queries*, March 1914, p.7.
2. WSRO, 1946/H6.
3. This is illustrated in John Harris, *The Artist and the Country House*, 1979, plate 92b.
4. *Ibid.*, plate 92a.
5. *Country Life*, 12 December 1931.
6. *Ibid.*
7. *Ibid.*
8. John Aubrey, *Brief Lives* (Folio Society edition, 1975), pp.145-7; 145.
9. *Ibid.*, p.146.
10. *Ibid.*
11. In *Arcadia* the 2nd Earl is thinly disguised as Basilius, King of Arcadia, 'being already well stricken in years'. Countess Mary is Basilius' wife Gynecia 'of noble beauty', 'great wit', 'of more princely virtues than her husband', but 'terrible' when crossed.
12. Aubrey, *Brief Lives*, p.145.
13. *Ibid.*
14. *Ibid.*, p.146, footnote.
15. Taylor's description of Wilton Garden I is quoted in Roy Strong, *The Renaissance Garden in England*, 1979, pp.122-3; 122.
16. *Ibid.*, p.122.
17. *Ibid.*, pp.122-3.
18. *Ibid.*, p.123.

19. *Ibid.*, p.122.
20. *Ibid.*
21. *Ibid.*
22. Aubrey, *Brief Lives*, p.284.
23. *Ibid.*, p.146.
24. Victor Skretkowicz (ed.), *The Countess of Pembroke's Arcadia* (Oxford, 1987), Book 3, p.317.
25. *Ibid.*
26. Edmund Spenser, 'Colin Clout's Come Home Again', lines 512-15.
27. *Ibid.*, lines 487 & 499.
28. *Arcadia*, Book 3, p.316.
29. Aubrey, *Brief Lives*, p.146.
30. Revd J.E. Jackson, 'Amesbury Monastery', *Wiltshire Archaeological & Natural History Magazine*, vol.x (1867), pp.61-84; p.83.
31. For the inscription and ground plans of both lodges see John Bold, *Wilton House and English Palladianism: Some Wiltshire Houses*, 1988, pp.118-19.
32. *Arcadia*, Book 1, p.17.
33. Edmund Spenser, *The Faerie Queene*, Book 2, Canto 12, verse 83.
34. For Elizabethan antecedents to park gate lodges see Timothy Mowl & Brian Earnshaw, *Trumpet at a Distant Gate: The Lodge as Prelude to the Country House*, 1985, p.xi & pp.1-7.
35. Possibly to designs by Henry Flitcroft who received a payment of £300 from the Duchess in 1761; see Bold, *Wilton House*, p.119.
36. For the Chelsea garden see Strong, *Renaissance Garden*, pp.176-80.
37. John Britton (ed.), *Aubrey's Natural History of Wiltshire*, 1847, p.93.
38. *Ibid.*
39. *Ibid.*
40. *Ibid.*
41. *Ibid.*
42. *Ibid.*
43. Sir Henry Wotton, *The Elements of Architecture* (1624 facsimile edition, Virginia, USA, 1968), p.109.

3 Wilton Garden II – a ghost that still haunts the park

1. For the complexities of attribution of Wilton II see Timothy Mowl & Brian Earnshaw, *Architecture Without Kings: the rise of puritan classicism under Cromwell* (Manchester, 1995), pp.31-47 and Timothy Mowl, *Gentlemen & Players: Gardeners of the English Landscape* (Stroud, 2000), pp.1-10.
2. The Magalotti view is illustrated in John Bold, *Wilton House*, 1988, plate 42.
3. *Ibid.*, plate 43.
4. This compilation appeared undated and without an author, 'to be sould . . . by Thomas Rowlett att his shop neare Temple Barre'. Twenty of its twenty-six plates were re-issued in 1654, so it was clearly popular; see Mowl & Earnshaw, *Architecture Without Kings*, p.34.
5. Roy Strong, *The Artist and the Garden*, 2000, pp.184-9; John Harris & A.A. Tait, *Catalogue of the Drawings by Inigo Jones, John Webb and Isaac de Caus at Worcester College, Oxford* (Oxford, 1979), plates 113-16.
6. Howard Colvin, 'The South Front of Wilton House', *Essays in English Architectural History*, 1999, pp.136-57.
7. John Aubrey, *Memoirs of Natural Remarques in the County of Wiltshire* (edited by John Britton), 1867, p.91.
8. *Ibid.*, p.91.
9. *Ibid.*, p.87.
10. *Ibid.*
11. *Ibid.*
12. *Ibid.*
13. *Ibid.* p.145.
14. In his *Diary* for 1655 (edited by E.S. de Beer (Oxford, 1955), vol.3, p.154) John Evelyn mentions an 'Amphitheatre Garden or Solitarie Recesse, being 15 ackers, inviron'd by a hill' at the Deepdene in Surrey. Chilworth in the same county retains a smaller specimen. See Mowl & Earnshaw, *Architecture Without Kings*, pp.206-7.
15. Lieutenant Hammond, 'Description of a Journey made into Westerne Counties', *The Camden Miscellany*, vol.XVI (1936), pp.66-7.
16. The illustrations were reversed in the printing of the 1644 book into mirror images of the originals.
17. From Evelyn's 'Elysium Britannicum', f.56; see John Evelyn, *Elysium Britannicum, or the Royal Gardens,*

edited by John E. Ingram (Philadelphia, 2001), and Therese O'Malley & Joachim Wolschke-Bulmahn (eds), *John Evelyn's 'Elysium Britannicum' and European Gardening* (Washington, Dumbarton Oaks Colloquium, 17, 1998).

18. *Diary*, 3, p.114.
19. Christopher Morris (ed.), *The Illustrated Journeys of Celia Fiennes c.1682-c.1712*, 1982, p.9.
20. These cartoons, attributed to de Caus but not signed, are in Worcester College, Oxford; see John Harris & A.A. Tait (eds), *Catalogue of the Drawings by Inigo Jones, John Webb and Isaac de Caus at Worcester College, Oxford* (Oxford, 1979), plates 94-7.
21. For comparison of the two layouts see Timothy Mowl, *Historic Gardens of Dorset* (Stroud, 2003), plates 10 & 11.
22. It was an amateurish but detailed composition 'delineated by the Lady of ye Seat', Mrs Margaret Weld.

4 Caroline formalism and the rude shock of Longleat

1. For Wotton see Mowl, *Gentlemen & Players*, pp.35-47.
2. For instance: WSRO, 944/1 (Amesbury), 1553/78 (Southbroom), 1300/372, f.38 (Tottenham Park), 740/2/1 (Sheldon Manor), 2027 (Littlecote).
3. See John Dixon Hunt, *Garden and Grove – The Italian Renaissance Garden in the English Imagination; 1600-1750* (Princeton, NJ, 1986), p.155.
4. *Country Life*, 10 September 1948.
5. *Ibid.*
6. Their later, eighteenth-century, house is now at the core of Devizes Comprehensive School.
7. WSRO, 1553/78.
8. For military symbolism in gardens of this period see Robert Williams, 'Fortified Gardens', in Christopher Ridgway & Robert Williams (eds), *Sir John Vanbrugh and Landscape Architecture in Baroque England 1690-1730* (Stroud, 2000), pp.49-70.
9. The full inscription was carved over the west door of the church in 1664.
10. WSRO, 135/20: 'Plan of the Estate of Joseph Dillon Esq.' of 1816 shows the cut-down relic of Hatch House facing the 'Terras Walk' and 'Summer House' as they now stand. What is now Blow's Croquet Lawn was 'Stables' and 'Barn'.
11. I am most grateful to the present owner, Sir Henry Rumbold, for showing me this photograph.
12. Local anecdotal evidence suggests that these busts were originally at Clyffe Pypard. There is some stylistic likeness to those emperors, which were set around Christopher Wren's Sheldonian Theatre in Oxford.
13. I am indebted to Jill and Peter Drury for my information on the family; see their *A History of Tisbury* (Tisbury, 1980), p.34.
14. Edward held Hatch from 1650-9; see *Victoria County History: Wiltshire*, vol.3, p.210; all subsequent references will be abbreviated to *VCH*.
15. A *circa* 1690 painting of the east front of Urchfont Manor with its garden is given as the frontispiece illustration to the *VCH*, vol.10.
16. Leonard Knyff & Jan Kip, *Britannia Illustrata*, 1707 (edition by John Harris & Gervase Jackson-Stops, Bungay, 1984).
17. See, for instance, the 1759 engraving by Luke Sullivan, illustrated in Bold, *Wilton House*, plate 112.
18. For a scholarly account of planting in the Longleat gardens see Michael McGarvie & John H. Harvey, 'The Revd George Harbin and his Memoirs of Gardening 1716-1723', *Garden History*, vol.11, no.1 (Spring, 1983), pp.8-36.
19. For the Partnership see Mowl, *Gentlemen & Players*, pp.48-61.
20. Longleat House Archives (hereafter abbreviated to LHA) 1st Viscount 275 01/01/1685i. I am indebted to the Longleat Archivist, Dr Kate Harris, for her help with the papers.
21. Colen Campbell, *Vitruvius Britanniucus*, vol.3 (1725), plates 63-4.
22. This was made by John Harvey of Bath: LHA 1st Viscount 275 19/02/1707.
23. For a complete list of this order see McGarvie & Harvey, *Garden History*, pp.30-1.
24. *Ibid.*, p.31.
25. LHA 1st Viscount 275 01/04/1687.
26. LHA 1st Viscount 275 01/03/1694.
27. LHA 1st Viscount 275 24/05/1705.
28. LHA 1st Viscount 275 19/02/1707.
29. LHA 1st Viscount 275 22/01/1709.
30. LHA 1st Viscount 275 26/11/1710.

31. LHA 1st Viscount 275 01/09/1711.
32. Aubrey, *Natural History*, p.93.
33. WSRO, 2664: surveyed by I Overton.
34. Robert E. Lassam, 'Lady Elizabeth Fox Stangways' Rose Garden at Lacock', *Wiltshire Gardens Trust Journal*, no.29 (Spring, 1994).
35. Illustrated in *Country Life*, 25 November 1965.
36. WSRO, 2027.
37. WSRO, 135/1. Surveyed by William Kirkland for the Hon. Laurence Shirley.
38. WSRO, 2478/1. I am most grateful to Martin McNicol for bringing these maps to my attention and for organising a site visit to Garsdon.
39. For the Shirleys see Derek Allen, *A Brief History of Garsdon Manor* (Garsdon, 1993). I am most grateful to Robery Lumley for this reference, and for his hospitality at Garsdon.
40. See Brian Carne, 'Some St John Family Papers', *Report of the Friends of Lydiard Tregoze 1994-96* (privately printed), pp.29-105. Subsequent quotations are taken from this source as they are quoted in the 'Lydiard Park Restoration & Development Plan', prepared by Nicholas Pearson Associates, 2003. I am grateful to Simon Bonvoisin and Sarah Finch-Crisp for their information on Lydiard.
41. Pearson, 'Lydiard Park', p.14.
42. *Ibid.*, pp.14-15.
43. *Ibid.*
44. *Ibid.*
45. *Ibid.*, pp.15-16.
46. These are shown on a map of about 1700 in the Warwickshire County Record Office, CR 162/714; it is reproduced in the Pearson Plan.
47. Aubrey, *Natural History*, p.93.
48. *Ibid.*
49. There is, however, an early eighteenth-century brick garden house with stone quoins in the garden of Portway House, Warminster, which overlooks the main town road.

5 Burlington, Bridgeman and the evolution of a garden for the Palladian

1. See Peter Willis, *Charles Bridgeman and the English Landscape Garden* (2nd ed., Newcastle upon Tyne, 2002).
2. Sir John, as the eldest, inherited his father's baronetcy. Sir Orlando was, though the second son, the 1st Baronet in a new creation engineered by his influential father; see The Earl of Kerry, 'King's Bowood Park', *Wiltshire Archaeological Magazine*, vol.41 (June, 1922), pp.502-521 & vol.42 (December, 1922), pp.18-38. The Bridgeman Pedigree is in vol.41, p.503.
3. The oil painting and the Powell map both hang in the Orangery at Bowood. I am indebted to Lord Lansdowne and his archivist, Kate Fielden, for allowing me access to inspect these.
4. The Whetham map is in the Bowood muniments.
5. See Timothy Mowl, *Historic Gardens of Gloucestershire* (Stroud, 2002), plate 30 and Timothy Mowl, *Historic Gardens of Dorset* (Stroud, 2003), colour plate 3.
6. WSRO, 1300/358 (around 1710).
7. WSRO, 1300/372, f.38.
8. The house is illustrated in John Harris, *The Palladian Revival: Lord Burlington, His Villa and Garden at Chiswick*, 1994, p.87; see also John Harris, 'Serendipity and the Architect Earl', *Country Life*, 28 May 1987.
9. WSRO, 1300/359.
10. Its true site is Mildenhall a mile to the east.
11. This is illustrated in Stukeley's *Itinerarium Curiosum*, 2 vols., 1724, 1, pp.60-1. It is also to be found in the Gough Collection in the Bodleian Library, Oxford (Gough Maps 33, f.9v) where there are many more rare engravings and maps pertaining to Wiltshire.
12. They are both in the Bodleian Library, Oxford, M.S. Gough Drawings a.3, ff.24-5; see *Country Life*, 13 February 1986.
13. For Eastbury see Mowl, *Dorset*, pp.53-6 & colour plate 3.
14. Bridgeman's 1738 plan for the park is in the Bodleian Library, M.S. Gough Drawings a.3*, f.32.
15. WSRO, 944/1.
16. John Britton, *Beauties of Wiltshire*, 1825, vol.3, p.151.
17. *VCH*, vol.10, pp.30-1.
18. Pevsner-Cherry, *Wiltshire*, p.572. In Pevsner's Herefordshire volume Newhouse Farm is described as having been built as a parsonage for the Revd Thomas Smith (p.138).

19. Copies of these three maps are in WSRO (no catalogue numbers). The originals are still at Newhouse.
20. I am most grateful to Andrew Eburne for biographical information on Kingsmill Eyre.
21. Horace Walpole, *The History of the Modern Taste in Gardening*, 1780 (Ursus Press, New York edition of 1995, edited by John Dixon Hunt), p.43.
22. Gwyn Headley & Wim Meulenkamp, *Follies, Grottoes & Garden Buildings*, 1999, p.537-8.
23. *Country Life*, 9 January 1909.
24. Sale particulars of 1870 for George Sampson then in residence: WSRO, 2454/6.
25. *Ibid.*
26. Also at Hackwood in Hampshire and Rousham in Oxfordshire: see Willis, *Charles Bridgeman*.
27. Quoted in Timothy Mowl, *Horace Walpole: The Great Outsider*, 1996, p.240.
28. *Ibid.*
29. I am indebted to Kate Felus for making available Roland Trafford-Roberts's *A Survey of the historic landscape at Spye Park, Wiltshire*, 2001.
30. Stephen Switzer, *An Introduction to a General System of Hydrostaticks and Hydraulicks*, 1734, p.80; quoted by Trafford-Roberts, p.4.
31. John Evelyn, *Diary* entry for 19 July 1654; quoted by Trafford-Roberts, p.4.
32. Switzer, *Hydrostaticks*, pp.412-13; quoted by Trafford-Roberts, p.5.
33. Quoted by J.C. Loudon, *Encyclopaedia of Gardening*, 1822; cited by Trafford-Roberts, p.5.
34. For Kent's work at Carlton House see Mowl, *Gentlemen & Players*, pp.116-17. For an illustration see Michael I. Wilson, *William Kent: Architect, Designer, Painter, Gardener, 1685-1748*, 1984, plate 73.
35. WSRO, 332/284: for Charles Penruddock.

6 Arcady on Avon – pioneering gardens of the mid-eighteenth century

1. For Benson see Anna Eavis, 'The avarice and ambition of William Benson', *The Georgian Group Journal*, vol.XII (2002), pp.8-37.
2. John Hutchins, *History and Antiquities of the County of Dorset*, 1861, p.45.
3. I am grateful to Carole Fry for alerting me to this complex system of sluices and channels.
4. WSRO, 944/1.
5. See Timothy Mowl & Brian Earnshaw, *John Wood: Architect of Obsession* (Bath, 1988).
6. John Wood, *An Essay towards a description of Bath*, 3rd edition, 1765 (facsimile, Bath, 1969), p. 238-9.
7. *Ibid.*, p.238.
8. *Ibid.*
9. Bodleian Library, MS. Top. Wilts.c.2, f.29: 'A Map of the Estate of Francis Yerbury Esq. lying at Belcomb Brook, in the Parish of Bradford in the County of Wilts'. I am indebted to Charlotte Gale for bringing this map to my attention.
10. It was re-routed in 1825-9; see Matthew J. Slocombe, *Clothiers to Gentlemen: The Development of the Yerbury Family and the Belcombe Estate at Bradford-on-Avon*, BA Dissertation, University of Sussex, 1987, p.45.
11. Slocombe, *Clothiers to Gentlemen*, p.50.
12. Wood, *Essay*, p.238.
13. See Timothy Mowl, *Palladian Bridges: Prior Park and the Whig Connection* (Bath, 1993).
14. William Stukeley, *Abury, a Temple of the British Druids*, 1743, Preface written on 1 January 1743. I am grateful to Andrew Eburne for this reference.
15. This is illustrated in Bold, *Wilton House*, plate 101.
16. For the Alderman's layout, captured in a 1755 painting by Arthur Devis, see Timothy Mowl, 'Inside Beckford's Landscape of the Mind', *Country Life*, 7 February 2002; see also Timothy Mowl, *William Beckford: Composing for Mozart*, 1998, pp.25-40. For the younger Beckford's collecting and patronage see Derek E. Ostergard (ed.), *William Beckford, 1760-1844: An Eye for the Magnificent* (New York, 2001).
17. See Mowl, *Composing for Mozart*, pp.36-7.
18. Joseph's best known work is the crystal grotto at Painshill Park, Surrey, made for Charles Hamilton, a cousin of Beckford's mother and a frequent guest at Fonthill.
19. I was escorted around the pleasure grounds by the Hon. Alastair Morrison, to whom I am greatly indebted for this inspection of the Beckford garden structures.
20. I owe this observation to Roger White.
21. For the 2nd Viscount see Timothy Mowl, 'Rococo and Later Landscaping at Longleat', *Garden History*, vol.21, no.1 (Summer, 1995), pp.56-66.
22. Longleat House Archives, Wilts. Maps 68.
23. LHA, 150 26/10/1734.

24. His theories were first propounded in *Landscape and Antiquity: Aspects of Culture at Stourhead 1718 to 1838* (Oxford, 1970); this was followed by his guidebook to the park, *The Stourhead Landscape* (1982).
25. It comes across much more persuasively in his later guidebook for the Trust.
26. Richard Colt Hoare, *History of Modern Wiltshire*, 1822, p.63.
27. From the unpublished Journal of Sir John Parnell, *Garden History*, vol.2, no.1 (1974), pp.59-70.
28. Letter of 17 September 1765 from Joseph Spence to Henry Fiennes Clinton, 9th Earl of Lincoln: University of Nottingham, Department of Manuscripts, Newcastle Papers, C2951. I am most grateful to Neil Porteous for alerting me to this letter.
29. From a letter Hoare wrote to his daughter, Susanna. The letter is quoted by Woodbridge, *Landscape and Antiquity*, p.57. Woodbridge's transcripts of Henry Hoare's original letters in the Tottenham Park papers in WSRO are at Stourhead House: Henry Hoare II, Box File 2 (Correspondence, family, 1760-81).
30. Remarked by Joseph Spence in his aforementioned letter of 1765: Newcastle Papers, C2951.
31. F.M. Piper's plan and section of the Druid's Cell is given in Woodbridge, *Stourhead Landscape*, p.54.
32. J Cartwright (ed.), 'The Travels through England of Dr Richard Pococke 1750-57', *Camden Society*, 2 vols. (1888-9), 2, p.135.
33. *Ibid.*, p.136.
34. Revd J.E. Jackson, 'Ambresbury Monastery', *Wiltshire Archaeological & Natural History Magazine*, vol.x (1867), pp.61-84, p.84.
35. Quoted in John Harris, *Sir William Chambers: Knight of the Polar Star*, 1970, p.196.
36. *Ibid.*
37. The Duchess was debating whether the Swiss Theodore de Bruyn should paint it and she was concerned that any acorns in the décor should not be 'big enough to disgust one'. Quoted by Harris, *Chambers*, p.196.
38. WSRO, 377/2, f.290: 'Inventory of items at Chinese House'.
39. WSRO, 282/3: The Bowden Park Account Book, 1780-88 lists Ezekiel's loans. His Letter Book (WSRO, 282/2) contains passages of shocking detachment from the fate of sick and mentally disturbed slaves and ends, after Ezekiel's death, in June 1788, with an estimate of his financial worth.
40. Pevsner-Cherry, *Wiltshire*, p.120.
41. See Timothy Mowl, *Historic Gardens of Gloucestershire* (Stroud, 2002), p.167.
42. See Mowl, *William Beckford*, p.110.

7 Lancelot Brown and Humphry Repton – minimalism and after

1. See Timothy Mowl, *Historic Gardens of Gloucestershire* (Stroud, 2002), p.90 & plate 41, and Mark Laird, *The Flowering of the Landscape Garden: English Pleasure Grounds 1720-1800* (Philadelphia, 1999), pp.127-8 & fig.71.
2. For Carlton House see David Coombs, 'The Garden at Carlton House of Frederick Prince of Wales and Augusta Princess and Dowager of Wales', *Garden History*, vol.25, pt.2 (Winter, 1997), pp.153-77.
3. The plan is illustrated in Laird, *The Flowering*, p.195, fig.113.
4. Quoted by The Earl of Kerry, *Wiltshire Archaeological Magazine*, vol.42 (December, 1922), p.19.
5. *Ibid.*, vol.41 (June, 1922), p.512.
6. There are three plans for the Mausoleum in Sir John Soane's Museum marked: 'For the Countess of Shelburne'.
7. Preserved at the house and illustrated in Fielden, *Bowood*, pp.4-5.
8. *Wiltshire Archaeological Magazine*, vol.42, pp.19-21.
9. Preserved at the house and exhibited in the Orangery.
10. The 5th Marquess (1845-1927) served a term as Viceroy of India and was impressed by the rhododendrons growing around the Viceregal Summer Lodge at Simla in the Himalayas.
11. See Stourhead Papers, WSRO, 1300/4280-99 for a further account of this statue in a letter of 23 October 1762 from Henry Hoare to his son-in-law, Lord Bruce.
12. See Frederick J. Ladd, *Architects at Corsham Court* (Bradford-on-Avon, 1978).
13. WSRO, Box File 47a & b.
14. WSRO, Box File 47a & b.
15. WSRO, 2027.
16. For Melbury see Timothy Mowl, *Historic Gardens of Dorset* (Stroud, 2003), pp.59-63 and colour plate 4.
17. For Cirencester see Mowl, *Gloucestershire*, pp.70-4.
18. WSRO, 1300/365: Rudolph Wittkower's typescript of 23 August 1946.

19. WSRO, 1300/1910-1952: Letters concerning alterations to the park by Brown, plan of the park, minutes of planting meetings (1764-72). Winckles was introduced to liaise on 13 January 1765 (WSRO, 9/35/52, 2302), and by 6 March he was made clerk of works (WSRO, 9/35/52, 1410).

20. WSRO, 1300/1937.

21. A letter of 12 February 1767 from Brown to Lord Bruce suggests that the master plan was still not complete, even though Winckles was in post to oversee the works: 'I am honoured with your Lordship's Letter and inform your Lordship that the Plan for Tottenham Park is nearly finished & that your Lordship will have it very soon' (WSRO, 9/35/52, 1410).

22. WSRO, 1300/1918.

23. WSRO, 1300/1933.

24. WSRO, 1300/362: 2 March 1773.

25. WSRO, 1300/360: 'A Plan of the Forest of Savernake and of Tottenham Park'.

26. It was first raised in 1760 at Brandenburg House by George Bubb Dodington to the memory of his wife. Letters concerning the erection of the column and its inscription are in WSRO, 1300/1870-1909.

27. WSRO, 1300/371.

28. WSRO, 2667/21/13: 'Plan of alterations at Wardour Park by Lancelot Brown, 1775'.

29. WSRO, 2667/21/10. For Woods at Wardour see Fiona Cowell, 'Richard Woods (?1716-93): A Preliminary Account Part II', *Garden History*, vol.15, no.1 (Spring, 1987), pp.17-26.

30. WSRO, 2667/18/21, Folder 1.

31. Uvedale Price, *An Essay on the Picturesque*, 1794, from a chapter summary on p.36.

32. See *Country Life*, 7 October 1993. I am also indebted to Fiona Cowell for her advice on Woods' work at Wardour.

33. Bodleian Library, MSS Beckford, c.47.

34. WSRO, G23/1/162: 'A Design for the Improvement of the Gardens of Pen. Wyndham Esq. of Salisbury, Wilts.' See Fiona Cowell, *Garden History*, vol.15, no.1 (Spring, 1987), p.44 & figure 63.

35. Britton, *Beauties*, vol.1, p.82.

36. *Ibid.*, p.81.

37. LHA, Thynne Papers, Box XXV, vol.LXXVII, fols.280-89. For Brown's work at Longleat see Timothy Mowl, 'Rococo and Later Landscaping at Longleat', *Garden History*, vol.23, no.1 (Summer, 1995), pp.56-66.

38. Heaven's Gate was planted with its wide-spreading arms on its new southern site in 1878 and 1879.

39. Horace Walpole, 'Visits to Country Seats etc.', *The Walpole Society*, vol.16 (1927-8), p.45.

40. Gloucestershire Record Office, D 1571, E396. I am grateful to Ruth Guilding for bringing these to my attention, and to John Kendall for his help in interpreting the site in the light of them.

41. LHA: 'Designs for Longleat by H. Repton'. I am grateful to Kate Harris for allowing me access to the book.

42. WSRO, Box File 47a & b: letter 6060 has an attached sheet of expenses dated 23 January 1798.

43. *Ibid.*

44. *Ibid.*, letter 6063: Specification of 23 September 1797.

45. *Ibid.*, letter 6060, 26 January 1798.

46. For the younger Beckford's plantations see Alexander Marr, 'William Beckford and the Landscape Garden', in Derek E. Ostergard (ed.), *William Beckford, 1760-1844: An Eye for the Magnificent* (New York, 2001), pp.137-53.

47. Lewis Melville, *The Life and Letters of William Beckford of Fonthill*, 1910, p.256.

48. *New Monthly Magazine*, vol.VIII (1823), p.370; quoted in Robert J. Gemmett, *Beckford's Fonthill: The Rise of a Romantic Icon* (Norfolk, 2003), pp.94-5.

49. John Rutter, *A Description of Fonthill Abbey and Demesne, in the County of Wilts: Including a List of the Paintings, Cabinets, &c.* (Shaftesbury, 1822), p.90.

50. Quoted in Mowl, *Beckford*, p.23.

51. Illustrated in Gemmett, *Beckford's Fonthill*, plate 28.

52. *The European Magazine and London Review*, vol.XXXI, p.105; quoted in Gemmett, *Beckford's Fonthill*, p.103.

8 An uncertainty of direction – nineteenth-century gardens

1. Sale particulars in the collection at Devizes Museum. I am most grateful to Lorna Haycock for bringing these to my attention and for many other helpful suggestions.

2. For Shenstone see Mowl, *Gentlemen & Players*, chapter 10.

3. For Bowles see June Wilson, 'A Georgian Eccentric', *Country Life*, 11 October 1956. I am also indebted to Chris Ellis for information on Bowles and for his hospitality at the Old Parsonage.

4. There is a delightful small watercolour of a fountain seen through a rocky arch at Bremhill in the Boodle collection at Devizes Museum.

5. William Lisle Bowles, *The Parochial History of Bremhill*, 1828, p.xi.

6. *Ibid.*, p.250.

7. *Ibid.*, p.ix.

8. See chapter III: 'Of King Bladud's Works at Bath, and their constituting the Metropolitan Seat of the British Druids'.

9. Revd George Gilfillen (ed.), *The Poetical Works of William Lisle Bowles* (Edinburgh, 1855), p.xii.

10. Bowles, *Parochial History*, p.254.

11. Thomson exhibited the original neo-Norman designs for the house at the Royal Academy in 1853 and published the design in *The Builder* of that year.

12. This is the most impressive nineteenth-century conservatory in the county, just eclipsing in scale that at Tottenham Park, which was added to the house when it was being altered in 1826 by Thomas Cundy: see WSRO, 1300/2827/E-L for Cundy's plans and elevations of the mansion and grounds. Cundy's cast iron conservatory is scimitar-shaped and supported by Doric columns.

13. See Timothy Mowl, 'A Taste for Towers', *Country Life*, 1 October 1987.

14. When Lady Caroline sued for her conjugal rights Neeld offered her rooms in a London hotel. She declined.

15. Robert of Normandy, the Conqueror's son, was imprisoned in it. Henry II brought it firmly into the Crown's possession. It had an aisled hall of six bays. See *Victoria County History*, vol.10, pp.237-45.

16. H. Brown divided it up into lots before the sale of 1961.

17. The original conception is illustrated in lavish sale particulars of 1888: WSRO, 130/78.

18. *Ibid*.

19. It is the Berks & Hants extension Railway to Hungerford in the north, but the Wilts, Somerset & Weymouth Railway to the south.

20. The Bishop's Gate was the Norman west door of St John's, which was being restored in 1862-3.

21. Robert Valentine replaced an eighteenth-century windmill with a massive circular tower.

22. WSRO, 1946/H12.

23. Christopher Hussey suggests Edouard André or W.A. Nesfield: see *Country Life*, 10 September 1964.

24. The original planting is illustrated in John Leyland (ed.), *Gardens Old & New: The Country House & Its Garden Environment*, no date (1920s), pp.67-70; see also *Country Life*, 10 September 1964.

25. Pevsner and Cherry in the *Buildings of England: Wiltshire* call it 'an extraordinary instance of Victorian self-confidence' (p.186). The Boodes married in 1834 so the Lodge, their honeymoon memento, will be of around 1836.

26. Their *Wiltshire* (p.248) confuses Fonthill House for the Morrisons with Fonthill Abbey for the Marquess of Westminster. This last was a Scots Baronial building by William Burn.

27. For an illustration of the house before its 1921 demolition see *VCH*, vol.13, p.160.

28. The formal terraced garden at Trafalgar House was commissioned in 1859 by the 3rd Earl Nelson and designed by William Butterfield. I owe this information to Fridy Duterloo. For the terraced gardens at Frankleigh, now mostly decayed, see *Country Life*, 14 July 1900.

29. See M.W. Thompson, *General Pitt-Rivers*, 1997, p.76.

30. For the site see Lt. Gen. Pitt-Rivers, *A Short Guide to the Larmer Grounds, Rushmore; King John's House; and the Museum at Farnham, Dorset* (Farnham, *c*.1907).

31. An account of his stay was reported in a local paper and is quoted in Florence Emily Hardy, *The Life of Thomas Hardy*, 1962, p.269. The paper actually insists that the gardens were in Wiltshire, but the Shire Stone is several yards inside the Gardens so the honours must be shared with Dorset. Hardy wrote at least nine poems on dance halls he had visited.

32. Their uniform was copied from Romney's painting of the last Keeper; see L.H. Dudley Buxton (ed.), *The Pitt-Rivers Museum Farnham: General Handbook* (Farnham, 1929), p.9.

33. The Dining Hall (1896) and Oriental Room (1898) have gone; see *Architectural Review*, March 1969.

9 The extended reign of King Edward VII – 1880-1923

1. Peto's own map of his Iford Manor estate is in WSRO, 2780/25. I am indebted to Elizabeth Cartwright-Hignett, her gardener, Leon Butler, and the garden historian, Robin Whalley, for their informed comments about Iford during the many visits I have made to the garden over the last twenty years.

2. For coaches Peto retained the old Brownian-style carriage entrance from a 'Saxon' lodge at the furthest eastern point in the grounds. This curls round through woods planted with box undergrowth to approach the house from the west.

3. Peto rescued one saint from a crude restoration of the front of Rheims cathedral, which was later devastated in the 1914-18 war. So this is a rare survival.

4. However, Sir Martin Conway has identified the wellhead in front of the Casita as a capital from the church of St Andrew of the Goths, built by King Theodorus at Ravenna.

5. Harold Peto, *The Boke of Iford* (Marlborough, 1993), p.49.

6. *Ibid.*

7. For a plan of Heale see David Ottewill, *The Edwardian Garden*, 1989, p.153.

8. *Country Life*, 5 April 1902.

9. For a full account of the mid-Edwardian fashion for Japanese gardens see Ottewill, *Edwardian Garden*, pp.55-7.

10. See *Country Life*, 24 October 1912.

11. *VCH*, vol.13, p.212, footnote citing WSRO, 135/20 & 2132/253.

12. Pevsner-Cherry, *Wiltshire*, p.272. It is unlikely that his co-author, Bridget Cherry, shared this blinkered view.

13. Illustrations of the garden in its prime are given in *Country Life*, 14 October 1933.

14. See Diana Baskervyle-Clegg's article in *Country Life*, 29 January 1998 for further gardens by Parsons; also Ottewill, *Edwardian Garden*, pp.130-32.

15. 14 January 1905 and 26 March 1904.

16. Tony Venison's irreverent article, 'Laughter over the Hedge', in *Country Life*, 7 March 1991, offers a helpful account of recent developments in the grounds of Hazelbury.

17. WSRO, 318/2. For an impression of this map see *Country Life*, 7 March 1991. There is also a useful map of 1832: WSRO, 1265/3.

18. This is illustrated in James Belsey, *Hazelbury Manor Gardens* (privately published by Hazelbury Manor, Box, no date), p.30.

19. *Country Life*, 7 March 1991.

10 The county's greatest garden age – the later twentieth century

1. For Pen Pits see *Country Life*, 29 August 1985. Alison and Peter Smithson, of the well-known architectural practice, built a weekend house at Upper Lawn, West Hatch, in a Brutalist minimalism for their own use in 1959. It had no garden, as the point the Smithsons were making was the need for minimal intrusion of the natural landscape. See *Observer Magazine*, 30 November 2003 for a full description of the experiment.

2. For an account of this remarkable lady and the *Shell Guides* in particular see Timothy Mowl, *Stylistic Cold Wars: Betjeman versus Pevsner*, 2000, chapter three.

3. For Whistler's relationship with Olivier see Laurence Whistler, *The Laughter and the Urn: The Life of Rex Whistler*, 1985, pp.102-17.

4. Cecil Beaton, *Ashcombe: The Story of a Fifteen Year Lease*, 1949; see also Stephen Calloway, *Baroque Baroque: The culture of excess,* 1994, pp.32-3; 86.

5. For an illustration of the painting see Beaton, *Ashcombe*, p.24.

6. This theory was proposed by Christopher Hussey in *Country Life*, 2 April 1938.

7. Michael Spens, *Jellicoe at Shute*, 1993 has detailed charts of all the flower planting; see also Michael Spens, *Gardens of the Mind: The Genius of Geoffrey Jellicoe*, 1992.

8. However, an article in *Country Life*, 21 August 1986, illustrates topiary four-poster beds planted by Lady Anne 'for late arrivals', which hints at a whimsical spirit that Jellicoe may have had to keep in check.

9. I am grateful to John Kendall for bringing Seend to my attention, and to Stephen and Amanda Clark for allowing me access; my guide was the gardener, Bill Painter.

10. The origin of this building is not recorded, but it looks very like the 1830s work of Henry Edmund Goodridge of Bath.

11. I was alerted to this garden by Jonathan Holt.

12. Nutmegs and snake seat are by Alison Crowther.

13. See *Country Life*, 23 April 1964, when it was the property of Mr & Mrs John Buxton.

14. The Pollards moved to Malmesbury in 1994 and the gardens first opened in 2002.

15. *Country Life*, 10 March 1928.

Index

Page numbers in bold refer to illustrations and captions